British animation:
The Channel 4 factor

D1438525

062123

THE HENLEY COLLEGE LIBRARY

First published in 2008 by Parliament Hill Publishing,
28 Parliament Hill, London NW3 2TN, UK
http://parliamenthillpublishing.co.uk

Co-published in North America by Indiana University Press,
601 North Morton St, Bloomington, IN 47404-3797, USA
www.iupress.indiana.edu

Copyright © 2008 Clare Kitson.

Clare Kitson has asserted her right under the Copyright, Designs and Patents
Act 1988 to be identified as the author of this work.

Unless otherwise specified, all illustrations are © Channel Four Television
Corporation.

All rights reserved. No part of this book may be reproduced, stored in or
introduced into a retrieval system, or transmitted, in any form or by any means
(electronic, mechanical, photocopying, recording or otherwise) without the
written permission of the publisher.

Cataloguing in Publication Data
A catalogue record for this book is available from the British Library.

ISBN 978-0-9560002-0-0

Book design by Mike Swift
Production by Martin Lee
Cover drawing © Joanna Quinn
Printed in Singapore by KHL Printing Co Pte Ltd

In memory of
Dick Arnall (1944-2007),
a major figure in Channel 4 animation,
an enormous help in researching this book
and a good friend

Contents

THE HENLEY COLLEGE LIBRARY

Foreword

When I was a boy there was no such thing as British animation.

Everyone knew back then that animation was American by definition. Everything I loved in the world of cartoons came from the States - whether it was Tom and Jerry celebrating Thanksgiving, or the Flintstones going to a drive-in movie. Animation was American - and if it wasn't, well then, it was probably a bit weird and not terribly funny. And even that wasn't British.

There was a British animation industry back in the mid-60s of course; it's just that most people didn't see much of it. What was visible was a scattering of children's cartoons, public information films and TV commercials - much of it trailing stylistically after its successful American sibling. There was the odd stand-out success of course. *Yellow Submarine* acted as a beacon for our generation of filmmakers but, beyond that, if you were interested in animation you had to work pretty hard to satisfy your craving. There wasn't a convincing animation culture, and there was nowhere to see the work.

And yet from this unpromising ground there suddenly grew a diverse and dynamic animation culture which in style, voice and content was aggressively, unmistakably British.

In the 80s, Britain took the world of animation by storm - winning the prizes, dominating the conversation and generally strutting its stuff with a burst of energy and creativity which has continued to the present day.

And how was this amazing feat achieved? Well from our perspective at Aardman the reason is simple - and I'm sure it applies across the whole industry: for the first time in our filmmaking lives we had an outlet for our independent work. We were nurtured, encouraged and - oh yes - *funded* by someone - by the new upstart television station of our age - Channel 4.

Clare's book illumines this culturally spectacular period. From a unique insider's perspective, and using her network of connections, she can tell the story of the filmmakers, the films and how they were made.

Animators are sometimes characterised unkindly as shy (if not socially inept) but as you'll see from Clare's book, the reality is far more entertaining. The actors in this cartoon revolution are diverse and opinionated as well as talented. Elsewhere in the world, animators have been discovered and reared inside a studio system. Not so in Britain. Here the filmmakers had to invent their own careers, carve their own niches and establish their identities. Every story is different and everyone is a true Independent.

Most of the careers that were launched in the 80s are still thriving today. The filmmakers have defined their styles, made their mark and, I'm delighted to say, been continually challenged by hordes of young upstarts determined to snatch their crowns. This book contains their stories. It celebrates a Golden Age, certainly, but not a lost one - the seeds planted are still growing strongly today.

Peter Lord CBE
Aardman Animations

Introduction

This book is something of a hybrid. The early and late chapters document events of which I was an interested observer. For the ten years and five chapters in the middle I was employed by Channel 4 to commission its animation. Paul Bonner, in his *Independent Television in Britain*, avoids this problem, nobly referring to himself in the third person and eschewing all anecdote and personal views. But his is the definitive reference work on the subject. My book is extremely personal. I just hope the grinding of gears is not too deafening.

Another part of this hybrid work, the 'film portraits' section, is no more nor less than a celebration - of individual works and of the circumstances which came together and unexpectedly provided a context for this work to flourish. Choosing was hard, verging on the heartbreaking, and my criteria were varied. Some films are the best-known, the most prize-laden, others are personal favourites, others have a particularly fascinating background story. It is an eclectic mix.

I hope my book contains something of interest to a wide spectrum of readers. Students or professionals in animation or the media should find food for thought in the narrative section: less specialised readers might want to skip the history and jump to favourite films or series in the 'portraits' section. It is your choice.

My memory is far from perfect and, though I was relieved, morale-wise, to discover that others share the same failing, this sometimes made it hard to adjudicate between differing recollections of the same events. And animation - surprise, surprise - is not documented in the literature, nor in the Channel 4 computer system, in the same detail as live action. So there may be errors, for which I apologise.

As well as being personal, this book is a team effort. And it was a large team. All the filmmakers mentioned - so many that I shall not name them again here - contributed time and patience, talking to me and going through ancient files for stills, sketches and storyboards. Without their care these would be lost to posterity.

Likewise, Channel 4 staff, past and present, have been ever willing to answer questions and scour files for me. Again, they are many, but I must single out Sir Jeremy Isaacs (who did not know me, but nevertheless gave up time to be interviewed at length), Paul Madden, Camilla Deakin, Ruth Fielding, Jan

Younghusband, Yvonne Taylor, Pamela Dear, Sally Stevens, Chris Worwood, Charlie Fearn, Nick Toon and Michael Palmer. Many with no C4 affiliation likewise gave their time, providing recollections or illustrations: Jayne Pilling, Colin Rose, Gary Thomas, David Curtis, Irene Kotlarz, Ben Weschke, Sian Rees, Alex Tham, Martin Pickles, Vernon Adams, Antoinette Moses, Michael Brooke and the British Film Institute. Other kind people agreed to read my texts and comment at various stages, notably Elizabeth Duff, Ruth Lingford, Gillian Lacey, Caroline Leaf, Joseph Pierce, Philip Bacon, Derek Hill, Deirdre Simms and Phil Davies.

Publishing this book represented a very steep learning curve and I needed a lot of help. Thanks are due to Mike Swift who designed and Martin Lee who produced the book, as well as Vivien Halas, David Gardiner, Richard Gollner, Richard Bates and Gerben Schermer who gave good advice.

Finally I have to thank Joanna Quinn for allowing me to use her homage to Muybridge on my cover, Clare Wilford, Gareth Evans and Nick Saltmarsh for help publicising the book and my husband, John Jordan, who has helped in various capacities, with an uncharacteristic display of patience.

I am also grateful to the many individuals and organisations who granted me permission to use their illustrative material. I have endeavoured to trace and acknowledge all copyright-holders and apologise in advance for any unintentional errors or omissions. I would be pleased to rectify these in any subsequent edition.

Clare Kitson

Note: Most of the films discussed in this book are available either on DVD or on the web. Go to www.britishanimationawards.com and www.4mations.tv.

1 Animation and TV

The Cartoon d'Or
Photo Clare Kitson

British animation has experienced several great moments. It was great for a while in the 1930s and again in the 1960s. But in the late 1980s the animation world had to acknowledge that it had hit its best form ever. By the 1990s it was getting embarrassing. From 1990 to 1995 the UK won the animation Oscar® every year except one, and even in that year it accounted for three of the five nominations. The story was the same with the Cartoon d'Or for best European animation. Some of these winners were student films, some were supported by the BBC or S4C, but the majority were Channel 4 commissions. In 1993, a year in which all five Cartoon d'Or nominations were British, when it transpired that C4 had commissioned four of the five nominees the Channel was given its own Cartoon d'Or, for its 'outstanding contribution to high quality animation in Europe'. Yet few at the time bothered to consider quite how extraordinary it was that a broadcaster should invest in these films, given that they were not standard TV half-hours, still less series, and very few were straightforward entertainment.

Animation, of course, is basically nothing more than a group of technologies which can create (rather than merely record) a moving image on a screen. They can be applied to any programming genre, from children's series to sitcoms, experimental to entertainment to factual formats. Some of these are natural TV genres: script-led, narrative-based, long-form such as feature films, adult comedy and children's series, but also extremely short-form genres such as commercials, title sequences and idents. All these are sent to animation festivals and the best of them - well scripted or stylishly designed as the case may be - win category prizes. But it is no surprise that television should commission these very natural TV products - indeed the real surprise is that UK television has largely failed to nurture home-grown longer form animation production, as American TV has. Channel 4's own entries into these genres - two features and a handful of series - are discussed in these pages.

But in festivals, historically, the short film category has been considered the main one and usually furnishes the Grand Prix winner. These films can vary in running time from infinitesimal up to half an hour and in genre from comedy to documentary, from narrative to abstract or any combination of these. Likewise they can be produced in any of the many technologies now accepted under the headword 'animation' or in a hybrid of these and other techniques. They often constitute an intense and sometimes challenging viewing experience (and hence their need of the short film format). In many ways the art of animation can be compared to painting which, for the last century, has been developing in different directions, some of which are not accessible to all viewers; modernist ways which often minimise and sometimes totally eschew figuration, ways which offer much to contemplate and demand to be seen over and over. Edwin Carels, in the Rotterdam International Film Festival catalogue (2001), came up with a convincing description of the short film at its best:

They are condensed and compact like a prayer, or abstract and open like a meditation. They were not made with a certain audience in mind, but are the result of a passionate belief, an interior dialogue between the artist and the medium.

But is TV the right vehicle for this art form, not made with a particular audience in mind? Short films are hard to fit into schedules based on half-hour units; television is a mass medium (and the general public will tend to prefer entertainment over challenge); and a brief single screening on TV will not satisfy that need to peruse and reflect that we feel after certain of the richest works. Yet one television channel, with an unusual remit from the government, struggled valiantly to make animation - and largely short-form animation - work on TV, with a degree of success which for a while convinced other broadcasters too that it could work. Between them they brought about a blossoming of British animation in the 1980s and 1990s which was acknowledged world wide.

This book examines the unique set of circumstances which led Channel 4 to embark on this endeavour in 1981 and the subsequent changes throughout a period of turmoil in the broadcasting world. But primarily it celebrates the unique body of work which resulted and the filmmakers responsible. Some names - Nick Park, the Quay brothers, Jan Švankmajer - are now known beyond the animation community. Some works - *The Snowman, Creature Comforts, Pond Life, Crapston Villas, Bob's Birthday, Alice, When the Wind Blows, Peter and the Wolf* - have become favourites with viewers and critics. Others remain well-kept secrets, which this book intends to illuminate.

2   Before C4

Rainbow Dance
GPO Film Unit

The success of the 80s and 90s was not, of course, conjured out of thin air. British animation already had a considerable history behind it, dating back to the origins of animation itself at the turn of the (19th-20th) century.

But, though Britain had been early on the world animation scene, its contribution was not at that stage particularly illustrious. While Emile Cohl in France, J S Blackton in the USA and Ladislas Starewicz in Russia were deploying extraordinary technical prowess in quirky, witty vignettes, the British pioneers were still enjoying the novelty value of getting things to appear, disappear and move a bit. The First World War produced some satire, but it was rather plodding. Cinema commercials began to thrive in the 1920s, to be dominated by Britain's answer to Disney, Anson Dyer. However, we have to wait till the 1930s for signs of real sophistication or any distinctiveness.

Two key factors brought this about. One was an influx of talent from overseas, some of it due to the rise of Nazism in Europe. The decade[1] saw the arrival in the UK of George Pal and John Halas from Hungary, Peter Sachs and Lotte Reiniger from Germany, Hector Hoppin from the USA and Len Lye from New Zealand. Some subsequently left for other destinations, but their presence had generated the energy and varied cultural perspectives needed to fuel a more original production. It launched a trend which has continued to this day: our animation community still benefits from a high proportion of foreign nationals.

But the second, and perhaps the major, factor was the creation in 1933 of the General Post Office Film Unit, set up by John Grierson who later went on to found the National Film Board of Canada. While with the GPO he recruited Len Lye and Norman McLaren among others and some key works of British animation resulted from their experimental techniques, including Lye's *A Colour Box* (1935), *Rainbow Dance* (1936) and *Trade Tattoo* (1937) and McLaren's *Love on the Wing* (1938), all selling various Post Office services. The GPO film unit was an early illustration of an eternal paradox of animation history (and perhaps that of the other arts as well): an artist is likely to enjoy more freedom when in the employ of a rich organisation, commercial or governmental, whose agenda happens to complement that of the artist, than when he suffers no restraints whatsoever but also has no funding. Such complementary agendas can be purely commercial, but they are more often tempered by other factors. Hence innovative animation has often thrived at the National Film Board of Canada, which was set up to promote the virtues of that country, and even under totalitarian Communist regimes - for, while it was fully funded by the state, it also managed as, supposedly, children's entertainment, to avoid most of the censorship to which other art forms were subject.

This ideal situation would recur in the UK from time to time, in various formats, up to the present day. But in 1939 the war brought an end to the idyll for the time being. Public information films were still needed, but there was neither funding nor time for artistic experimentation. After the war these and industrial films continued to be a mainstay, with funding suddenly forthcoming from new tax reliefs to industry and some even from the Marshall Plan in its efforts to promote European unity as a defence against totalitarianism; and there was also a resumption of cinema commercials. Some of the work was in a modernist style, especially that of Halas & Batchelor, given John Halas's European roots and especially the fact that he had worked briefly for Moholy-Nagy in Budapest. Some of the studio's government information films - *Dustbin Parade* (1941), *Robinson Charley* (1948) - were classics of the genre and, unusually for the time, the studio was already investing in art films such as the ambitious allegory *The Magic Canvas* (1948).

Dustbin Parade
© Halas & Batchelor Collection Ltd

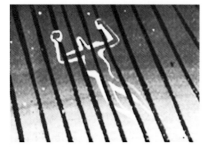

The Magic Canvas
© Halas & Batchelor Collection Ltd

A pattern was beginning to emerge. As far as the cinema was concerned the general public now wanted features, but a programme of feature production would have represented a massive investment. Significant investment in British animation has rarely been forthcoming, and in this case demand was being satisfied by American imports. It was far simpler to continue importing. Even in these early days, when cinemas were able to include short cartoons, and even after the Eady Levy was established in 1950 to channel a proportion of cinema ticket sales back into British production, the need for entertainment shorts was also largely satisfied by product from the US majors. By and large it was only the animated commercials on our cinema screens that were made in the UK, and this did indeed provide the only regular work for the few existing studios.

From the 1950s the British Film Institute was valiantly financing a small amount of experimental animation, notably two films - *A Short Vision* (1956) and *Animated Genesis* (1960) - by another Hungarian import, Peter Földes, and his English wife and collaborator, Joan. One entertainment feature was produced in the period, Halas & Batchelor's *Animal Farm* (1954), financed by the American Louis de Rochemont. Nowadays we know that the funding actually came from that great benefactor of the arts the CIA, whose campaign to promote Western democracy and discredit communism was obviously very lavishly funded[2]. But with those few exceptions it was plain that British animation had to survive on government or industrial information films and on commercials. Clients would only pay for films designed to sell something.

The television situation was no better where entertainment films were concerned, for TV schedules were already based on half-hour programmes, which did not leave much room for shorts and - like the cinema - television

Animal Farm
© Halas & Batchelor Collection Ltd

could purchase any it needed from the USA. Yet it was television that brought about a sudden proliferation of studios from 1954, just as the demand for industrial films started to decline. What saved British animation - and offered its greatest opportunity - was the advent of commercial television[3]. Halas & Batchelor was crucial at the period for it alone had established a studio large enough to train up the legions of young animators who would be required. The two London studios already existing in 1954 became ten or so by 1958. This was the period when two complementary elements entered the British animation scene, both of which were to invigorate it and typify it for the foreseeable future. They arrived in the persons of Bob Godfrey, who set up shop in Soho in 1954 as one quarter of Biographic Films; and the Canadian George Dunning, who was sent to London in 1956 to set up a branch of the American studio UPA. After it collapsed, he stayed on to found TV Cartoons.

Bob Godfrey is often classed among our exotic foreign imports - but in fact the Australian nationality he's sometimes credited with is illusory. He happened to be born there, but his (British) parents decided to return to the UK when he was 6 months old. So the 'Australian' raunchiness and irreverence are in fact London East End humour and this was a gift which would remain with British animation. It would be enhanced by the appearance on the scene of scriptwriter Stan Hayward in 1958. He was hired (by TV Cartoons, though later working with all the top studios) on the basis of having written for the popular 50s radio comedy series, *The Goon Show* - though he did not at that stage reveal that his *Goons* input had amounted to only a few lines, plus a title: *Seven Snowballs That Shook the World*[4]. As for Dunning, Richard Taylor characterised his contribution to the British scene as:
a sort of Yankee know-how which made us conscious of how comparatively amateur our methods were. The transatlantic acceptance of technology embodied in a man whose artistic capacity was unbounded. The pithiness and energy of the films TVC produced lit a rocket under the rest of us[5].
At this period another Canadian, this one something of an infant prodigy, Richard Williams, was associated firstly with Biographic, before joining fellow-countryman Dunning in the early days of TVC, and then setting up his own studio in the 1960s.

The injection of 'Yankee know-how' now brought the UK commercials industry up to US standards as regards craft and production processes; and the new input of quirky humour from Godfrey and Hayward and experimentation and artistry from Dunning and Williams made animation a far more attractive option. Given, additionally, that animated commercials are usually cheaper than live action (stars and locations eat up budgets), UK animation was suddenly irresistible to advertisers at home and abroad. In the UK about a quarter of TV commercials at the period were animated and British commercials took prizes around the world. Animators were not only earning well but were also having fun, for commercials production in those days was not so tightly controlled by the advertising agencies as it is today, so studios had a major input into ideas and gags. Thus, in the 1950s and 1960s, this pleasurable activity afforded its producers a financial cushion and allowed them to invest in their own, personal short films. Despite the Eady Levy, very few of these had any commercial success, but they did gain recognition for their directors (especially since international animation festivals began to proliferate from 1960).

Among the key works of the period were Richard Williams' *The Little Island* (1958); George Dunning's *The Flying Man* (1961, Annecy Grand Prix) and *The Apple*[6] (1962); John Halas's *Automania 2000* (1963, the UK's first-ever Oscar® nomination for animation); and Bob Godfrey's *Do It Yourself Cartoon Kit* (1961). This golden age continued until the late 1960s, and even into the early 1970s, with Richard Williams' *A Christmas Carol* (1971, financed by US television and an Oscar®-winner), George Dunning's *Damon the Mower* (1972) and Bob Godfrey's *Henry 9 'til 5*[6] (1970) and *Kama Sutra Rides Again*[6] (1972). The latter was the only short of the period to make any money, because Stanley Kubrick demanded that it be shown with *A Clockwork Orange*. During this period Halas & Batchelor was continuing its support of British animators, funding a good few personal shorts and thereby launching the careers of filmmakers such as Tony White, Paul Vester, Geoff Dunbar, Ginger Gibbons and Gillian Lacey.

There was even a second British animated feature. TV Cartoons was commissioned by King Features - which owned most of the famous American comics - to make *Yellow Submarine* (1968). This was an extraordinary enterprise, directed by Dunning and using the design talents of Heinz Edelman and a staff of 200 people at the peak of production. It was a critical triumph and remains an icon of Britain's 'swinging 60s'. The Queen, it seems, nominated it as her favourite film[7]. However, the production was apparently a fairly chaotic affair, the studio had badly miscalculated its costs and was almost ruined financially. And it did not do UK animation much good either, for advertisers, lacking in imagination, demanded only *Yellow Submarine* clones for a good few years and not everyone was willing to go down this route.

By the early 1970s times were getting harder, largely due to the global recession caused by the 1973 oil crisis, and commercials work was drying up. Miraculously, however, a few award-winning shorts were still appearing. Bob Godfrey's *Great* (1975) was the UK's first home-grown Oscar®-winner, and this half-hour documentary on the engineer Brunel was, unlike *A Christmas Carol*, financed in the UK, partly from the *Kama Sutra* profits. The 1970s also offered a couple of straws in the wind indicating that women animators might now be ready to play a more prominent role. Before this period women had been largely relegated to the mechanical work of tracing and painting or, if allowed into the animation area, simply 'inbetweening', ie filling in the intermediate stages of movement between key poses provided by the animators. There were of course some honourable exceptions, but they were few: Gillian Lacey found she was

The Apple
© TV Cartoons Ltd 1968, 2008

the only female guest at the Tours festival, where her Halas & Batchelor-funded film *Up* (1971) was screening. But this began to change in the mid-1970s. Alison de Vere managed to get funding from Wyatt Cattaneo, where she was employed making commercials, to make *Café Bar* (1975), which questioned sexual relations from the female point of view, while Thalma Goldman's self-funded *Stanley* (1979) explored female sexuality more graphically.

There was also some success in other branches of animation, notably Richard Williams' celebrated feature film credit titles and Bob Godfrey's *Roobarb* (1975), a very rare UK-produced animated series for TV. But notable short films were few and perhaps the recession was not the only problem. Writing in 1973 Ralph Stephenson surmised that possibly 'the success of *Yellow Submarine* has made shorts seem less of an achievement'[8]. He seemed to sense a waning of inspiration and determination among the short film stars of the 1960s. Stephenson also wondered whether 'new thought will come from schools and colleges, where film-making and film appreciation are increasingly finding a place in the curriculum - though not often, alas, animation'[9]. He was to be proved correct.

It seems there had been some animation quietly going on at the Royal College of Art - an exclusively postgraduate institution - since 1963, within the school of film and television. However, there had been no official teaching, just the use of a rostrum camera and as much exposure to different disciplines as students wanted. The late 60s and early 70s saw such diverse talents as Paul Vester, Vera Neubauer, the Quay brothers, Phil Mulloy and Anna Fodorova pass through the hut which housed the animation camera. 'We learned from one another,' says Vera Neubauer. 'It was a wonderful playground.'[10] In 1974 the National Film School[11] - also for postgraduates - opened its doors to the first animation students, Derek Hayes and Phil Austin. Again there was no regular animation teaching but a course covering all other filmmaking disciplines. Derek and Phil would be followed by David Anderson, Nick Park, Alison Snowden, David Fine, Tony Collingwood, Joan Ashworth and Mark Baker. Soon afterwards, the first full-time animation BA course was instituted at the West Surrey College of Art and Design[12], a development from the part-time course Bob Godfrey had run at the Guildford School of Art. Here there was tuition, notably from course leader Roger Noake and animation academic Irene Kotlarz. But early students remember it as pretty chaotic, and from that chaos arose the likes of Michael Dudok de Wit, Mark Baker (before graduating to the NFS) and pop promo stars Annabel Jankel and Rocky Morton.

All three centres, perhaps thanks to the laissez-faire set-up of the early days, produced some real individualists, many ahead of their time in the use of new and hybrid technologies. But they may equally have turned out a good few students with little idea of how to make an animated film - their careers are not recorded. Starting in around 1985, all three would clean up their act and initiate structured and comprehensive animation courses. The other notable undergraduate course of the pre-C4 era was the antithesis of the disorganised norms of the time. Set up at Liverpool Polytechnic in 1980 by eccentric modernist artist Ray Fields, it was run with military precision, though with an active disdain for the orthodoxies of the animation industry. Again, some maverick talents were nurtured, including Jonathan Hodgson, Susan Young, Stuart Hilton and Sarah Cox.

The Decision
© Vera Neubauer

It was in the late 1970s and early 80s that women animators really started to come into their own, seeming to be better placed to make genuinely innovative films than were their sisters in the live action sphere. Firstly, in live action, feature films are the be-all and end-all; and they demand enormous budgets and consequently masses of confidence and contacts - which it is hard for any newcomer to muster, let alone a woman, given our gender's former role assumptions. (Animator Candy Guard expresses this succinctly: 'A lot of women can't bear to be thought of as horrible, forceful, to appear bossy, while men don't give a shit.'[13]) Live action short films are often a means to an end, a help in getting feature film funding. But this is not usually the case in animation, where shorts are considered a fine genre in their own right. And they are far more attainable than features in terms of funding. Not only that: the kind of funding that is required is - in contrast to live action with its actors, large crews, locations and varied equipment - largely in the form of payment to the animator(s) for their very labour-intensive efforts. Women, having concentrated on innovative, auteurist work as students, sought to continue making such films, putting in most of the labour themselves, sometimes in home-based studios. In a perceptive *Sight and Sound* article, Jeanette Winterson called animation 'a safe place', which

can provide an artistic haven away from the demands of the cash register and outside the monolith of film production. [...] For women the combination of absolute control over their material and the financial capacity to make their project has resulted not in complacency but in experiment.[14]

But even low-budget filmmakers need a bit of funding, and at the time only public bodies such as the British Film Institute and the Arts Council were funding such personal work. Furthermore, this was an era when some funding bodies were highly politicised. As Jayne Pilling, who worked at the BFI at this period, concedes: 'We recognised that it was tough luck if you were a woman filmmaker who didn't happen to want to do a film about feminist issues.'[15] Vera Neubauer, for one, most certainly did want to, and was in the vanguard of the feminist onslaught, with two films, *Animation for Live Action* (1978) and *The Decision* (1981), both dealing with such issues and both funded by the BFI. Another crucial development in women's animation in this period was the founding, by Gillian Lacey in 1976, of the Leeds Animation Workshop, initially funded by the Yorkshire Arts Association, the Arts Council Community Arts scheme and various job creation schemes of the period. This all-woman group had an equally political but utterly practical orientation: their films were cartoony and designed to raise women's consciousness on matters close to their hearts, such as nurseries, the nuclear threat and health and safety at work.

Animation was now thriving in the UK, the only fly in the ointment being the scarcity of funding for personal shorts. Even the animated commercials industry, despite the recession of the early 1980s, was doing rather well. Jerry Hibbert, now perhaps the most successful in the field, was then just starting out, and perceived a distinct thrust by advertisers to 'advertise their way out of the recession'[16]. Their only concession to harder times was to move from high-cost live action advertising, using stars and exotic locations, to more economical animated spots. Another flourishing area was that of pop promos, a genre which was virtually invented in the UK, by the young generation of animation graduates. As well as Rocky Morton and Annabel Jankel, Matt Forrest, Felix Films and Speedy were also using mixed techniques, new technologies and rapid pacing.
In many ways it was these companies that dragged animation away from the perceived view that it was a medium solely for kids, and therefore kids' products, and made it a trendy medium that was under-explored.[17]

Furthermore, interest in animation was now fuelled by a succession of initiatives designed to bring it to the public and to foster communication between animators. The BFI was putting animated films into distribution and touring packages round the country, while in Cambridge the Animation Festival, which had expired after two distinguished editions under Dick Arnall's leadership in 1967 and 1968, was revived in 1979 by Antoinette Moses, providing an ideal forum for viewings, exhibitions and discussion events. Irene Kotlarz would take up the baton from 1985, moving the festival to Bristol in 1987 and Cardiff in 1992.

There was thus a growing enthusiasm for the art, a greater sophistication and appreciation of its potential and a growing number of graduates qualifying. The pool of talented British animators had reached critical mass. But these young animators had ambitions beyond that of a diet of commercials and pop promos only. In 1979, in a crucial if tiny first move into adult animation for television, BBC Bristol had produced a series entitled *Animated Conversations* (of which more later); but this low-budget series was not followed up at the time. The BFI and Arts Council remained the targets of the majority of innovative proposals being floated but their budgets were unable to satisfy the burgeoning demand. A new source of funding was needed, and badly. That source of funding was liable to reap significant rewards in terms of prestige, but probably not commercially. As luck would have it, a television channel with a strict remit not to gauge its success in commercial terms was about to be born in the UK.

3 The new channel

For years there had been discussions about the possible creation of a new TV channel. That then-precious commodity, wavelength spectrum, would stretch to one more, and it had been noted that the advent of BBC2 had worked well to complement the more popular programming on BBC1. Thus many felt that a fourth channel, were it to be created, should stand in a similar relationship to the ITV network of commercial companies and be run by it. A succession of lobby groups were formed by independent producers from the early 1970s onwards, their main aim being to oppose this assumption.[18] One of the first formulations of the unique structure under which the channel would actually be set up almost ten years later came from Anthony Smith, then director of the British Film Institute but previously working in broadcasting. In a 1972 article in *The Guardian*, he proposed a National Television Foundation to act as an 'electronic publishing house'.[19] The existing channels, he was sure, had become too predictable, an inevitable consequence of the same, limited, number of TV executives deciding what the public should see and originating programmes in-house. He wanted a channel which could operate like a publishing house, open to the ideas of a multiplicity of different voices and, once programme ideas had been accepted, finance their originators to make the programmes themselves, as independent production companies. Although this precise proposal foundered due to weaknesses in its suggested funding provision, its basic demands as regards programming struck a chord with many, not least the future new channel's future chief executive Jeremy Isaacs:

Why need transmission schedules be fixed and repetitive? Why need programme durations conform to regular slot lengths? Why could no programme express a point of view? Why should all broadcasting aim at an audience of millions, and not reach out to small self-selecting audiences? Why, above all, if we were to extend the volume of British broadcasting, should we be offered more of the same?[20]

The Annan committee tried to crack the problem in 1974 but its solution to the funding issue was also inadequate. The funding formula which was eventually accepted and would function well for many years was actually the brainchild of a Conservative MP, the then shadow home secretary William Whitelaw, without whose enlightened thinking and strong conviction the new channel would certainly not have prospered. The channel should, Whitelaw said, be regulated by the Independent Broadcasting Authority (the government body which already regulated the ITV) and funded by the ITV. In May 1979 the Conservatives, under Margaret Thatcher, came to power, her cabinet an interesting mix of right- and relatively left-wingers. The discussions about the fourth channel rumbled on.

That same year Jeremy Isaacs was invited to give the annual McTaggart Memorial Lecture at the Edinburgh Television Festival on the subject of 'TV in the Eighties'. His outline for the most desirable format for the fourth channel was detailed and impassioned, and made the point that even if the new channel was to be regulated by the IBA and funded by the ITV, 'to have a different flavour it needs a different chef'[21]. It is hardly surprising, then, that it later came to be referred to as his 'McTaggart Memorial Job Application'[22].

The structures began to fall into place. The IBA would set up a non-profit-making company to run the new channel, with funding from the ITV companies, the latter taking on the job of selling Channel 4's advertising and retaining the income. This would be aggregated with the advertising income of the ITV companies themselves, and a percentage of the net total paid over to cover Channel 4's running costs. The exact proportion - in the early years at least – was to be decided by the IBA on an annual basis. This way, C4 could concentrate on producing innovative programming with no fear of being led downmarket by the need to appeal to advertisers. The IBA itself would regulate the channel and see that its schedule complemented that of ITV.

William Whitelaw's 1980 Broadcasting Act incorporated the famous, and wonderfully vague, remit which was to produce some extraordinarily innovative television over the years and which, as an unintended side-effect, would put animation on a sure footing in the new channel. Rather than specifying minimum hours per week of specific programme areas it instead required the IBA to ensure that 'a suitable proportion of the programmes was of an educational nature', that the schedule would contain 'a suitable proportion of matter calculated to appeal to tastes and interests not generally catered for by ITV' and that it must 'encourage innovation and experiment in the form and content of programmes.'[23] And that was all.

Jeremy Isaacs became chief executive on 1 January 1981 and the Channel was to launch on 2 November 1982. As Rod Stoneman points out in a *Screen* article of 1992[24], what was being launched in 1982 was, thanks to its long gestation period, actually the late fruit of 1960s radicalism. But the 1980s world into which it was born - into an intimate relationship with ITV and under a Thatcher government - was a very different one. So much so that the chosen chief executive came from a traditional TV, in fact ITV, background and his reaction, when asked at the Edinburgh festival how different his model for Channel 4 would be, was: 'different, but not that different'. It was not an answer to please the radicals. Isaacs enlarges on it in his memoir of the Channel's early days, *Storm Over 4*[25]:

An artist - writing, painting, making music - can be, can afford to be utterly true to the singularity of his or her vision, almost irrespective, at least for a time, of whether that particularity is communicated to others or not. Such an artist is not dependent on reaching audiences, except to pay the bills. Broadcasting, though

Jeremy Isaacs
Photo Matt Prince

it can certainly be a medium for artistic expression, is not a solitary art. If the Channel were to carry innovative work, and that was its explicit purpose, it must somehow find audiences for that work, either by the work itself reaching out to viewers or because other more familiar work the Channel broadcast brought in those audiences and dared them to expose themselves also to the shock of the new. [...] To offer nothing familiar, to house only experiment, would be a brave way to die.[26]

One manifestation of the diversity of voices Isaacs required was his selection of commissioning editors and acquisitions team. Determined to avoid the old brand of executive, bound up in traditional TV convention, he placed an extraordinary job advertisement:
DO YOU KNOW A GOOD IDEA WHEN YOU SEE ONE?
Television production experience may be an advantage but is not essential. Whether your passion is angling or cooking, fringe theatre, rock, politics, philosophy or religion, if you believe you can spot a good idea and help others realise it on the screen, we are looking for commissioning editors, and would like to hear from you.[27]

There were six thousand replies. While not the most focused means of recruitment, this ad certainly proclaimed a different approach. In the end about half the initial commissioning body did come from television but the others did not. Liz Forgan (current affairs) had been editing *The Guardian*'s women's page and was offered the job after interviewing Isaacs for her paper; Naomi Sargant (education) came from the Open University; Andy Park (music) from radio; Paul Madden (with initially an archival function) from the British Film Institute's television archive; Michael Kustow (arts) from the Institute of Contemporary Arts; Alan Fountain (independent cinema and community) had been a member of the Independent Filmmakers' Association and Derek Hill (independent film acquisitions) ran his own film distribution company. All would contribute to the freshness of the new channel's voice, though few could be considered dyed-in-the-wool radicals. Alan Fountain, who had been vocal in lobbying for the new channel to be independent of ITV, was probably the most politically committed and his early contribution of highly political programming would be an extraordinary departure for television. His department would also, later on, commission a unique slate of avant-garde film and video art.

Animation, being not a subject area but a technical approach, did not appear in anyone's job description. Furthermore, one could imagine good reasons why animation should not be actively sought, given that several categories of animation simply work best for the viewer in short formats. Even in those days, this would have constituted a disincentive to TV channels, for the half-hour grid was already king. Yet Jeremy Isaacs 'was dogmatic that we would not be controlled by slot lengths and everything would not come out of the same sized can'.[28] He was initially determined to challenge the supremacy of the half-hour:

'It's too short for any discussion, for most current affairs and a lot of comedy. We'll have many more programmes in 45-minute slots.'[29] In the event, though, it proved hard to pursue that aim too rigorously, since the arrangement with ITV was for complementary scheduling, ie providing at least two common junctions per evening where viewers could switch between the two channels without missing bits of programmes. But nevertheless a good few short slots were created by this policy.

The other trait which made the Channel potentially hospitable to animation was the Broadcasting Act's requirement that it should provide for 'tastes and interests not generally catered for by ITV', which certainly implied that large audiences were not the be-all and end-all. This was enthusiastically endorsed by Jeremy Isaacs and even fashioned into a sales pitch to advertisers. We *could*, of course, target mass audiences - so the pitch went - but these were easily reachable already via ITV. We would instead mainly be targeting groups not catered for elsewhere and thus unreachable by advertisers - ethnic minorities, gays and lesbians, disabled people, and even young adults and women in general were in those days badly served by television, as were fans of all manner of exotic sports. And animation of course. None of these groups would, it was thought, initially translate into high viewing figures, but the Channel's rates for air-time sales to advertisers would be correspondingly reasonable. A cost-effective way to reach the previously unreachable. What was more, according to this ingenious pitch, 'we will not be a minority channel, but a mass television channel which will be selected at some time or other by around 80 per cent of viewers during the course of any one week'.[30]

The process of launching a new channel, in new premises, would be hard at the best of times. But launching a new channel which also aspired to such different programming values, and was partly manned by TV virgins, made things harder. Great excitement was generated both among the staff - Paul Madden, future commissioning editor for animation, would dye a multicoloured '4' logo on to the back of his head as the launch neared - and among the independent production community. According to Isaacs:
Nowhere was one safe from the programme proposal. I was accosted twice one afternoon by men with scripts between Warren Street and Tottenham Court Road, and followed by another, treatment at the ready, into the urinals at Brompton Road.[31]

Somehow the programmes would come together and the Channel would launch at 4.45pm on Tuesday 2 November. The event was not a conspicuous success. Due to a dispute over repeat fees between the Institute of Practitioners in Advertising and the actors' union, Equity, there were no commercials where they were supposed to be, the gaps being graced by nothing more than a title card reading 'Next programme follows shortly'. A good few of the programmes were a bit boring, if well-intentioned, and some a touch amateurish. Press reviews were dreadful and the headline writers had a field day. Initial verdicts of 'Channel Bore' and 'Channel Snore' only gave way at the end of the first week to 'Channel Swore' and 'Channel Four Letter Word', after the Burt Reynolds American football film *Semi-Tough* was inadvertently purchased without anyone screening it first, and scheduled without warning at 9pm on Sunday, treating viewers to a non-stop stream of locker-room expletives.[32]

Walter
© ITV plc

Yet most of those early programmes were innovative, thought-provoking and exactly what the remit ordered - once a few rough edges were smoothed down. And some were truly groundbreaking, auguring extremely well for the future. This book is not the place to go into non-animation programming in detail, but we can get a general flavour from a few examples from the first weeks of transmission. *Walter* was a brave C4-commissioned film for the opening night programme, directed by Stephen Frears and starring Ian McKellen as a young man with learning disabilities. *Five Go Mad in Dorset*, also on the opening night, was an extreme parody of the Enid Blyton children's books and caused controversy by an outrageous portrayal of the racist and right-wing views pervading England in Blyton's time. It also helped launch the comedy careers of Dawn French and Jennifer Saunders. *The Animals Film* (on the third night of transmission) was a shocking exposé of the suffering of animals in the interests of profit in factory-farming and pharmaceuticals. Dickens' *Nicholas Nickleby*, adapted as a 9-hour Royal Shakespeare Company production, was considered a theatrical landmark - so Channel 4 re-staged it for television and did not flinch from liberating a 9-hour slab of the schedule for the show. I do not know much about the education department's offering, *Quilts in Women's Lives*, save that it portrays a group of American women who are ace quilt-makers, and that no other channel would have risked such a programme or such a title.

Critics and audiences gradually warmed to the Channel - it was mainly feature writers who made such a meal of the odd problems the infant network was encountering. The advertisers and even ITV would come to find that the Channel worked for them too. C4-generated advertising revenue would increase to such an extent over the years that the ITV companies, far from subsidising their junior partner, would end up making a good profit from its advertising. This situation was only to be remedied when, on the expiry of the 1980 Broadcasting Act, Isaacs' successor Michael Grade negotiated a beneficial new deal for the Channel whereby it would sell its own advertising.

However, this is long into the future. For the moment, let us return to 1981. The Channel Four Television Company has just been created. Neither in Jeremy Isaacs' McTaggart lecture, nor in his actual job interview, nor by his choice of commissioning editors, nor anywhere up to page 58 of *Storm Over 4* has animation as yet been mentioned.

4 Uncharted territory

Paul Madden at Channel 4
Photo Tim Roney

The new channel had been set up with a commissioning body designed to generate the kinds of programmes for which there was a perceived need. The commissioning editors' titles covered specific subject areas. There was, understandably, no commissioning editor for animation, but why should there be, given the varied subject areas in which animation could be deployed? Animation proposals were to be sent in to whichever of the CEs handled the relevant area, be it comedy, drama, education, factual or arts. Yet animation is different from live action, in almost every way (budget, production schedule, aesthetic considerations, audience expectations…). One can imagine non-specialist commissioning editors feeling nervous of such an unfamiliar area with its concomitant challenges, and often-marginalised animators feeling diffident about submitting their ideas. And yet the proposals did start coming in, and amazingly (as it would seem now) the commissioning editors did start commissioning them. After a short while, animation was added to the many duties of an inspired generalist, Paul Madden, though other editors continued to commission occasional films up to 1990.

Yet it is perhaps not so surprising after all that this particular team of commissioning editors was prepared to commission work in this foreign area. Risk-taking was in the C4 air at that period, budgets were not such a problem (and though the cost per minute of animation is high, the products were mainly of short duration), and the schedule was flexible enough to accommodate one-off programmes, even of non-standard lengths. What is perhaps initially more surprising is that British animators somehow just happened to hear about the new channel, find out what its policies were, research the programme areas and send in proposals. It may sound uncharitable, but to me one of the most endearing traits of animators is that many of them are without commercial ambition, political nous or much in the way of organisational skills. This phenomenon needed a bit of research.

It turns out that behind the scenes there was a great deal going on to promote the cause of animation within the Channel and, outside, to alert animators to the new opportunities. Not that there was any actual opposition to it in the higher echelons of the Channel. Jeremy Isaacs was very much aware that television was - and is - a visual medium, yet at the time 'there were very few programmes on screens anywhere whose essence was to give visual pleasure or convey ideas in a visual way'[33]. Hence the Channel's instant espousal of *film*, as a refreshing change from studio-bound TV style. He was certainly very keen on art, especially abstract art. Also, given that he was acquiring and, initially, commissioning various features, dramas and documentaries of non-standard lengths, he did have a need for short fillers, a role typically filled by animation. But that did not amount to a policy to seek out and commission major new animation.

One of animation's behind-the-scenes benefactors was Derek Hill, one of the Channel's two film purchasers in the early days. One prong of his attack - and one which would hugely influence Isaacs - was his insistence on the importance of acknowledging a broad film culture. Film was not just Hollywood: it was world cinema, silent film, experimental film and, of course, animated film. His second was a more specific promotion of animation. His recommendations for purchase[34] were extremely adventurous and even spilled over into programming suggestions (none of which materialised though). He insisted on paying licence fees which were way above the pittances which television had previously paid for the despised 'fillers'. In his notes of 8 January 1982 we find: *I urge an annual round-up of the best international animation, and separate national histories of the past all using the expertise of animation enthusiasts and, above all, involving animators themselves. Animation has been abominably abused by television. Let's do it right.*
This did not happen either, or not until many years later, but it nevertheless contributed to an awareness and very gradual acceptance of animation within the channel.

Derek Hill was also behind a campaign involving Eileen Baldwin (then teaching animation at Croydon College of Art) and David Curtis (a specialist in artists' film and video, who was to become the moving force behind animation funding by the Arts Council). These two visited Jeremy Isaacs in the Brompton Road office and harangued him about the importance of animation in our culture and - briefed by Derek about the structure of the new channel - demanded a commissioning editor for animation. Eileen was not greatly mollified to learn that Isaacs had decided to give this responsibility to the 'commissioning editor for odds and sods'[35], Paul Madden, whose business card already listed archive programming, single documentaries, media and community. She admits that she 'went berserk' at what she saw as a typical British response to a great art form[36]. Jeremy Isaacs responds well to passion and still remembers the Baldwin onslaught fondly - but, understandably, he could see no justification for making animation, which would take up a tiny proportion of the air-time, a full-time job. Subsequent meetings were arranged and various schemes proposed, though all bit the dust. What did happen was a questionnaire to the animation community asking them what they expected of the new channel. No one can remember the results, still less any action resulting, but the very sending of the questionnaire must have alerted animators to the new possibilities.

Meanwhile, C4's channel controller Paul Bonner was being subjected to similarly aggressive lobbying on the animation front. This time Bob Godfrey was the aggressor - that purveyor of saucy (but not only saucy) cartoons has

Derek Hill was a long-standing supporter of the animation community. Seen here supporting the 1972 Zagreb Animation Festival picnic.
Photo Clare Kitson

always been a very effective spokesman for the animation community - and his mission was to get Isaacs and Bonner to attend the Cambridge Animation Festival that September (1981) and to announce the Channel's intentions to this, often marginalised, group. Not only did Isaacs and Bonner indeed attend the festival; they also placed a full-page ad in the catalogue wishing the festival luck and announcing that 'The best of British animation will appear on Channel 4'. Not, at this stage, 'will be commissioned by Channel 4', but it was a start. Furthermore, as a result of this first contact, festival director Antoinette Moses managed to negotiate sponsorship of £20,000 from the Channel, which was double the festival's original budget.

Down and Out
© BBC MCMLXXVII

Perhaps the most historically important incident at Cambridge that year, though, was a chance meeting in Clive Sinclair's rose garden. The millionaire inventor had been persuaded to host a festival party in his garden; a clutch of animators had been invited as had, of course, Isaacs and Bonner. Derek Hayes[37] was one of a group of tongue-tied young animators daring each other to approach the great man and finally pushing David Sproxton forward, he being the only one they considered to have the gift of the gab. But they kicked themselves at the sight of Isaacs and Sproxton wending their way, deep in conversation, among the roses for what seemed to them like hours. Isaacs was apparently enquiring about the lifestyle of a freelance animation producer, and asked David for a showreel.

Aardman Holdings' net profit for 2006 was very nearly £6 million[38], but in 1981 David Sproxton and Peter Lord were two of the 'cheap animators'[39] who had been recruited by Colin Thomas for his groundbreaking 1979 BBC series, *Animated Conversations*. A documentary producer, Thomas had wanted to experiment with giving animated visuals to real-life conversations. Another 'cheap animator', Bill Mather, had made a pilot using his son's audition for the St Mary Redcliffe church choir. There were five films in the final series, but it was the plasticine characters in Sproxton and Lord's films, *Confessions of a Foyer Girl* (usherettes talking about boys) and, especially, *Down and Out* (a confused old man trying to get a meal out of a charitable institution) that fired Jeremy Isaacs' imagination. Isaacs, not very well versed in the painstaking processes of stop-motion production, excitedly asked for 'ten of those please for our first week of transmission'[40]. Given that the first week of transmission was, at that stage, only eight or nine months away, David and Peter were slightly more cautious and offered him 'five now and the rest later'. In fact, the five *Conversation Pieces* were delivered a year late and ended up gracing the channel's celebratory first anniversary week. ('The rest' became the *Lip Synch* series, including *Creature Comforts*, which did not arrive until 1989.) The pair have always considered this Channel 4 commission one of the major lucky breaks of their career. The Channel 4 budget formula meant that the production crew would always get paid for their work (originally at union rates) and in addition a mark-up would be added, a sum specifically intended to give the studio a bit of paid time to think about their next project. The difference between C4 and normal practice at other networks was, in David Sproxton's words, that 'Channel 4 wanted us to survive'[41]. Not only did they get better paid for the *Conversation Pieces* than they had for anything previously: the prominent slotting, stripped across a whole week at 9pm, got them noticed by a host of advertisers, all anxious to get hold of Aardman-style, crudely executed but vibrantly alive characters for their own products. The studio was made.

While Aardman had made the first contact via Jeremy Isaacs, others were taking different routes. Glasgow-based animator Lesley Keen somehow found her way to Naomi Sargant's education department with her proposal for *Taking a Line for a Walk* (completed 1983). This 12-minute work, relating Paul Klee's famous dictum to his actual working practice and his theories about colour and movement, was an early festival success and was given tremendous prominence in the Channel's schedule, broadcast at 8pm on a Thursday, followed by a half-hour documentary on how the animation was created and then by a repeat of the film ('because it was very dense and visually exciting'[42]). Isaacs was apparently bowled over by the film and its presentation, to such an extent that Lesley Keen's next film, *Orpheus and Euridice*, was presented in the same way, with a documentary about various portrayals of the Orpheus myth between two screenings of the film.

But among the various (non-animation) areas of the Channel it was David Rose's fiction department which commissioned the most animation in the early days. This is the route taken by producer Keith Griffiths. He is a rare exception in the animation world: a highly professional producer, tenacious builder of co-production partnerships and canny political strategist. Furthermore, well versed in a wide variety of genres, live action as well as animation, he has never accepted and certainly never personally experienced the marginalisation which others in the animation world have perceived: he has always seen animation as simply a part of the independent, experimental filmmaking culture in which he is involved. He is the regular producer of the films of Jan Švankmajer and the Quay brothers. At the time that Channel 4 was set up the latter, identical twins from Philadelphia who had studied illustration at the Royal College of Art, had made some experimental films with the support of the BFI and the Arts Council. The drama department's script associate Walter Donohue had heard about them and invited Keith in to discuss a possible project. In accordance with Isaacs' predilection for film as opposed to studio-bound TV programmes, David Rose's department was charged with commissioning feature films as well as drama series, and Film on Four would of course contribute to, if not single-handedly bring about, a renaissance of British cinema over the next decade. According to Paul Bonner[43], it was at one stage the Channel's intention to produce or co-produce one animated feature a year. This policy would not be long upheld, for all sorts of practical reasons, and in fact only two were ever supported by the Channel. But this, it seems, was the background to Keith's visit to the Brompton Road office while the Channel was 'still in five packing cases' to meet Rose, Donohue and money man Colin Leventhal.

At that stage, however, the twins did not feel confident enough to embark on a feature, having only four short films to their credit, all produced in their flat with a 16mm Bolex camera. In fact, they would perhaps not ever have thought of graduating to feature films, given the poetic nature of their shorts, their low-tech methods and their habit of working alone (as identical twins they possess a telepathy which makes communication far simpler than between a whole team) if the prescient Griffiths had not sensed future problems for animated shorts on TV. Anyway, for now they proposed two 25-minute films, one a tribute to Janáček and one to Stravinsky. Perhaps because of Jeremy Isaacs' background in documentary and his love of classical music, especially opera, these proposals were accepted and the films were completed and transmitted in 1983.[44] The Quays' magisterial *Street of Crocodiles* (1986) would also result from a fiction department initiative, but as part of a co-production formula with the British Film Institute.

Two other early callers on the drama department were recent National Film School graduates Derek Hayes and Phil Austin, who had also been among Colin Thomas's 'cheap animators' on the BBC's *Animated Conversations*. Hayes and Austin were in many ways typical of the new generation of British animators, 'who had expectations and who had style'[45]. Their company Animation City was, as Roger Noake points out in his obituary to Phil Austin, who tragically died in January 1990, 'born out of that great release of energy which was punk'[46]. Filming, it seems, had stalled on the Sex Pistols' film *The Great Rock 'n' Roll Swindle*, and since Sid Vicious was in jail at the time there seemed little chance of completing it with the planned documentary footage. So Animation City was called into existence to fill the gaps and finally 'over a third of the film was animation and the resulting onslaught of images and ideas signalled that happy conjunction of animation and music, of fantasy and reality that marked the new animation'[47]. The pair consolidated their reputation with a series of classic commercials and music promos. Even so, being animators, they were initially convinced that the new channel could not possibly be interested in them, until they were persuaded by other Film School alumni, who had already been commissioned, that it was in fact interested in some pretty weird things and they could very well fit in. Given that one of these alumni knew someone who knew David Rose… they fetched up in the fiction department. It was Walter Donohue who looked after them and discussed several ideas with them before steering them towards the science fantasy genre and *Skywhales* (1983), another early festival success for the Channel. It was allocated a prime transmission slot on Christmas Day 1983 plus - such was the semi-chaos that reigned in the Channel's early days - an unexpected 'preview' of about half the film, preceding *Conversation Pieces* in the first anniversary week. (*Brookside*, it

Skywhales

seemed, had come in under length and for some reason it was thought that half of *Skywhales* would be just the job to fill the gap.) The directors were not best pleased. However, they did later return to the Channel with their proposal for *The Victor* (1985), a comic-strip style, extraordinarily prescient critique of past and potential abuse by an army of its soldiers.

Producer John Coates was also early on the scene. He had a long history on the business side of cinema (with the Rank Organisation) and television (with Associated Rediffusion) before setting up TVC with George Dunning in 1957. In 1980, still bearing the scars of the *Yellow Submarine* debacle and still living off TV commercials, he was bitterly critical of British television of the period, which swamped our screens with kids' cartoons from the USA and almost never gave UK studios a chance (and when the BBC did, exceptionally, commission *Roobarb* from Bob Godfrey, 'he was paid peanuts'[48]). But for the kinds of things John wanted to do you needed rather a lot of money. So, out of desperation, and for the first time in his life, he read a White Paper, the White Paper which would be enacted the following year, thereby creating Channel 4.

As it happened, on his desk at the same time as the White Paper, but several strata below (the desk is always buried under a precarious mountain of papers and books) was Raymond Briggs' book, *The Snowman*. Animator Jim Duffy, who by this time had long since returned to his native America, had given it to John almost a year earlier, telling him it would work wonderfully in animation and hinting that he himself would like to direct it. Miraculously - and partly because John had taken out an option on it which was about to expire - the book now emerged from the pile and was read in conjunction with the White Paper. Luckily, the latter gave no detail as to the future channel's programming areas, so he was blissfully unaware that the first chief executive would decree that children, adequately catered for on the other channels, would have no department at C4 to service their needs. What it did make plain was that innovation would be the order of the day. John chose to interpret 'innovation' commercially rather than aesthetically: other UK channels did not commission animation very much at all, let alone high quality, expensive work and least of all one-off programmes as, according to the received wisdom, these cannot make money. (He laughed merrily as he told me this. Including merchandising, *The Snowman* has netted Snowman Enterprises over £10 million to date.) Anyway, if he could get hold of a large enough budget to emulate the pencil-rendered technique of Briggs' images, and if he could crack the technique needed to achieve it, the look of the film would also be pretty innovative.

So he made an 8-minute animatic[49], sent it in to the channel and it was duly allocated to the recently-created animation editor, Paul Madden. The animatic - which already had, as its soundtrack, a miniature version of Howard Blake's memorable score - was magical. It helped, of course, that the new animation supremo was already a fan of both Raymond Briggs and of TVC's *Yellow Submarine*. Despite initial concerns from Jeremy Isaacs over the budget, the commission (Paul's first) went ahead and *The Snowman* graced Channel 4's first Christmas schedule. As it would every Christmas schedule except one, right up to the present day.

And there was yet another department of the Channel where, during this pre-launch period, minds were concentrated on animation; and this was the department most crucial in dictating Channel 4's image. The presentation department was responsible for everything that appeared on screen between programmes: the trailers, of course, but more importantly those little idents which would provide the clearest indication of the Channel's personality. It seemed to augur well for the future of animation on C4 that channel controller Paul Bonner had, in the summer of 1981, approached various graphic design companies, large and small, soliciting their proposals for a contemporary-looking animated visual identity for the future channel. Two proposals made it through to the final round, one by a long-established brand consultancy and the other by young designer Martin Lambie-Nairn. The latter's proposal was a multicoloured, computer-generated, three-dimensional figure 4 splitting into its individual parts, which then rotated before returning to form part of the whole. It was a bold and simple representation of the Channel's policy of seeking new voices and making them part of a whole, and the idea was much liked by the

Channel 4 ident, 1982

Channel. But producing this animated ident was not so simple. Tony Pritchett, one of the UK's computer animation pioneers, produced the basic, wire-frame animation of the desired sequence, but UK technology was at that time not able to put a solid surface on to this skeleton to a sophisticated standard, with the reflective highlights required by the design, so the rendering had to be done in Los Angeles. It was completed just one week before the new Channel went on air on 2 November 1982. As Bob Swain observed in a publication on computer animation later produced by Channel 4:

These days it is hard to appreciate the impact of such a logo. But just remember that, at that time, the BBC's own spinning globe was just that - a globe constantly spinning round in front of a camera in a room deep inside Television Centre. Most ITV companies used static cards or crude animated graphics.[50]

The logo was a major success in branding the Channel, which, as Paul Bonner points out, from that time came to be more usually referred to as 'Channel 4', even though its name was, and remains, 'Channel Four'. It also made Lambie-Nairn's career: he went on to design similarly characterful logos for other major companies, notable among them the BBC, whose mischievous BBC2 idents seemed to mark a renaissance for that channel. It also changed the face of the whole ITV network, which realised that, as it was funding Channel 4, it had better try to emulate the freshness of the young channel's approach - with the result that within a few years computer-animated logos were everywhere. The fresh idea became stale. Channel 4 would stay ahead of the game for a while, with its animated logo being wittily adapted as stings for various different programming strands, but would eventually, in 1996, bow to the inevitable and replace its old multicoloured 4.

On 2 November 1982, however, Channel 4 had just managed to brand itself not only the channel of the many voices, not only the channel of the latest technology but also the channel of animation.

5   Animation gains a foothold

Despite Eileen Baldwin's fury at animation being given to someone with no previous experience in the field, Paul Madden in fact did a superb job, in difficult circumstances. Paul had previously headed up the television section of the British Film Institute's National Film Archive and in 1981 was dividing his time between freelance writing on television issues and a consultancy for the BFI. Thanks to his all-round knowledge of television and especially archive material, he was one of the people Jeremy Isaacs phoned when recruiting for the new channel. At first his role was limited to programming seasons of archive work. But Isaacs was determined not to allow the Channel to grow into an impersonal bureaucracy as other broadcasters had and so, as the volume of proposals increased, instead of hiring new commissioning editors he split up the already-allocated job areas which were proving too unwieldy for the incumbents - and handed two of these to Paul Madden. He inherited a part of single documentaries from Liz Forgan and began working with Alan Fountain on community issues. Bear in mind that all these areas were generating a huge quantity of proposals and he had only half a secretary in the way of help. Then, some time in late 1981 or early 1982, he was also given animation. Animation commissioning, that is. Animation acquisitions were by this time no longer handled by Derek Hill but by Richard Evans, who had been recruited by the light entertainment department. Madden's innovative commissions and Evans' fillers would somehow never manage to gel: the Channel was thus denying itself a valuable programming opportunity.

Given that single documentaries took up the majority of Paul's budget and time, and that he had no previous experience of animation, and given that he had considerable flexibility to move money between his various budget heads, it seems little short of miraculous that such a plentiful, varied and sometimes downright outlandish crop of animation programmes was commissioned. People new to animation often retreat along well-trodden paths - Paul on the contrary revelled in some extremely unorthodox ideas, encouraged by Jeremy Isaacs, who granted his commissioning editors considerable freedom. In those early days, and indeed under Isaacs' successor, Michael Grade, the 'right to fail' - in fact, the need to fail from time to time - was consistently stressed. It was recognised that the most innovative ideas are always going to be high-risk. Some will succeed triumphantly; others will fail; and you are unlikely to get much that is mediocre. A further bonus was Isaacs' devotion to one-off programmes as opposed to series and his insistence that the schedule should not be a strait-jacket. Non-standard lengths must be accepted and the schedulers must manage to make up a schedule with whatever strange products and odd running times the commissioning body handed them.

Dreamless Sleep
Photo David Anderson

Yet Isaacs' schedule was of course a mixture and from the very beginning he had required a proportion of regular programmes - soaps, quiz programmes, comedy series - to satisfy a certain strand among viewers and, of course, to keep the ratings reasonable. This was important for the advertisers and for ITV, which was selling the Channel's airtime and paying its running costs. Animation was never seen as capable of delivering large audiences, which was actually an error of judgement - as has since been demonstrated by various US series, notably *The Simpsons* - but at least it meant that the commissioning editor was free to commission according to criteria of quality and originality without being pressured to produce ratings-focused work.

One particularly striking group of films Paul commissioned - certainly no turn-on for mass audiences - was the *Sweet Disaster* series proposed by a versatile Bristol-based producer/director, David Hopkins. This was a series of five reflections on nuclear war, each one made by a different Bristol animator - of which, since Aardman's early success, there were a growing number. David Sproxton and Peter Lord's *Babylon* (1984) was an extraordinarily ambitious work, using no fewer than fifty plasticine puppets to recreate an arms-dealers' convention. Another in the series portrayed the home life of US politicians with their fingers on the nuclear button, another focused on the clichés of political speechwriters, another on a lone post-holocaust survivor. But the most memorable of this group was David Anderson's *Dreamless Sleep* (1986), a mixed-media, wordless evocation of the timeless moment before the bomb goes off. Innovative techniques added to the atmosphere, with puppets made of translucent wax and an agitated natural world rendered grainy by a complex, multi-stage process. It took a good few prizes including, fittingly, the 1987 Hiroshima festival Peace Prize.

A similarly brave choice, and one not calculated to achieve high ratings, was *When the Wind Blows* (1986) which, unexpectedly, TVC now proposed to Paul to follow *The Snowman*. Another, very different Raymond Briggs best-seller, it was the tale of a simple couple who put their faith in 'the authorities' and their futile safety instructions during and after a nuclear attack. A feature film, very much of its time (Chernobyl and the breakdown of arms limitation talks at Reykjavik had happened between the book being written and the film being released), it was well received by the critics but - probably thanks to its uncompromising subject matter - failed to recoup its budget.

At this period, in the early to mid 80s, interesting animation projects were still originating in departments other than animation. The youth department's contribution to the Channel's animation was extremely lively, though its first endeavour, in 1984, gave rise to an almighty row and the films were never transmitted. These were two commentaries on Thatcher's Britain by *Guardian* cartoonist Steve Bell, which were commissioned for the summer period when Friday evening youth music show *The Tube* was off the air. *Beaks to*

Beaks to the Grindstone

the Grindstone was about youth unemployment (the youths being played by Bell's trademark penguins) and *The Journalist's Tale* about cynical Fleet Street newspaper tycoons and the role of the National Union of Journalists in defending employees. Both were produced by the Trade Union Resource Centre, which had also raised 20 per cent of the funding, the rest coming from Channel 4. When I arrived at the Channel in 1989 I was told that the films had not been transmitted because they were not good enough. This struck me as strange because I had seen these films, and it was obvious that they actually had quite a lot going for them. They were very entertaining - especially *Beaks to the Grindstone* - and they reflected the mood of a large swathe of the population. They were, after all, commissioned by John Cummins, who had got the youth editor's job at the improbable age of 25 and had, according to Paul Bonner, 'an innate understanding of the language of young people, their aspirations, their aesthetics'[51]. Given that Steve Bell was already a big name, it was clear that these films would have gone down a treat in that *Tube* slot. They were, of course, not subtle. In fact they were undisguised anti-Thatcher propaganda - but surely nothing else could have been expected from a Steve Bell and Trade Union Resource Centre commission.

I was not alone in suspecting that political influence had been brought to bear, for the Channel was undoubtedly walking a political tightrope throughout the Isaacs period. It was, basically, brought into being by a Thatcher government which, since winning a second general election in 1983, had now moved further to the right. Indeed one or two C4 board members were staunch Conservatives. Most of those submitting programme proposals, on the other hand, were of a different persuasion. Jeremy Isaacs now cheerfully concedes that censorship did happen at the Channel and confirms that he personally does not like Bell's cartoons.[52] But he strongly encouraged me to investigate this incident. He himself did not remember it but suggested that Liz Forgan or Paul Bonner might. I set off in search of government pressure and a boardroom battle. But Forgan and Bonner did not remember any such thing - or indeed the films at all - and the latter, who had scoured the minutes of Board meetings fairly recently for his history of the Channel[53], is fairly certain the matter never even got as far as the board. Steve Bell, however, has the incident 'vividly implanted in my brain'[54]. Isaacs himself had, apparently, told Bell at the 1985 Cambridge Festival that he did not want a situation where the militant left could buy airtime, referring to the 20 per cent funding from TURC.

The whole debacle begins to look like a major misunderstanding, possibly not helped by the three somewhat intransigent personalities involved. John Cummins had commissioned two pieces of classic agitprop and almost certainly not referred them upstairs in the early stages. Jeremy Isaacs and Steve Bell would be surprised to discover that they have at least one thing in common: their opinion of the commissioning editor for youth programmes. Isaacs thought him 'the most arrogant young man I think I had ever met'[55] and had already decided against broadcasting another Cummins commission which he considered misjudged, *Sex with Paula Yates*. Steve Bell felt that Cummins made no effort to support him in this conflict. His actual comment on Cummins has not, as far as I know, been previously published, so I shall exercise a bit of discretion here. I can, however, contribute my own experience of working with Steve himself several years later on a series marking the 20th anniversary of Mrs Thatcher's arrival in Downing Street[56]. Below his diffident charm lies a steely determination which neither my requests nor the more strident urgings of my director of programmes could dent. Bob Godfrey, who as director of the series was in the middle of all this, was heard to remark that it might be easier to work with Mrs Thatcher on a series about Steve Bell than vice-versa.

In 1985 the music department had a giant hit with *Max Headroom: 20 Minutes Into the Future* ('as good a movie as we ever made' - J Isaacs[57]) and its 'computer-generated' hero. It was dreamed up by C4 commissioning editor for music Andy Park, record producer Peter Wagg and animators Rocky Morton and Annabel Jankel, stars of the music video industry. Music was provided by Midge Ure and Chris Cross (of Ultravox). It even made the cover of *Newsweek*. Sadly, though, Channel 4's greatest animated hit turned out not to be animated at all. The 'computer-generated' tag had been attached by the press office. 3D computer animation, now sometimes criticised for draining life from characters rather than bringing them to life, was thought very sexy in 1985. Yet I wonder whether we might indeed classify those sequences as animation nowadays. With the plethora of different technologies now deployed, the previous narrow definition (which insisted that the movement itself must be created by the animator) seems a bit old-fashioned. These days anything that appears on a screen and moves but is not a record of real life - including creatures moved by motion capture[58] - tends to fall under the animation umbrella. Max Headroom was indeed a live actor (wearing a pre-fabricated suit and tie, bits of latex in his make-up and hair and contact lenses). But a fair bit of technology was applied as well. He was shot against blue screen with light sources to simulate the computer-generated images of the period, and the blue screen was replaced in post-production with an animated, computer-generated moving background grid; every other frame was removed, and the remaining frames doubled, to simulate the effect when animators 'shoot on doubles'; and, finally, various frames were repeated to simulate faults.[59] The current popular synonym for animation, 'manipulated moving image', seems to be made for Max.

Between drama department commissions - the Janáček and Stravinsky diptych and *Street of Crocodiles* - the Quays were commissioned by arts editor Michael Kustow to make a pilot for a proposed series inspired by the ancient *Epic of Gilgamesh* entitled *This Unnameable Little Broom* (1985). One would have thought the arts department might be an ideal home for the Quays' brand of visual poetry, but Kustow declined to commission the full series, and this reflects the major problems thrown up for a television channel by this extreme form of avant-garde animation: how accommodating or how challenging should programmes be vis-à-vis viewers? I recently asked the Quays themselves whether they ever considered the needs or expectations of viewers when making their films. 'No, never,' was the response, and for two very good reasons: firstly, that it is impossible to gauge what an audience will respond to and, secondly, that if audiences are asked they will invariably want what they already know, thus precluding the possibility of challenge and innovation[60]. Absolutely logical, but it still left commissioning editors with some headaches.

Jeremy Isaacs was from day one eager to seek out and commission films by women and depicting the world from a female point of view. The days when women were confined to only mechanical tasks in animation were long gone by the time C4 came about. Young women were now directing their own films, many of them comments on some aspect of the female condition. Animation seemed to be a perfect medium to convey their sometimes shocking, sometimes allusive thoughts and feelings. And, as Jayne Pilling explains, women tend to approach filmmaking in a different way from men: in a way which is eminently suitable for animation:

Ideas, feelings, issues can be presented not as linear arguments - to be accepted or rejected by the viewer - but imaginatively embodied, enacted, literally played around with for the viewer to experience and interpret for themselves.[61]

This Unnameable Little Broom
© Koninck Studios Ltd

This was exactly the kind of filmmaking seen in the explosion in British women's animation in the mid-1980s. Graduates were buoyed by the confidence instilled by their art school training, inspired by the political mood of the era (and especially the women's movement) and equally by visionary course leaders such as Roger Noake and Ray Fields and notably a large number of women teachers including Irene Kotlarz, Gillian Lacey, Marjut Rimminen, Christine Roche, Vera Neubauer and Anna Fodorova. All this gave them the confidence to tackle serious subjects never broached before in animation, or subjects we already knew - but had previously seen only from the male point of view. Or to make quiet, observational films of the kind many male students would reject as too uneventful to succeed. Thus at the National Film School Alison Snowden (with, admittedly, fellow-student David Fine as co-writer) made S*econd Class Mail* (1984), a parody of Bob Godfrey's *Dream Doll*, in which a woman sends off for an inflatable male companion, and Joan Ashworth produced a classic of gothic animation, based on Mervyn Peake, *The Web* (1987). At the Royal College Emma Calder made *Springfield* (1986), with a heroine half-woman and half-vacuum cleaner and Karen Kelly railed against apartheid in *Egoli* (1989). At Middlesex Polytechnic Joanna Quinn made *Girls Night Out* (1985/88)[62], in which some middle-aged female factory workers enjoy a night on the town which rebounds on the male stripper they are ogling, and at West Surrey Karen Watson's *Daddy's Little Bit of Dresden China* (1987) tackled child sexual abuse. Two Liverpool alumnae, Susan Young and Susan Loughlin, who had gone on to the RCA and National respectively, continued in the minimalist, observational mode encouraged by Ray Fields, to produce *Carnival* (Young, 1985) and *Grand National (*Loughlin, 1989).

These films had a tremendous impact nationally and internationally, winning not just the student prizes at festivals but major awards, including an Oscar® nomination for *Second Class Mail*. It was a vibrant mix and its timing was impeccable. A few years earlier and this talent would have been diverted into commercials and series. But Channel 4, coming on the scene in the early 1980s with substantial funding, finally made women animators' personal projects viable.

Second Class Mail
© National Film and Television School

The World of Children

At the Channel, Alan Fountain's independent film and video department had been in the vanguard and Vera Neubauer was one of the earliest to benefit. Her first animated films, for the BFI, had dealt with concrete female concerns but in an open-ended, allusive and sometimes contradictory way. C4 would allow her to expand these ideas in what became a quartet of films about the stages of human life, the four drawn together by various internal strands as well as their overall subject. They used a variety of media and genres, the first and the third being largely animated. The first, *The World of Children* (1984) used both drawn and cut-out animation, in a resolutely unfinished style, as well as live action to reflect on attitudes to race. The predominant 'story' among a wealth of other motifs featured a grandmother telling her grandson a bedtime story about how she came to give birth to his father and the problems the child's mixed race had seemed to present her with. *Undercut* praised its 'colourful, sometimes bizarre layers of signification and symbolism' and its 'complex and witty collection of pictures and ideas'.[63] It challenged accepted animation styles, techniques and themes: indeed Leslie Felperin Sharman characterised Neubauer's films as the 'terrorist branch of an already often subversive art form'[64]. So it says a lot about the early days of Channel 4 that it saw fit to programme it on Christmas Day 1984, in a family slot occupied for the previous two years by ratings-winner *The Snowman*.

The third film in Neubauer's series, the equally allusive (and elusive) and many times more mischievous *Mid Air* (1986) observes that housewives can get bored and surmises that, according to a boldly-daubed and mis-spelled graffito: 'WAR = MENSTRUTION ENVY'. So why should these bored housewives not go to evening classes to learn witchcraft and prepare a potion to make their hapless policeman and soldier husbands menstruate? The form is again novel. This time live action mixes with (mainly) flat puppets of grotesque design and the story is told in the words of the spoof - one imagines anyway that it's a spoof but you can never be sure with Neubauer - modern opera which is stridently and discordantly sung throughout. The film has been widely seen - it even had a run at the Ritzy cinema - and was extremely influential.

Blind Justice: Some Protection

In 1984 Alan's department took another step which would benefit women's animation, among other groups of independent filmmakers. A Workshop Declaration and Agreement was drawn up between C4, BFI Production, a group of left-wing local authorities and some trades unions and NGOs, which would fund regional filmmaking cooperatives for a specific period. Channel 4, the major funder of the scheme, had no input into the kind of work produced but, equally, was under no compulsion to transmit everything that resulted. The Leeds Animation Workshop was one of the earliest units to be adopted under the Agreement and Gillian Lacey recalls the procedure whereby this happened: a meeting over spaghetti at Alan's house and the gift (to the Workshop) of an old Steenbeck editing table. The films would continue in their previous, rather unsubtle and propagandist way, very much products of their time[65]. But they fulfilled an important role and had a distinct influence on future work. When Gillian had set up LAW, in 1976, there had been very little other issue-based animation of any kind, still less animation which confronted issues in a more innovative form, but in the 1980s this was changing and she became disenchanted with the LAW films' lack of ambition in this area, seeing the collective way of working as partly responsible:

…collectives can reduce everything to the lowest common denominator, unacknowledged hierarchies may emerge, equality is difficult to achieve and commonly held political beliefs do not necessarily make for good working partnerships.[66]

By 1985 Vera Neubauer and a band of women animation students were challenging that format. Lacey now felt there must be a way for women to work together and offer each other support and stimulation but without submitting to the reductionist tyranny of the collective, and in a way which would allow for more innovative formats than had been seen in the LAW productions. In 1985 she left the Workshop to work on such formats.

She approached Paul Madden for funding to develop a project along these lines, in which a group of women animators would produce individual films with a common theme - aspects of women and the law - and assembled a team of like-minded women to work on the project: documentary-producer Orly Bat Carmel (now Yadin) as producer and coordinator and animators Monique Renault, Marjut Rimminen and illustrator and cartoonist Christine Roche to direct the films along with Lacey. The overall title was to be *Blind Justice*: one film would relate the gender inequalities of Western law back to its origins in ancient Greece; another would look at the prejudices of mainly male, white, middle class and middle-aged judges; another was a theatrical version of an actual case in which a man was accused of murdering his wife. The final film, *Some Protection* by Marjut Rimminen, would attract the most accolades. Based on the true story of one Josie Dyer, whose life was devastated by a legal system which had put her into detention for her 'own protection', the film gains immeasurably from the damaged voice of Dyer herself on the soundtrack and a variety of visual styles expressing the girl's emotional states. The creative process for these films was far more what Lacey had had in mind.

The series was completed in 1987 and the films were widely seen at festivals. But no appropriate transmission slot was on offer, for some at Channel 4 felt one or two of the individual films were behind the times in their approach to feminist issues, a bit heavy-handed perhaps. In February 1990 they would find a home in the Women Call the Shots season but, unfortunately, by that time the BBC had already broadcast a high-profile drama series, co-devised by Helena Kennedy QC and starring Jane Lapotaire and Jack Shepherd. Like the C4 series it dealt with inequalities in the law and like the C4 series it was entitled *Blind Justice*. So the animated *Blind Justice* suffered the indignity of a last-minute title change, to *In Justice*.

As we shall see later in this book, veteran animator Alison de Vere now followed up her 1975 *Café Bar* with another very idiosyncratic take on woman's lot, *The Black Dog* (1987). But there was a new generation of female animators coming on the scene in the late 1980s and they seemed to feel that the struggles of the older feminists had been more or less won. Or perhaps it was just that the culture of the time was more oriented towards humour as a weapon, with a generation of female comedians now suddenly very high-profile. Whatever the reason, the new approach was far more light-hearted. Candy Guard never felt oppressed by men during her formative years. From the age of 7 she grew up in a single-parent household, the parent being an actress who had done comedy sketches in revue, with two older brothers who were happy to associate with their tomboy sister. So when, in the mid-1980s, she went to Newcastle Polytechnic to study fine art with film and video, she felt no inclination to join in the feminist debates still being aired. Not only was she unmoved by such ideas in the abstract, she was also entirely unaffected by the animation of the older generation of women, as she had actually watched no contemporary animation before herself becoming an animator - nor indeed until after she had made her first animated films. Candy also discounts any possible influence from the women comedians such as French and Saunders who were so popular at the period. She certainly felt a kinship with them, being interested in the same kinds of subjects and prone to the same 'silliness'. But she had heard those kinds of gags at home all her life from her mother, obviously a far greater influence.

After her Newcastle degree and a spell at St Martin's School of Art, she found herself at the age of 25, with none of her ambitions achieved, temping for Ealing Council. By a strange and complex coincidence (which involves her sister-in-law's brother and a chance meeting with a still unknown woman), a production company, Scarlet TV, happened to see the animated film she had made at Newcastle and asked to purchase it for inclusion in a documentary series *Woman in View* (1988), which they had been commissioned to make by C4's current affairs department. This student film was nowhere near broadcast

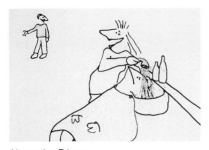

Alternative Fringe

standard, and Candy ended up being commissioned to make four 3-minute films, which were themselves barely broadcast standard, since she knew very little about animation at the time and the women of Scarlet TV knew even less. Candy now charitably qualifies the terribly earnest *Woman in View* as 'very 80s'. But Jaci Stephen's contemporary *Daily Mail* review[67] hit the nail on the head, likening it to 'a send-up of *Blue Peter*'. She found Candy's animated segments 'brilliant', though. The four films were *Alternative Fringe*, *Fatty Issues*, *Wishful Thinking* and *A Little Something*; extraordinarily accomplished first works, *Alternative Fringe* winning both best script and best use of humour at the 1988 British Animation Awards and *Fatty Issues* taking best film at the Ottawa Animation Festival of the same year. The films dealt with stressful situations, such as going to the hairdresser and trying to lose weight, and wherever there is serious analysis of the films - their director finds such analysis hilarious - the consensus seems to be that these are 'women's problems', relating to a social structure in which women do things to please men. Candy is saddened by such reductionist interpretations. For her, *Alternative Fringe*, while it may deal with an ordeal at the hairdressers, is about 'insecurity, hope, self-delusion, fantasy, optimism, assertiveness, disappointment. I was never trying to say anything about women or men, but about human beings.'[68] Such controversies would be revisited, with a vengeance, in 1996 in relation to her series *Pond Life*.

Candy's Newcastle Poly contemporary, Sarah Kennedy, was not far behind in reaching Channel 4. Sarah had followed her Newcastle course with an MA from the Royal College of Art, where her ribald stories and primitive model-making technique made one cringe - but roar with laughter at the same time. Graduating in 1989, she had immediately been commissioned by production company Stephens Kerr and C4 youth editor Stephen Garrett to make an animated short in the same unbuttoned vein - *Family Favourites*, an account of a typical family Christmas - for inclusion in the youth magazine programme *The Survivor's Guide*. It was already clear that Sarah's style and inclination would eventually lead her, like Candy, into series work rather than auteur shorts. Her visual style was fairly rudimentary (not too much for viewers to take in, nor too complicated for animators to achieve in industrial amounts) and the script was of paramount importance. Stephen Garrett would commission her again for one of his *He Play - She Play* series, and I would later channel these talents into two series.

If the nurturing of women's animation has been a Channel 4 constant, so too have been various attempts to improve the standard of writing for animation. Short films do of course need good scripts - a good, original idea and a structure which will reveal that idea to its best advantage - as much as longer formats. But this is often not realised by animators, who tend to see the script as a subsidiary to the visuals, something they themselves can dash off in no time. Trained in the animation departments of art colleges, they are certainly encouraged to think about the time-based nature of their medium, but it is undeniable that these young people have arrived where they are through a talent in the visual arts, and the art college environment is unlikely to decrease the primacy of this element in their minds.

Binky and Boo

Paul Madden perceived this problem in the 1980s, as did animators Derek Hayes and Phil Austin, and the latter were commissioned to investigate a way of working with writers. Some illustrious names, including Brian Aldiss, Julie Burchill and Michael Moorcock, showed some interest in the project and two scripts were finally commissioned, one from Angela Carter and one by a stand-up comedian, Bernard Padden. Both scripts were based on pre-existing works, Carter's on her short story *Overture and Incidental Music for A Midsummer Night's Dream* and Padden's, *Binky and Boo*, on a sketch for the one-man show he had just written and performed. There was only funding at the time for a single production and thanks, presumably, to some crossed wires, it had to be the Padden since C4 was already involved in coproducing another animated film based on the *Dream*[69]. Padden's sketch was intriguing - a spontaneous-sounding riff on the notion that a comedy duo (the film was narrated by Jimmy Jewell, of Jimmy Jewell and Ben Warris fame) has ranged through history in a quest for gigs, appearing at venues as diverse as the court of Louis XIV and London in the Blitz. In the final film (1988) the cut-out animation and unsettling design looked fantastic. Yet the transfer from a verbal to a visual art form was not totally successful. It felt as if there were either too many words or too many visuals or not enough action - something did not quite fit. Perhaps an original script, rather than an adaptation from another medium, would have worked better. This would not be the Channel's last venture into writing for animation.

Paul's full-time contract expired at the end of 1984. Jeremy Isaacs had always maintained that there should be a healthy turnover in commissioning staff, so the contracts of four commissioning editors were not renewed on expiry. Isaacs was actually somewhat erratic in his adherence to this self-imposed rule - though in Paul's case perhaps there was some logic. The major part of his job was concerned with single documentaries; yet film buyer Derek Hill, with his boundless enthusiasm and seemingly boundless budget, had somehow managed to purchase such a massive stock of these that there was no point in commissioning any more until they had been transmitted. This would keep them going for several years. Yet Paul himself believed that the non-renewal owed more to the controversy stirred up by his commissioning of Ken Loach's *Questions of Leadership*. This documentary series charting the failure - as Loach saw it - of 'right-wing' trade unions to respond to Thatcherism was, in the end, never transmitted.

Paul agreed, however, to remain as a consultant for animation and for Christmas archive nights. As a consultant he would continue to commission films but he was not in a position to exert any pressure on the scheduling

Lip Synch:Next. Director Barry Purves
© Aardman Animations Ltd 1989

The Stain

department. The slots given to animation - which were deteriorating anyway thanks to a constant drive towards the half-hour grid - seemed to reduce even more rapidly after that date. When Paul finally decided to resign these last two vestigial roles in order to develop his career as an independent producer, he campaigned (successfully) for his successor not only to be full-time but also to handle animation acquisitions, with a view to presenting coordinated seasons of commissioned and acquired programmes.

Ironically, the films which appeared towards the end of Paul's time at the Channel were among the very best that British animation has ever produced. They included Alison de Vere's *The Black Dog* (1987), Marjut Rimminen's *Some Protection* (1987), Joanna Quinn's *Girls Night Out* (1988), Erica Russell's *Feet of Song* (1988), Aardman's *Lip Synch* (1989), including *Creature Comforts*, *War Story* and *Next*, and David Anderson's *Deadtime Stories for Big Folk: Deadsy and Door* (1990). He also partnered the European co-production of Jan Švankmajer's *Alice* (1987). (Many of these works are dealt with in more detail elsewhere in this book.) Towards the end of his term he also developed *The Stain* (completed 1991), brought to him by two of the *Blind Justice* team, Marjut Rimminen and Christine Roche, which would use psychoanalytic methods to hypothesise the roots of a double suicide they had spotted in a newspaper.

The Channel 4 commissioning system was very simple. It amounted to: going with filmmakers' proposals rather than the Channel's, nurturing those filmmakers with development time and funding if necessary, checking on progress only when called for by the contract terms (ie at the payment stages), or more frequently where filmmakers welcomed an extra sounding board; but also demanding complete professionalism in the technical and administrative areas. In the late 1980s, in the UK, in an animation milieu of abundant talent, this system was generating an extraordinarily diverse range of work in a multiplicity of interesting techniques and dealing with subjects hitherto not tackled in animation. The somewhat ragged structure of the early days, whereby a whole range of commissioning editors would happily commission a bit of animation from time to time, contributed to this diversity.

Michael Grade arrived in 1988, eager to smooth down some of the rough edges of Isaacs' Channel 4 and give it a more professional gloss. One element of this appears to have been a neatening up of the commissioning structure, with each editor's province more clearly defined. Although I cannot imagine anyone was specifically told not to commission any animation, this kind of venturing into unfamiliar territory was now no longer the order of the day. When I arrived, in June 1989, I alone would be responsible for maintaining the track record.

6 Four-Mations

In June 1989 animation acquired a champion, employed on a full-time basis and responsible for both commissioning and purchasing. But I, like Paul, was not supposed to spend the whole of that time on animation. It was thought, and with some reason, that so little air time could never justify a full-time post. Although the initial job title was 'assistant commissioning editor, animation' (there was, of course, no 'commissioning editor, animation'), it was felt that I needed to do something else as well to earn my keep. It had been decided that animation should migrate into the purchased programmes department, partly because a proportion of the job was to be acquiring animated films as well as commissioning them and partly because, as I had come to Channel 4 from a programming job at the National Film Theatre, it was thought I could also programme the old black-and-white feature films that ran in the afternoons. This was probably the reason I got the job over the other applicants. Yet I had had little to do with Hollywood during my time at the NFT. From day one I had been regularly packed off to the capitals of Eastern Europe to select these countries' Film Weeks, because this was the one area in which the BFI did not already have access to a myriad expert film buffs desperate to organise seasons. I had gradually (and more and more willingly) become the 'Eastern Europe expert' as well as the 'animation expert', but had acquired no expertise in the area Channel 4 now needed in addition to the animation.

However, it soon transpired that the animation activities alone would, in fact, constitute a more than full-time job. Firstly, I had no television background whatsoever and had to learn the hard way the nuts and bolts of commissioning programmes. It was perhaps less than helpful that I had been placed in the only department of the Channel which did not itself commission programmes on a regular basis. Understanding the situation I had inherited also proved harder than expected. I was handed all Paul Madden's files, which were quite honestly not the best-kept files in the world, but Paul was always willing to fill in any gaps. The real problem was with Richard Evans' animation purchases. Whatever parameters I would feed into the Channel's computer system, all that came out was a contract number with a running time. No titles or other form of identification. It seemed that, whatever records Richard had kept, he had kept them to himself. There were rumours that he maintained a red card index containing all this information. In the absence of that index, I started the laborious process of ordering tapes up and viewing everything. Finally, the good news came that the card index had been found on the ground floor. The less good news was that Richard was still attached to it. Nowadays Channel 4, in common with most companies of any size, has Fort Knox-style security, with magnetic key fobs for staff of which they are, I am sure, unceremoniously divested once the job goes. In the old days, though, anyone known to the receptionist could walk in. Although Richard's contract had not been renewed, he was still coming into Charlotte Street and, universally well-liked in the Channel, had been offered an unofficial cubby-hole somewhere in the programme management department. No one knew quite what he was doing there. I started to visit Richard's cubby-hole. In due course he came to see me upstairs, and together we would consult the card index. Finally he presented me with the red box and left, never to be seen again.

In other respects, however, Channel 4 offered a breath of fresh air after life at the BFI. There I had been surrounded by people who were not very well paid but could find no other organisation with a need of their particular knowledge and talents (which in most cases were considerable), so they had stayed too long in the same job. I had been one of them. Television, however, was a thriving industry where the pay was good and there was a healthy turnover of staff. The commissioning structure that Jeremy Isaacs had set up situated the lawyers and the programme finance teams in separate departments. Although each commissioning editor was allocated one contracts lawyer and one programme finance specialist, these reported not to the commissioning editor but to their own respective head of division. Some commissioning editors found this unsatisfactory and felt that the finance people especially assumed too much responsibility and that they sometimes tried to cut the commissioning editor out of the loop. In my case, perhaps because of my ignorance of their areas, I was grateful for their willingness to shoulder this responsibility. Furthermore, if ever a project needed some kind of unusual financial or legal formula, or if ever I myself had an unorthodox idea, and asked about the feasibility of said idea, I would regularly see faces light up at the prospect of a challenge and off they would go to crack the problem. At the BFI most ideas had been tried before and had failed: the answer there was more often 'no'. I was also unused to the mutual respect among the various departments. Even if I did not know the first thing about commissioning programmes, nor even initially about television (I had been taught at the NFT that it was the work of the devil), I did know a lot about animation[70] and was given tremendous credit for that, by bosses, lawyers, accountants and assistants alike. The supportive atmosphere was conducive to good commissioning.

Michael Grade, a flamboyant character and scion of a showbiz family, had arrived at the Channel about eighteen months before me. He had, it seems, encountered considerable hostility at first, largely because of the tremendous affection and esteem in which the staff had held Jeremy Isaacs; and his previous pronouncements on the subject of Channel 4 cannot have helped. He had even told a Royal Television Society conference in Cambridge that he thought C4 should be privatised (though he had been working for the BBC at the time and simply doing his job, for a privatised Channel 4 would clearly have been to the BBC's advantage)[71]. When he actually landed the C4 post his views

Michael Grade at Channel 4
Courtesy Channel Four Television Corp

changed and he would later fight a magnificent campaign to save the Channel from privatisation. But he did see his immediate mission as getting rid of the amateurish look of some programmes. He also came in gunning for certain commissioning editors who 'pursued artistic and cultural aims so lofty that they thought it vulgar to consider such sordid matters as ratings and money.'[72] Yet the Channel's funding formula had been deliberately devised so as to remove commercial considerations from the commissioning editors' choices, so these particular editors were absolutely right in their attitude.

Or they had been right in the Isaacs era. Grade, however, was prescient and could see that the Channel had to become competitive. The 1980 Broadcasting Act was coming to an end just as he arrived at the Channel and a new White Paper was published exactly a year later. Significantly entitled *Broadcasting in the 90s: Competition, Choice and Quality*, it offered three possibilities for the survival of the Channel in the new multi-channel age which was obviously round the corner. None of these choices was to retain the status quo, with ITV selling the Channel's air-time, for the Thatcher government could no longer countenance ITV's monopoly in this area. The three possibilities were: privatisation; a merger with the soon-to-be-created Channel 5; or a continuation of the previous structure but with C4 selling its own air-time. What would emerge at the end of lengthy negotiations was more or less the third of these, with C4 being given a safety net of 14 per cent of terrestrial net advertising revenue (as suggested by Grade), but with the unwelcome appendix that this safety net would be granted by ITV, not the ITC[73], and that, just as ITV would have to make up any shortfall below 14 per cent in C4's advertising income, so C4 would have to split equally with ITV any income above the 14 per cent. It was not a perfect solution, and it later led to Channel 4 subsidising ITV - but it was far better than the dreaded privatisation and it set the Channel on a firm basis for broadcasting in the 1990s. We would start selling our own air-time on 1 January 1993.

Thus it was that Michael Grade began steering the Channel into the new, competitive broadcasting age. It is undeniable that his policy of professionalisation of the Channel did make it begin to look more like other networks. Jeremy Isaacs had recruited a large proportion of commissioning editors from outside TV, because he did not want accepted TV lore to seep into the programming. Instead, he hoped that editors would exercise the hands-off role of book publishers, recognising something original if it was offered and encouraging the realisation of the programme-maker's vision. Most of Michael's new recruits on the other hand did have solid broadcasting backgrounds and they were not averse to intervening in productions. This somewhat conflicted situation was not helped by the fact that the country went into recession in the early 1990s. Advertising revenue was down and most commissioning editors' budgets were frozen, some cut.

Dawn Airey at Channel 4
Courtesy Channel Four Television Corp

Strangely enough, animation suffered none of these depredations. Partly, of course, because my activities and budget constituted such a small part of the whole that they were hardly worth cutting. But, even more strangely, not only did animation avoid cuts but it actually flourished under Michael Grade. Animation was now considered to merit a full commissioning editor and I was duly promoted out of the programme acquisitions department and for several halcyon years I reported direct to the head of arts and entertainment, first the amiable Andrea Wonfor and then the even more supportive Dawn Airey. With the encouragement of these two women and the benevolent presence of Michael in the background Channel 4 animation continued to thrive.

It took me some time to fathom why some of my most experimental and lowest-rating offerings received such support from two of British television's biggest popularisers. Dawn, who later went on to senior roles at Channel 5, BSkyB and ITV, was, I believe, equally supportive to all the commissioning editors under her. She did not claim to know anything about animation but appeared to trust me implicitly, as she did the whole of her team. She would back us all to the hilt in what she presented as a battle for funding and slots waged against the factual and drama divisions. It was her way of getting the best out of us. Michael likewise did not seem to know much about animation or to take an enormous interest in it. Yet at a time when other departments' budgets were being cut he intervened more than once in my annual budget meeting (he sat in on all these meetings, which were run by programme director John Willis) to remind John that we were 'the channel of animation' and that perhaps he should give me the funding I was asking for. Once he suggested, quite out of the blue, that extra funding should be found so that I could commission some animated trailers for a particular season I was planning.

Gradually I realised what this largesse was about. The Channel's newly competitive spirit had of course been interpreted in some sections of the press as 'dumbing down'. *The Daily Mail* in particular waged a long-lasting vendetta culminating in an article in 1995 dubbing Michael the 'pornographer-in-chief'. No one at C4 took this anti-Grade campaign too seriously, though Michael himself did seem stung by it and felt a need to defend himself against these charges. I realised that animation was the perfect argument in his defence. It was very expensive (per minute, though the minutes were few), attracted rather low ratings (sometimes because of poor and erratic slotting, but sometimes because work was challenging) and won enormous numbers of prizes for its innovative nature. Quintessential remit programming, in other words, to counter the complaints. I was not offended that the support emanated from strategic considerations – I was just disappointed when later it transpired that Michael's successors did not, by and large, subscribe to the same strategy.

Though posterity will judge a funding body by its commissions rather than by its scheduling, nevertheless scheduling was perhaps the most pressing problem that I inherited, especially given that scheduling considerations had a considerable bearing on commissioning policy. In truth the scheduling of animation must have been something of a problem since the early days of the Channel. Very little animation could be produced as standard, half-hour programmes, partly because the high per-minute cost of animation would have made such programmes prohibitively expensive in large quantities and the animation budget was not geared to such production; but also because the personal animated film tends to work better at shorter lengths. So there was an obvious mismatch. Yet in the early days of Channel 4 there had been a great deal more flexibility than there was later. Then, it had not only been the animation department that was handing the schedulers non-standard length programmes: in those days feature films and foreign buy-ins of strange lengths would be shown in peak time, and the Channel itself even commissioned a few programmes which did not fit standard half-hour or one-hour slots. The schedulers were coping manfully with this situation. It was after all their job to find slots for whatever the commissioning body presented them with, and they managed quite ingeniously to fit animated shorts into the overall jigsaw. This would change over the years and the scheduling department would later exercise considerably more power, even being mandated to propose to the commissioning body the types of programmes that they felt would work in their ideal schedule. And one requirement of their ideal schedule was the elimination of short slots.

When I arrived at the Channel, non-standard length slots were still fairly plentiful during the daytime and late at night, but the only short evening slots remaining were the 5-minute slot at 7.55 every weekday, after the *Channel 4 News*, and the 15-minute slot once a week at 9.45 after the current affairs series *Dispatches*. Both seemed to me ideal for animation, and not only because of their length. The main problem the Channel had with animation was that it rarely achieved the high ratings now required for peaktime slots. Whereas the original remit had been to cater for light TV viewers and people with minority interests - small groups of viewers who would be switching on only to watch a particular programme and then turning off again - the overall strategy now was to attract viewers as early as possible in the evening and hang on to them as long as possible. Animation was seen as a turn-off to mass audiences. However, the wonderful thing about the above-mentioned two slots was that both followed serious, quintessential remit programmes, which themselves attracted relatively few viewers and both were followed, after the vacant short slot, by predominantly entertainment-oriented programming. Thus, at both these junctures, it was expected that the viewers of the first programme would nearly all be lost, to be replaced by a different, and larger, group for the entertainment show. So these were the slots where one could afford to take risks.

Unfortunately, however, the 7.55 slot was supposed to be reserved for ultra-low-budget risk-taking, so it was rare that we could get animation, which is, or was, almost by definition expensive, into these slots. They were also hotly contested by all departments. Everyone had a short-format experiment to try out there - which seemed a bit unfair to a department whose output consisted almost entirely of short format material constantly seeking a home. We would have more success with the post-*Dispatches* slot.

It was plain that slotting was the major problem - especially since it transpired that many of Paul Madden's commissions had not yet had an airing and that many of Richard Evans' acquisitions contracts were not long off expiry. We really had to use some of the transmissions we had paid for. The only way to make use of an array of disparate short slots was via the 'festival' format: throughout a short-ish period animation would be slotted into whatever slots were available. Thus an Animation Festival was swiftly arranged, for 22 to 29 October 1989. It took its inspiration and title from that month's Bristol Animation Festival (which, as the successor to Cambridge, was still sponsored by the Channel) and celebrated it with an introductory half-hour documentary about the festival, but the rest of our 'festival' had only incidental connections with Bristol. Instead, it premiered a batch of commissions and acquisitions which the schedulers had been unable to slot thus far, as well as some repeats. Almost all the slots were pre-6.30 or around 11pm or midnight, which seemed a tad late at the time, but considering the ad hoc nature of the whole thing, they were much appreciated. And there was an exception to this afternoon/late-night arrangement, the very Hitchcockian *Last Respects*, made by animation prodigy Mole Hill when he was only 14 years old: this was honoured with a 9pm slot preceding Hitchcock's *Rear Window*.

The following year, we were able to piggyback on a season of women feature-film makers (February to April 1990) with our celebration of women animators and had another 'festival' on the go from 7 to 19 April - and this one was also a bit of a mopping-up exercise. It premiered Jimmy Murakami's moving *When the Wind Blows* and a few more of Paul Madden's commissions, including Nick Park's *Creature Comforts*, which we decided to rush out ahead of its scheduled transmission as part of the *Lip Synch* series later in the year. Another strand to this season was a rather wonderful look at Czechoslovakian animation, with a documentary, three features and some classic shorts. The third element was a complete ragbag of world animation, responding to the challenge of expiring contracts, and this contributed films from the Zagreb studio, from France, Belgium and Italy as well as a few Betty Boops, Mr Magoos, Woody Woodpeckers and one by Tex Avery. Again, few peaktime slots were on offer, but *When the Wind Blows* and *Creature Comforts* were both prominently housed at 10pm.

Messy as this all was, it was very much in the spirit of an actual animation festival, where one might dip into a dozen different cultures before lunch, and we hoped this approach would catch viewers unawares and maybe convert a few. At the very least, the programming of animation in the interstices of the afternoon and late-night schedule would enjoy the advantage of freedom from ratings pressure.

The schedulers, however, finding it hard to slot the shorts, encouraged us from now on to package as many as possible into half-hours. So the final season of this 'festival' design, a very thorough snapshot of current British animation, in late November 1990, included five half-hour documentaries-cum-packaging exercises under the title *State of the Art*, produced by Redwing, which focused on, respectively, women's humour, David Anderson, Aardman, recent developments, and a new proclivity among young directors towards an Eastern European sensibility. These were shown in irregular but good slots, varying from 9.30 to 11.20pm. The whole of the *Lip Synch* series was now shown, also in irregular but good slots around 10pm, and the season was completed - in afternoon and late night slots - by another batch of Channel 4 commissions, as well as an excellent array of student buy-ins featuring the dazzling generation of Susan Young, Jonathan Hodgson and co.

This arrangement seemed ideal to me and to animation audiences. We had, at last, a substantial presence in the schedule and we even coined a name for it, 'Four-Mations'. David Anderson produced a logo film, bursting with vitality. Despite some derision from my colleagues - too obvious, they said - the name proved admirably memorable as far as animation enthusiasts were concerned, and has now been revived for C4's new broadband channel. Sadly, this greater visibility turned out to be a catalyst for more scheduling problems further down the line.

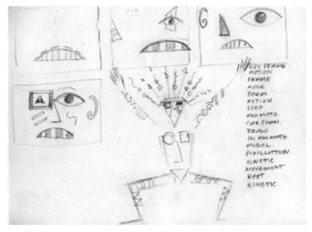

David Anderson's sketches for the Four-Mations indent

7 Missionary zeal…

In parallel with these early scheduling experiments, I was trying to shape a coherent commissioning policy. We were still in the period when the commissioning editor for animation was largely left to his or her own devices. Animation was not a high priority for our superiors: its presence on the screen and cost as a proportion of the Channel's overall programme budget did not warrant too much concern - and this relaxed attitude was also supported by the Channel's secure advertising income. Furthermore, our production schedules were so much longer than those of C4's regular programming that it was extremely hard to involve the animation department in any of the pan-Channel seasons which were mounted from time to time. So there was little pressure to conform.

Not that this isolation was necessarily a good thing, and we would, whenever circumstances did make it possible, co-operate enthusiastically with such seasons. Tim Webb's *A Is for Autism*, for example, was already in development when the 1992 Disabling World season was announced, with a long lead time, so that it was possible (just) to get the film completed in time. Sarah Kennedy's *Nights* series was not specifically commissioned for the 1993 Love Weekend, but that event happened to offer a brilliant occasion for its first transmission. In later years, when time-saving new technologies were within everyone's reach, budgets were rather lower (inviting simpler techniques) and most of the slots on offer could only accommodate 3-minute programmes, such involvement in seasons would become far easier. In 1998 the Channel ran a season marking the 30th anniversary of legalised abortion in the UK and the education department wanted a low-budget, partly-animated contribution. Marjut Rimminen and Gillian Lacey directed *Mixed Feelings*, four 3-minute live action interviews about people's experiences of abortion with overlaid animation and video trickery to penetrate the emotions expressed. Likewise, in 2000 Channel 4 was able to give good notice of its Caribbean Summer season marking Britain's five-match Test series against the West Indies, so Camilla Deakin could commission a week of 3-minute films showcasing black talent in the post-news slot.

But back in 1989 animation was a world apart, and I was given no guidelines as to the kind of films I was to commission. So I could accept whichever proposals I felt had the most merit and not worry too much about the conundrum of scheduling them. But although, along with the rest of the commissioning body, I was not overly sympathetic with the plight of the schedulers, I did feel a sense of responsibility towards viewers. Television is a mass medium and even a channel addressing itself to light viewers and people with minority interests, as

What She Wants (1994). Female sexual
fantasies. From Animate
© Ruth Lingford

required by the C4 remit, is nevertheless talking about figures counted in the hundreds of thousands rather than the small but super-receptive audiences of animation festivals. I wanted films which could communicate with rather more viewers than only art school students, for example, who inhabited the same hothouse atmosphere as the makers of the most abstruse films. At the other extreme, a large proportion of world animation and of festival schedules consisted of little bits of whimsy or rather weak gags, and we needed to avoid these. Animation budgets were far too high and the input of labour far too great to waste on material of that kind. We needed films with a point to them.

This did not, I hasten to add, mean that films had to have a clear-cut narrative, as long as they either had something interesting to say - in whatever visual or verbal language the filmmaker felt appropriate - or were engrossing pieces of visual art in their own right. I did not object to difficult films, addressing the more confident of our viewers, as long as such works had something else going for them as well. In the case of the Quay brothers' films, for example, the quandary mentioned earlier, which arts commissioner Michael Kustow had faced regarding This Unnameable Little Broom, would not go away. Yet when watching certain of their films, even while experiencing a slight sense of panic at our failure to follow a supposed narrative, we can still get swept along by the palpable atmosphere, the tension, the exhilarating camera movements, the textures, the music and so on. I tried to be alert to such qualities.

I was anxious to nurture the whole range of genres, from popular to experimental, and practitioners, from large studios to newcomers. Our attempts to reach different animation communities would sometimes involve partner organisations. One area which seemed to fit well with C4's remit was the more experimental end of the animation art. Thus, shortly after I arrived, David Curtis, film and video officer at the Arts Council[74] visited me at Charlotte Street, accompanied by producer Keith Griffiths, who had had a hand in many of the experimental works commissioned by the C4 independent film and video department and was of course the Quays' producer. The Arts Council had already partnered the Channel on various schemes, beginning in 1981 with a slate of arts documentaries and continuing with a scheme for avant-garde works run jointly with C4's independent film and video department, so there was a tried and tested template on offer.

Thus the new Arts Council/Channel 4 Animation Awards scheme (as it was originally named - it became the zippier animate! and, later, Animate) was set up quickly and proceeded painlessly. The Channel contributed cash, with the Arts Council putting in less cash but adding staff and facilities to make the contributions roughly equal. We would solicit proposals from anyone in any area of animation but also from practitioners in other visual arts who had an unusual idea they wanted to pursue, the unusual element being either in the form of the piece or the content or both. Selected projects would be awarded a

15th February (1995). A rejected Valentine's card provokes a violent reaction. From Animate
© Tim Webb

Withdrawal (1997). Family members disappear and the landscape becomes ever sparser. From Animate
© George Barber

Feeling My Way (1997). An annotated walk into the studio. From Animate
© Jonathan Hodgson

rather small budget (the maximum was £20,000) and the scheme would provide a production consultant to give technical, budgetary and organisational back-up but very definitely not take a hands-on role. These were to be original artists' pieces bearing no trace of an Animate mould. This and the fact that filmmakers would retain all rights should compensate, we hoped, for the low budgets. The matter of who should be that production adviser was easily settled. Dick Arnall was our unanimous choice. His production skills were a bit out of date and he immediately set about educating himself in the new technologies. But the skills he had acquired latterly - house-building and childcare[75] - would certainly not come amiss.

What would C4 get out of this scheme? In contractual terms, not much at all: two transmissions of the completed films and no share in rights, a deal which benefited the filmmakers and was almost unheard of in those days, when the Channel would normally have expected to retain all rights. A 2003 Act of Parliament has meant that all independent filmmakers retain rights in their work nowadays, no matter how much of the budget a broadcaster has paid, but Channel 4's schemes with the Arts Council were very much ahead of their time in this respect. So, no rights. And neither was the Channel expecting high ratings - though in the event these works have consistently attracted a surprisingly high proportion of the late-night TV viewers. We were simply fulfilling our remit to encourage innovation and in a wholehearted way few might have expected of any television channel. The committee - comprising David Curtis and me, together with three invited artists from various areas of animation and other disciplines - was single-minded in this pursuit.

Why bother to innovate, though? Of what relevance are these artists working on the fringe? Plenty, we felt: for in the world of the moving image what is marginal today tends to constitute the cutting edge of tomorrow's mainstream. It was (and still is) such opportunities for experimentation which have given Britons a lead in commercials and music videos. And even the budget limitations of the Animate scheme have proved influential. On these budgets, traditional, hand-drawn animation throughout is a tall order, so over the years Animate filmmakers have been in the forefront of developing ingenious new methods. Ruth Lingford, until that time a traditional animator, decided to investigate the potential of her family's Amiga computer for her Animate film *What She Wants*, partly as a means of saving time and money and having greater personal control over the project. Likewise, other cheaper media such as live action, pixilation and still photos have been mobilised and often combined into weird and wonderful hybrids. In this world, hybrids - whether resulting from budget inadequacies or from experimental imperatives - are definitely the way forward. Experimental multi-media artist and filmmaker Jo Ann Kaplan refers to herself as a 'mixed old bag' and praises Animate as offering 'another means to practise without squashing myself into an arbitrary box of skill or genre'.[76]
The Animate artists would come from a variety of milieux. Some were already

3 Ways to Go (1997). Reflections on death.
From Animate
© Sarah Cox

Love Is All (1999). Evocation of a bygone
age, shot on film with complex optical
effects. From Animate
© Oliver Harrison

Furniture Poetry (1999). Based on
Wittgenstein but funny: household objects
transform at speed. From Animate
© Paul Bush

low-budget experimental filmmakers, and some had had considerable
exposure in the field (notably the Quays). Others came from specific areas
of experimentation (William Latham from high-end computers, Tim McMillan
had developed the time slice technique). AL+ AL were installation artists and
David Shrigley an underground artist who had tackled most disciplines. The
scheme also attracted animators much in demand for commercials (such as
Mario Cavalli, Jonathan Hodgson and Sarah Cox), who saw it as an opportunity
for some R & D as well as R & R: a means of leaving the treadmill for a while
to recharge the creative batteries and think outside the narrow constraints
imposed by commercials production.

The work produced would be as varied as the artists. The scheme would really
blossom, achieving a far greater public profile, after 2000 thanks to changes
at ACE (see chapter 11): as this book goes to press, it has been going for 18
years, a record among such collaborations.

It also seemed important to nurture young talent, thereby investing in a future
for British animation. But it would have been hard to commit the large budgets
required by animation to newly graduated animators unless some protective
structure were in place to help the animator and reduce the risk to the Channel.
But this conundrum had been solved for me even before I reached Charlotte
Street. Just before I left the British Film Institute, a meeting was convened of
all the BFI staff who had any interest in animation, to discuss the problem of
the glass-fronted studio in the Institute's Museum of the Moving Image. This
tiny studio had been incorporated into the Museum's animation section, with
the idea that young animators could come in and use the facilities without
payment in return for forming a living exhibit, showing museum visitors how
an animated film was made. But it had become apparent that this was an
extremely unreliable way to man the studio. Independent animators needed
more than just facilities to make their films. They also had to live, and so were
constantly disappearing to earn a bit of cash before returning to their project.
The meeting had been called by Paul Collard, the Museum's administrator, and
the problem was explained by David Watson, its researcher, and the ubiquitous
David Curtis, who had been engaged to advise on the animation section. What
was really needed, they said, was a sponsor, an organisation which might
itself gain from this nurturing of animation talent, a TV company perhaps… My
dramatic announcement that I had that very week been offered the animation
post at Channel 4, and that I thought there was every chance that I could make
this scheme happen provoked a gratifyingly enthusiastic response - though
I discovered recently that news of my appointment had already leaked. I had
been set up.

Nevertheless, like Animate, the Animator in Residence scheme would obviously
benefit both parties and was put into action as soon as I arrived at the Channel.
We would fund four new graduates per year to spend three months each

Growing (1994). Director Alison Hempstock.
From AIR

The Broken Jaw (1995). Director Chris
Shepherd.
From AIR

developing a film in the Museum's animation booth, after which we would put into production any developments which achieved the required standard. All that remained was to advertise for candidates and to find an experienced, and ultra-motherly, production adviser. Lisa Beattie was our first, to be followed by Yvette Burrows, Chris Shepherd, Louise Spraggon (both Chris and Louise having themselves been AIR animators), Adam Pugh and Deb Singleton. Our focus here would not be on experimentation, but on easing the way for young filmmakers into a professional milieu. In practice, the scheme came to focus on films with a strong narrative.

At first we simply short-listed candidates on the basis of past work and their proposal for the new project, and then selected the four winners after interview by a panel of industry people as well as C4 and MOMI representatives. In later years we noted that many proposals suffered from specific problems which we thought we could help put right. So we began offering the short-listees a consultation with a friendly animator or writer (most of the problems turned out to be in the writing), before the final interview and consideration of the improved proposal. We were intending to treat these final proposals like any others arriving on my desk and only commission those of the necessary quality. But in the event we were so unsure as to what quality we could expect in the case of first-timers that we perhaps incautiously commissioned all the early films, which set an expensive precedent. By the time the scheme got into its stride, we realised that the quality was often easily comparable with professional work and we could have afforded to be more discriminating. But the regime turned out to be excellent, if sometimes tough, for aspiring filmmakers. Some development packages were returned time after time and new consultations arranged, until finally we felt the project was professional enough to transmit. The industry rallied magnificently, with people donating time, advice and equipment and agreeing to house the ultimate commissions in an appropriately nurturing way.

Filmmakers reacted differently to life in the booth. Some enjoyed the role of museum exhibit, coming out to talk to visitors about their film and the techniques used: others wrote down whatever they thought necessary and stuck it on the glass wall. Some added a complete storyboard, to ensure that they themselves remained invisible.

Sadly, MOMI closed its doors in 1999 - the BFI could not find funds for necessary refurbishments or new exhibits - and we were offered space in another BFI venue, the nearby Imax cinema. Never as congenial, it sufficed for a while. But we had always recognised a metropolitan problem with the scheme. Young filmmakers turned up from all over the UK for their three months in the booth, complaining loudly about the expense of London and the lack of regional AIR schemes. Then, when the film was commissioned, they would move into a professional studio for the production, often in London.

Andares in Time of War (1997). Director
Alejandra Jimenez Lopez. From AIR

The Cat with Hands (2001). Director Robert
Morgan. From AIR

When the film was completed they would look for work and, usually, find it in London. Our scheme was perpetuating the problem, and I was anxious to give it a more regional angle. In 1999 chief executive Michael Jackson agreed an increase in the funding and we hoped to open regional schemes parallel with London, the first to be somewhere in Scotland, the second, if all went well, in Bradford, at the National Museum of Photography, Film and Television, and hopefully later on a third centre. In the event these ambitious plans would not come to pass. I left the Channel later that year and shortly afterwards the scheme was transplanted from London to Bradford. The Museum there was a far more pleasant home than the Imax cinema, though young animators turned out to be less keen on the idea of three months in Bradford than three months in London, and applications dipped somewhat.

But throughout the scheme's life a steady stream of outstanding work has emerged - in fact three AIR films are given particular focus elsewhere in this book - and its alumni are now prominent in the industry. The top UK studios have taken many, and one of the first year's crop, Sam Fell, co-directed and co-wrote Aardman's 2006 feature *Flushed Away*. Brian Wood's *Cramp Twins* books were made into a TV series for Nickelodeon. Chris Shepherd's company, Slinky Pictures, has twelve animation directors, five of whom are AIR alumni. Others have opened their own successful studios and yet others have crossed the Atlantic: both Anthony Hodgson and Boris Kossmehl animated on *Shrek*.

Another initiative for young animators originated in Michael Grade's suggestion, one year, that I should be given funding to commission some animated stings to complement one of our animation seasons. The funding was, however, anything but lavish, so we decided to kill two birds with one stone and hold a student competition which would give young filmmakers, while still at college, the experience of putting together proposals and completing commissions in a professional context. We were able to recruit one of animation's most creative and philanthropic producers[77], Phil Davies, who initiated this competition in 1995. A resounding success, it was to provide punctuation for a further three animation seasons, in 1997, 2000 and 2001 - only to come to an end with the demise of animation seasons themselves.

In the mid-90s it became plain that there was another need we could answer: new technologies were obviously the way forward for all areas of animation, but most of these facilities were at that time beyond the budgets of the majority of animators. The Arts Council, this time in the person of Rodney Wilson, its director of film, video and broadcasting, had marshalled a group of high-end facility houses and persuaded them to make their machines available to six bursary holders per year, financed again by C4 and the Arts Council. The aim was to allow them a period of research, exploration and development with, theoretically, a potential work for television as the long-term goal. There were some exciting experiments done, but it transpired that the scheme did not have legs. The technology changed so rapidly and became so much cheaper that many hi-tech effects could now be done on home computers. Our scheme no longer seemed necessary. From now on auteur filmmakers who did need more advanced hardware would forge individual relationships with the facilities companies, which would happily offer them access during the evenings, when the machines were not in use for more lucrative purposes, in exchange for the opportunity to widen the product range on their showreels.

We also pursued the campaign to engage good writers with animation, which had been initiated by Derek Hayes and Phil Austin and resulted in *Binky and Boo* (1988). Now, in the mid 1990s, a proposal in this vein was brought to me by Dick Arnall, with Richard Gooderick of the Arts Council, who was proposing to share in the financing. The idea was again to approach predominantly novelists and poets rather than scriptwriters, but this time we would not accept adaptations from already-existing works, nor would we commission scripts, to be handed over complete to the animation team - for we had found that even the most original of writers would, if left to their own devices, often default to traditional, hackneyed forms when writing for animation. What we hoped to create was a set of true partnerships, in which writer and animator would nourish each other's ideas to transcend the limits of both art forms.

Dick approached a 'wish list' of writers and animators, the latter group not being quite as obvious as the former, for we wanted animators who read novels and would be confident discussing ideas with men and women of letters. He finally identified fifteen or so interesting and interested animators; and a broad range of writers, including Will Self, Ted Hughes, Ian McEwan and Lavinia Greenlaw, were issued with a compilation of some of the most exciting of recent British animated shorts and briefed as to the kind of partnerships we were seeking. We were hoping for six of these pairings; but there were many disappointments. Some of the writers just did not get it. Finally two collaborations struggled into being. Simon Pummell - who had taken an English degree before getting into animation - got on well with science fiction and fantasy writer M John Harrison. Dick Arnall recalled a Soho dinner where, suddenly, 'a light went on. Mike Harrison jumped up and rushed round the room in excitement as he realised they were on to something'[78] - though even there the first draft script appeared to me to smack slightly of an outsider's realisation of some of the more obvious visual tricks that animators had been exploiting since time immemorial. However, subsequent drafts tightened *Ray Gun Fun* (1998) up into a spooky tale of worlds within worlds using live action and digital effects.

Dick, having made enquiries at Virago and at a feminist bookshop, came up with the suggestion of Sara Maitland to partner Ruth Lingford. It turned out that Lingford already knew and liked her work. This was a marriage made in heaven. Maitland is a novelist and short story writer, and a radical Christian who

Pleasures of War
© Channel Four Television Corp/Arts Council England

has published several works on theological issues as well as interpretations of Bible stories. Lingford had just completed *Death and the Mother* (1997), an adaptation of Hans Christian Andersen, and was looking for something completely different. *Pleasures of War* could not have been more different in nature (though it did share *Death and the Mother*'s woodcut look and desktop computer technique). Luckily they had started work before it became obvious just how popular this previous film was going to be: 'If I'd realised the prize-winning power of *Death and the Mother*, I'd have been tempted to make *Death and the Mother 2*, *Death and the Mother 3*…'[79]. Instead, the pair settled on a story from the Apocrypha, that of Judith, a beautiful widow who saves her town from the attacking Assyrian army by seducing and beheading its general, Holofernes. But was Judith the undisputed patriotic heroine that our Sunday schools painted her? Lingford and Maitland saw that the moral issues were far more complicated than that, and they weave in some interesting questions and contemporary parallels. As Lingford explains[80], being a victim gives you the moral high ground but brings dangers too. Judith was a victim and so have Jews been throughout history - but does that justify her actions in liberating Bethulia, or Israel's in the current conflict? The other key motifs were women and violence (an early title was *The Worst Thing*) and a link between warfare and sexual gratification - both hotly disputed issues.

Achilles (1995). Barry Purves' film focuses
on Achilles' relationship with Patroclus.
Photo Paul Smith

Go West Young Man (1996). From Animate
© Keith Piper

Britannia (1993)
© S4C/Channel Four Television Corp

The collaboration with Maitland was exemplary. Unlike the many writers who write 'down' for animation, Maitland was fully intellectually engaged, exploring and uncovering the layers of the story along with Lingford. There was a constant process of discussion and, interestingly, no demarcation of roles: everything was shared, with Maitland often suggesting images and, likewise, Lingford words. Lingford, having worked in an earlier life as an occupational therapist in a psychiatric hospital, gave me the technical name for the phenomenon whereby - contrary to the myth that group decisions tend to be gutless compromises - collaborators egg each other on and encourage excesses which maybe the individual members would shy away from alone. The seduction scene, ending up with Holofernes' sword thrust into his back passage, exemplifies this phenomenon, the 'risky shift'. Apart from anything else, the fact that a committed Christian was prepared to handle a semi-Biblical story in this way smoothed the way for Lingford's wilder flights of fantasy. The collaboration of a male animator, Ron MacRae, also enriched the scene.

The film attracted a clutch of awards, the greatest honour perhaps being its inclusion in a work[81] highlighting '150 masterpieces of world cinema selected and defined by the experts'. In among the *Potemkins*, *Psychos*, *Alphavilles*, etc, animation academic Paul Wells was allocated twelve places for animation. Half went to classics of the past, but Ruth was there with *Pleasures of War*, along with only Norstein, Švankmajer, Miyazaki, Nick Park and John Lasseter representing the greatest living exponents.

Alongside the various schemes we put into place and areas we tried to foster, certain types of programming developed almost spontaneously, probably thanks to our well-known government remit. In the animation output we were pleased to reflect minority interests whenever we could, commissioning several gay films, for example, and a couple relating to disabilities. There were few proposals on multicultural subjects, but those we had were enthusiastically received, notably Maybelle Peters' *Mama Lou*, Shilpa Ranada's *Naja Goes to School*, about a family of untouchables, and Keith Piper's *Go West Young Man*. Current affairs were hard, given that animation's long production schedules militated against topicality, but we did encourage political comment, in Joanna Quinn's *Britannia* for example, and Phil Mulloy's *Eldorado*, and we marked the 20th anniversary of Margaret Thatcher's arrival in Downing Street with a short - but biting - series by *Guardian* cartoonist Steve Bell.

Perhaps because of this obvious concern with more serious issues than much of world animation, proposals with a documentary, even journalistic basis, began to arrive on my desk. Contrary to appearances, animation is in many ways the most honest form of documentary filmmaking. As Orly Yadin, co-director of the animated documentary *Silence*, points out[82], live action documentary footage appears transparent but can discreetly offer new meanings by means of framing, lighting or editing. Animation, on the other

Gotta Get Out (1995)

hand, is completely upfront about the filmmaker's intervention. Secondly, animation is less exploitative of its subjects. Live action documentaries about living people often penetrate personal areas and sensitive subjects, tending to provoke a voyeuristic response in viewers. Animation avoids this searching physical portrayal of its protagonists.

This animation genre, often using real, first-person narratives, had I believe first been seen in the UK with Colin Thomas and Bill Mather's pioneering work for the BBC on *Animated Conversations* and continued with Aardman's *Conversation Pieces*. While Aardman gradually moved into the comedy arena, the journalistic baton was taken up by Marjut Rimminen with *Some Protection* (1987, for Paul Madden) and, later, by several filmmakers under my watch. *Silence* (about a holocaust survivor), *A Is for Autism* and *Abductees* (alien abductions) all crammed more emotional truth about their protagonists into their 11-minute running time than one would expect to find in a standard half-hour documentary. Others did not use the real voice of the film's protagonist, using instead actors and scripts; but they were nevertheless factual accounts of a real personal experience. Robert Bradbrook's *Home Road Movies* dealt with his relationship with his father and Jonathan Hodgson's Animate film *Camouflage*, about the effects that mental illness can have on the sufferer's family, was based on his own childhood. Gillian Lacey's claustrophobia film, *Gotta Get Out*, was an expression of her greatest fear. Likewise, Marjut Rimminen's *Many Happy Returns* is an oblique account of her own past and its long-lasting effect. Several other MOMI and Animate films also took the same approach, as did a good few student films, making it a UK speciality, much-admired at festivals during a certain period.

The extraordinary record of festival prizes, which had kicked off in 1990 and 1991 with an Oscar® and a Cartoon d'Or for *Creature Comforts*, continued at the 1993 Cartoon d'Or ceremony when C4's *The Village* (by Mark Baker) took the award and the jury, noting that four of the nominees were Channel 4 commissions, decided to break with precedent and present a second award, to Channel 4 itself. *Bob's Birthday* took an Oscar® in 1994, and these high points were supported throughout the period by numerous other Oscar® and Cartoon d'Or nominations, a succession of BAFTA (British Academy) nominations, best British animation prizes in Edinburgh (Post Office/McLaren) and London (Mari Kuttna/ BFI), major prizes at international festivals and two Dick awards. This latter, for the 'the most controversial, subversive and innovative short film of the year', was a rare distinction for a public service broadcaster and one I especially cherished.

8   … And pragmatism

Famous Fred
© Channel Four Television Corp/S4C

Prince Cinders
© Longreturn Ltd

But the short films were only a part of the story. Paul Madden had established the Channel's reputation for world-beating half-hour specials, TVC's *The Snowman* and *Granpa* (Dianne Jackson 1989, based on John Burningham) being classics in the genre. And this was a genre which garnered ratings as well as kudos. I tried to follow his lead, with four more from TVC, who usually seemed to turn up with the best properties: *Father Christmas* (Dave Unwin 1991, again based on Raymond Briggs), *Tales of the Night* (Michel Ocelot 1992), *Famous Fred* (Joanna Quinn 1996, based on Posy Simmonds) and *The Bear* (Hilary Audus 1998 - Briggs again). Iain Harvey, who had executive-produced for TVC on several specials, now joined with director Derek Hayes to bring us a delightful animated version of Babette Cole's *Prince Cinders* (1993). The rule at Channel 4 was that, whenever a project was a candidate for co-production, we should seek such funding rather than spend Channel 4 funds unnecessarily. The family specials were prime candidates for co-production, and partners presented themselves from Europe, Japan and the United States. A very regular and amiable partner (and one which, unusually, was sometimes prepared to partner us on short films as well) was our Welsh sister-channel S4C. The animation department, headed by Chris Grace, had worked hard to promote animation in Wales and to attract non-Welsh animators to Cardiff. In this way he could justify supporting most of Joanna Quinn's films and a large part of Candy Guard's. It would have been a pleasure to work more frequently with S4C, but sadly (for us) their main activity was making very popular half-hour animated versions of the classics - Shakespeare, Chaucer, operas - and this did not coincide with our own remit.

Adult comedy series were an area I was very anxious to get into. I first saw a pilot for *The Simpsons* at a TV market in early 1990. I seem to remember a divine scene with Homer staring in desperation at a Scrabble board and the letters he had been given - O,X,Y,M,O,R,O,N (do they play with eight letters in America?) - and wondering what on earth he was going to do with that 'load of crapola'. It showed that cartoons can be witty, intelligent, subversive as well as highly entertaining to both adults and children. My boss, Mairi Macdonald, head of programme acquisitions, had already seen it and was equally enchanted, though sadly the amount the Channel was able to offer at the time did not get us the series.

My own enthusiasm to commission adult series stemmed from a recognition that it could be a brilliant genre, and the knowledge that it was also a genre which, unlike shorts, would fit very happily into a television schedule. There was a bit of *esprit de corps* in it too: I hoped that if we produced something to generate good ratings these more commercial exploits would perhaps help subsidise the production of shorts and put me in better odour with my bosses. I also hoped that adults, unused to watching animation of any kind, might come to it via comedy series, discover its many virtues and so think of giving the auteur shorts a try. The main problem was that, with a budget which barely covered the annual slate of expected shorts, it would take some stealth and considerable negotiation to embark on a slate of series.

The first opportunity presented itself in 1991, when Stephen Garrett, commissioning editor for youth programmes, commissioned a series of 11-minute pieces, *He Play - She Play*, highlighting the work of first-time filmmakers. Aware of Sarah Kennedy (also known as Sarah Ann Kennedy) from her student films and later contribution to *The Survivor's Guide*, he now commissioned her to write one of these pieces. *First Night* was the live action talking head of a woman (Lesley Sharp) regaling her chum with details of a magnificent night of passion with a new boyfriend. Animated inserts (also by Sarah, while the live action sections were directed by Cindy Irving) revealed the actual, unvarnished, horribly recognisable truth of the encounter.

This mixed format seemed to be a good, and inexpensive, way of testing the water for animated series, and in 1992 I commissioned a further four episodes charting the progress of this doomed romance, as it should have been (in live action, with Nick Hancock playing the boyfriend) and as it actually was. It was sufficiently successful to merit another project with Sarah, so I immediately commissioned her to make what could, if the worst came to the worst, be transmitted as a one-off 11-minute, puppet-animated film about the inhabitants of a dilapidated house in a seedy part of south London. If successful, I would propose it as a series for the coveted 9.45 post-*Dispatches* slot. It would be produced by the famed satirical puppet company, Spitting Image.

Around the same time as this, Candy Guard - an equally talented writer, who had studied together with Sarah at Newcastle Polytechnic and had then enjoyed some success with early shorts for the Channel - also proposed a series idea. The heroine was to be one Dolly Pond, who plans a future escape from her 'crap' family, friends and ex-boyfriend with such intensity and in such time-consuming detail that she never progresses beyond the cul-de-sac she so despises. Again, the first step would be a transmittable short, but the hope was that it would go to series. Again, it fulfilled the criteria: script and dialogue were paramount, the visual style rudimentary.

Pond Life. Dolly's crap family, friends and ex-boyfriend
© Channel Four Television Corp/S4C

By 1993 both these shorts were completed and both seemed to me to be eminently suitable for series, though I did worry about Sarah's *Crapston Villas* for the 9.45 slot. It had somehow transmuted during production into something exceeding even Sarah's vague conception of the boundaries of good taste and it felt to me like something for the late night schedule. However, somewhat to my surprise, the head of scheduling said yes, both would be just fine for 9.45, and added that of the two he preferred *Pond Life*. My own instinct was also that *Pond Life* would probably get the go-ahead first, since surely no one could help but recognise his or her own weaknesses in Dolly's.

We were by now into the era of the focus groups, so slotting and indeed decisions as to whether or not a project should proceed were no longer the exclusive preserve of TV executives and their hunches. The conclusion for *Crapston Villas* was perhaps predictable: though many participants in several groups (notably the females and the middle-aged) disliked it intensely ('I'm shell-shocked', opined a lady in one of the 35-44 year-old groups), the 18-24 year-old men all liked it a lot and felt it fitted the Friday night, post-pub mood. Given that young men are the demographic group most courted by advertisers, the Channel decided to put the series into production straight away. Since, given the extreme nature of much of the material, we would have little hope of finding a co-production partner, C4 happily agreed to put up the entire budget. The *Pond Life* groups also reacted very much as predicted. The pilot was much liked by a far broader spectrum of participants, with the women of all ages being particularly enthusiastic and only some of the young men reacting badly. ('Crap', was one verdict from this quarter.) The overall warm reception meant that this project would also get the go-ahead. But there were two hitches. One was that my small series allocation for the year had all been put into *Crapston Villas*; the other was that due to *Pond Life*'s gentler, broader appeal, it seemed likely that co-production partners could be found - so the hunt was now on. The funding would not be in place for another two years, with scripts commissioned in 1995 and the series only getting made in 1996, a time when, as we shall see, the climate for animation projects would not be as propitious.

As well as Sarah and Candy, there were yet more potential providers of character-based comedy. British animator Alison Snowden and her Canadian husband David Fine (who together had made two Oscar®-nominated shorts, *Second Class Mail* at the National Film School and *George and Rosemary* at the National Film Board of Canada) had decided to return from Canada to the UK. They came up with a proposal for a short film about a dentist with a mid-life crisis. The resulting film, *Bob's Birthday* (1993, co-produced with the NFBC), was a textbook illustration of the multiple talents of this couple: their narrative structure is as good as any sitcom writing, their comic timing that of the best comedian and - the big plus, unique to animation - they complete the picture with visual gags involving dogs, plants, greenflies… This time, they won the Oscar®. A series seemed inevitable.

On the scheduling front, we gradually mopped up the untransmitted commissions and acquisitions of my predecessors, but were generating new material all the time. As well as showcasing new British animation talent, Four-Mations also brought an international and historical dimension to our programming, with focuses on legends such as Norman McLaren, George Dunning, Yuri Norstein, Oskar Fischinger, Bob Godfrey, Ray Harryhausen, Zbig Rybczyński and John Lasseter. In most cases, their films were shown along with a specially-commissioned documentary. But as the seasons became more ambitious, the schedulers felt there was too much animation packed into too short a time, and that this was bringing our ratings dangerously low for that week or fortnight - so the period of the animation 'festival' was over. The deal now was that the work had to be packaged into half hours, to be transmitted weekly over a longer period, in fairly good slots, with some of the more challenging work scheduled the same evening but in late-night slots. Most of these packaging exercises were now produced for us by Paul Madden's company, under the title *Secret Passions*.

Half-hour programmes were of course a fact of life by now, so there was no arguing with that. In the case of packaged animation shorts, half hours could sometimes work well, as for example when David Anderson's *Deadsy* and *Door* (both only 5 minutes) had been enclosed within a really stimulating documentary about their production, or when Paul Vester's or Alison Snowden and David Fine's films were now packaged into an extended interview about their makers' life and work. But sometimes the links between films could appear tenuous, manufactured, as indeed they were, the only thing really linking the works being compatible running times.

At first these seasons happened twice a year but later they became fewer. And the promised peaktime slots got later and later. Animation programmes starting at 10.30 or 11.00pm could attract good audiences, but by the end of 1996 they would be starting considerably later. In 1997 we changed the format: *Dope Sheet* (produced by Illuminations Television) was a fast-paced, irreverent magazine show covering news and issues in the animation world. It was immediately followed by a substantial block of animated shorts, starting with work referred to in the preceding programme but then diverging into whatever interesting paths seemed to beckon. It was a satisfying formula, and concentration into a single block enabled animation fans to set their videos and thus assemble a fine collection of diverse work. But, since *Dope Sheet* itself did not start until midnight, ratings were obviously not going to be too impressive.

We managed to break into the peaktime post-*Dispatches* slot twice, with runs of our most popular commissions and acquisitions in June-August 1993 and April-June 1996. These were highly successful, attracting phone calls of appreciation in the duty log and even a few reviews in the dailies. The 1996 run, sandwiched between *Dispatches* and the US blockbuster *ER*, achieved ratings of over a million for most programmes, and over two million for one. I doubt it was the animation that attracted the viewers, but this rare exposure to large audiences did raise awareness of our medium.

Everything in the garden seemed rosy, though with the benefit of hindsight it is now clear that this period of high hopes was also a time when the seeds of future problems were sown.

Some key works 1982 - 2006

The Snowman

1982/26mins

Director
Dianne Jackson
Supervising director
Jimmy Murakami
*Music composed and
conducted by*
Howard Blake
Animation
Roger Mainwood
Dianne Jackson
Alan Ball
Dave Livesey
Eddie Radage
Hilary Audus
Arthur Butten
John Offord
Joanna Fryer
Tony Guy
Stephen Weston
Robin White
Backgrounds
Michael Gabriel
Paul Shardlow
Tancy Barron
Joanna Fryer
Design supervisor
Jill Brooks
Editor
John Cary
Senior cameraman
Peter Turner
'Walking in the Air' sung by
Peter Auty
Producer
John Coates
Executive producer
Iain Harvey
Production Company
Snowman Enterprises for
Channel 4

James and the snowman take off on their flight

Christmas. James wakes up to find it has snowed. In the absence of any friends around, he makes a snowman. That night, the snowman comes to life.

In 1980, TV Cartoons was living off commercials but studio head John Coates wanted to get into broadcast television. Animation funding by British broadcasters was paltry at that time - they were happy to import what they needed from the US - and, as already mentioned, in desperation John was driven to read the 1980 Broadcasting White Paper which would create Channel 4. He realised that his only chance of making Raymond Briggs' *The Snowman* into an animated half-hour special would be to persuade the new channel to fund it. So he asked animators Hilary Audus and Joanna Fryer to produce a short animatic, using images cut out of the Briggs book plus one or two new episodes. The main addition was the journey to meet Father Christmas. It had been clear that *something* had to be added to the flight over Brighton pier, because the Briggs story would never have stretched to a half-hour, but Father Christmas…? 'Raymond was very iffy about it, but now he admits it works very well'[83]. Just as this silent filmed storyboard was due to be submitted to Channel 4, John was introduced, quite by chance, to composer Howard Blake. Despite the latter's illustrious cv (choral and orchestral music, many 'big' film scores including Ridley Scott's *The Duellists* and Chabrol's *Blood Relatives*) he was willing to do a piano track for this piece in a single week and for an extremely reasonable price, because the music already existed. He had written it for another film on which he had failed to get the commission. It already included what was to become 'Walking in the Air'.

Paul Madden, a convinced Briggs fan, had no trouble convincing Jeremy Isaacs and head of programme finance Colin Leventhal that it was just what the Channel needed for its first Christmas on air. There was, however, a problem with the size of the budget. TVC thought it would come to £200,000 - a woeful underestimate of the actual cost of such an elaborate film, but even that was far higher than usual for animation and also much more than the Channel was paying for the rest of its programming. So, at this period when C4 usually fully-funded its commissions, and thus ended up owning the programme, in this case it could come up with only a part of the budget. Hamish Hamilton, the publisher of the book, and TVC would account for the balance. As a result, Channel 4, to its eternal chagrin, only acquired a limited number of transmissions, which have to be renegotiated periodically, and Snowman Enterprises (jointly owned by TVC and Hamish Hamilton, now Penguin) control all film and merchandising rights.

Once Channel 4 had given the go-ahead, John began crewing up the production. It had been decided that veteran director and regular TVC associate Jimmy Murakami should be supervising director, but both Murakami and Coates felt this film needed a woman at the helm. There were not too many women directors around at the time, especially with the talent and experience required for a project of this kind. They decided on Dianne Jackson, who had first worked at the studio on *Yellow Submarine* in 1968 and had returned frequently to do commercials.

Dianne set about expanding the 8-minute piece to a detailed, 26-minute storyboard, timed down to the last detail, and handed it to Howard Blake to produce a finished music track. This was unusual: more normally the music would be added at the very end. However this film had no dialogue: Howard's score would have to communicate ideas, emotions and even sound effects. The animators would have to 'mickey-mouse'; to follow the music absolutely rigorously. The idea that the 'Walking in the Air' theme should become a song was John's. He was satisfied that the story could be compellingly told without dialogue, but nevertheless felt the need of a human voice somewhere, to make closer contact with the audience. Legend has it that he suggested this to Howard Blake over lunch, whereupon the latter scribbled down the lyrics, Hollywood-style, on a napkin.

Father Christmas hosts a party

Storyboard panel.
The snowman cools down by the fridge

Fun with a model railway

Dianne's main visual challenge was to find a way of emulating Raymond Briggs' crayon rendering in a moving image. The problem was that when the still images were animated the individual crayon-strokes could not be properly aligned so there was a risk of the rendered surfaces 'boiling'. But *Pink Floyd: The Wall* had featured a similar kind of rendering, so Jill Brooks - who had cracked the problem on *The Wall* - was now appointed to art direct *The Snowman*. She just had to figure out how this could be done in massive quantities. Many thought it couldn't - but it could and was. However, the process was extremely labour-intensive - averaging 45 minutes per cel, with even the backgrounds pencil-rendered[84] - and, with Christmas fast approaching, more and more staff had to be recruited. By the end there were 60 or 70 people working on it. In all the rush, a few errors made it into the final version. James and the snowman look out of an upstairs window and see a snow-free tarpaulin covering a motorbike. By the time they get downstairs it is under four inches of snow. Another error affected the credits, with choirboy Peter Auty, who had sung the song so angelically, unaccountably omitted. The original £200,000 budget was easily exceeded. No firm figure is available, but it seems to have doubled, at least. Hamish Hamilton was finally persuaded to provide a bank guarantee for a very considerable sum and, as a last resort, John borrowed £50,000 against his house to add to the pot. 'Somehow we weren't that worried about money. We were just going to make that film come hell or high water'. Iain Harvey - who was at that time working for Hamish Hamilton - was, however, very worried. He was fully expecting to lose his job over it.[85]

By some miracle the film was finished in time for Christmas. Jeremy Isaacs' verdict on seeing the rough-cut: 'You've made a dreadful mistake'. After a shocked silence he mischievously pointed out that the TV in the film was equipped with only three buttons - how would James and family find Channel 4? In fact he thought it 'a knock-out piece of entertainment, a child's-eye view of the world as a happy place. I couldn't believe our good fortune in getting something like that'[86], and he threw a Christmas party for Channel 4 employees with children, showing them *The Snowman* before it went on air. The reaction was overwhelming. It had its TV premiere at 6.15pm on Boxing Day 1982 to, frankly, a tiny audience. C4 ratings were, anyway, low at that time, and as the Channel had no children's department and was by now known for its more abrasive fare it was not seen as the place to look for the next children's classic. But the reviews were excellent and by the following year word had got round and the audience increased massively. And not just in the UK - over the 1983 Christmas period it aired in 22 other countries as well. Apart from 1984, when it was held back for the video launch, it has been shown annually on C4, reaching, in its heyday, ratings around the 3 million mark. As I write, 25 years later, it is still reaching over a million viewers. As a result of its success one-off, half-hour TV specials, which had previously been considered commercial madness, became flavour of the month with the BBC and even ITV.

After Raymond Briggs, then David Bowie, since 2003 it is Father Christmas who introduces the story. Roger Mainwood directed this scene

Animation drawings for James and the snowman's dance

But it was not only on television that *The Snowman* thrived. It won a clutch of major awards, including a BAFTA for best children's film, a Prix Jeunesse and an Oscar® nomination. Merchandising also took off and Snowman Enterprises has done extremely well out of it. It is, in fact, the basic source of income which has sustained TVC and kept it going until now, alone among the host of studios which set up in the 1950s to make TV commercials. *The Snowman* has conquered other media too. Howard Blake[87] had considerable success with an album and a concert version of the film score, as a result of which 'Walking in the Air' was used for a commercial. Since the original soloist, Peter Auty, could no longer do the job as his voice had broken, Howard suggested Aled Jones - and also proposed that he record a single of the tune at the same session. The record went to number 3 in the UK pop charts. The snowman melted 25 years ago, but has since been reincarnated - in a ballet, a stage musical and a film of the stage show. There are even rumours of a feature-length sequel…

Images reproduced by kind permission of Snowman Enterprises Ltd.
The Snowman © Snowman Enterprises 1982, 2008

The Victor
1985/14mins

Directors/script
Derek Hayes
Phil Austin
Producer
Mandy Groves
Design
Lin Jammet
Animation
Anna Brockett
Bill Hajee
Gary McCarver
Gaston Marzio
Kevin Molloy
Backgrounds
Denis Ryan
Camera
Terry Handley
Music
Dirk Higgins
Voices
Shaun Curry
Robert Llewellyn
David Tate
Production company
Animation City for
Channel 4

Jimmy's nightmare

A soldier embarks on an assault course. As he progresses, the scene becomes more and more horrific. The soldier, believing this to be a nightmare, embarks on a killing spree.

Derek Hayes and Phil Austin had studied and made an animated film together at Sheffield Polytechnic before becoming, in 1974, the very first animation students at the National Film School - where 'nobody knew what to do with us'[88]. They had a room and a rostrum camera and painted the legend 'Animation City' on the wall outside, to give themselves - and succeeding generations of animation students - a presence in this somewhat chaotic world. It would later become the name of their company. At the Film School they were given regular lectures in all the filmmaking disciplines except animation: this they had to make up as they went along, using their film budget to buy in a day's tuition here and there from the likes of Bob Godfrey and Terry Gilliam. The result was an ambitious fantasy, *Max Beeza and the City in the Sky*. This calling card - plus being friends with Julien Temple, a student in the year below them at the Film School - won them a major role animating a large part of Temple's punk epic *The Great Rock 'n' Roll Swindle*. After that they were made, and at a time when animation was booming, their new company was kept busy with pop videos, commercials and TV graphics.

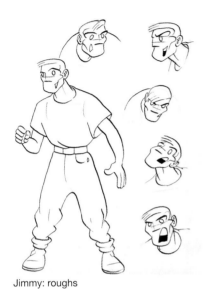

Jimmy: roughs

Jimmy: animation drawing

Jimmy: final version

Derek and Phil's first contact with Channel 4 had been with the drama department. There, they had been steered firstly in the direction of science fantasy, resulting in the hugely popular *Skywhales* (1983). But back in 1976, while still at the Film School, Derek had seen a Granada TV *World in Action* documentary about the US army's experimental administering of drugs to its soldiers. His memory was stirred later when a friend with mental health problems had been prescribed two drugs which, between them, caused him to hallucinate. His doctor's comment, 'I wondered if that might happen - I haven't used those two drugs together before', would actually make it into the film. The title would be *The Victor*, both an acronym for the on-screen computer message 'Violence Induced, Control Terminated, Operative Reaction?' and a reference to a boys' comic of Derek and Phil's youth - as well as an ironic comment on the outcome of the plot. It was in Cambridge, while attending the 1983 Animation Festival, that they wrote the script to submit to Channel 4. As with *Skywhales*, it was the drama department that commissioned the film. It had been intended as a 100 per cent commission, but 'one thing we hadn't learned at the Film School was how to assess the length of a script in terms of screen time, and we went over length and were sure to run out of budget before the film was finished'. David Rose was sympathetic but unable to translate this into any additional funding, so the directors approached British Screen, which granted them enough to finish the film.

Traditional cel animation was used, in a comic-book style - reminiscent of the 1950s but back in vogue in the 80s - courtesy of a young designer, Lin Jammet, who walked in off the street one day bearing a dazzling portfolio. The pacing is hectic, but without ever losing its strong narrative structure, which made the film especially appealing to a young audience. Furthermore, the choice of popular comic-book style seemed to promise harmless entertainment - rendering the final revelations all the more shocking. Animation City's regular and very versatile composer, Dirk Higgins, was asked for something that would evoke 1960s action-adventure series such as *The Avengers* or *The Persuaders*, with which he duly obliged. Despite the top-up funding received, the film went way over budget, the main reason being that the animators were being paid a weekly rate rather than one based on footage delivered. Since some of them were not that experienced it took them a long time to get things right - one single shot cost £1,000 just for the animation, which in 1983 money was a lot. 'That put a kink in our finances for a long time.'

The film had a tremendous impact on the animation world, winning a special award for its graphics at the 1985 Annecy Festival and taking the Mari Kuttna (BFI) Award for best British animation of the same year (ex aequo with Susan Young's *Carnival*). It obviously made a big impression too on the organisers of the Los Angeles Animation Celebration, who invited the studio to submit the film but then failed to enter it into the competitive section: 'it was too bleak and depressing'. Derek speculates that the festival may not simply have been

Billy Bunter design

Bunter appears at the promenade café

Nightmare dodgems

using optimism as a criterion. The film, he suspects, 'may not have gone down well in *Rambo*-land'[89]. It had a run at the Scala cinema in March-April 1986, supporting the horror pic *The Return of the Living Dead*. Kim Newman in *City Limits* compared it favourably to the 1981 animated fantasy/horror classic *Heavy Metal*. 'The Victor', he continued, 'is remarkable mainly because of the clarity of its science-fictional vision, the boldness of its imagery, and the general weirdness of the plotline. Very neat.'[90]

Delivered in 1985, the film did not make it on to our TV screens until October 1989. It had possibly been held back after completion until the film had had its theatrical run and then fallen victim to scheduling problems. The film was finally scheduled in October 1989 within an animation 'festival', assembled to complement the Bristol Animation Festival which was happening over the period. *The Victor* went out at 11.30, a late but in this case perfectly suitable slot, making it into *Time Out*'s selections as 'Virtuoso cartoonism which demands to be taken seriously'[91].

When the Wind Blows

1986/85mins

Director
Jimmy T Murakami
Voices
Peggy Ashcroft
John Mills
Title song
David Bowie
Film score
Roger Waters
Art director
Errol Bryant
Script
Raymond Briggs
Storyboard
Jimmy T Murakami
Richard Fawdry
Joan Ashworth
*Special effects sequences
planned and animated by*
Stephen Weston
Producer
John Coates
Executive producer
Iain Harvey
Production company
Meltdown Ltd in association
with the
National Film Finance
Corporation/Film Four
International/TVCLondon/
Penguin Books

Hilda and Jim: drawn characters in a stop-motion environment

Retired couple Jim and Hilda live in the country, only vaguely aware of an increase in international tension. Hearing on the radio that a nuclear war is on the cards, Jim picks up the appropriate literature from the library and follows the instructions for building a 'core refuge' from doors and cushions...

One Christmas, John Coates took to his bed with a dreadful cold and took advantage of the enforced leisure to read the new work by Raymond Briggs, creator of *The Snowman*. But *When the Wind Blows* could not have been more different, and John 'cried buckets'[92].

The idea for the book had come to Briggs - who was not a particularly convinced nuclear disarmer - as the result of a 1980 *Panorama* programme, which inspired him to look a bit more closely at how very unprepared the UK was for a nuclear attack. 'When I got the government leaflets I saw they were ready-made comic material'.[93] He decided to set his black comedy in the beautiful Sussex countryside where he lives and base Hilda and Jim on his parents. *Protect and Survive*, the Home Office leaflet Jim Bloggs follows when constructing his 'core refuge', was indeed preposterously inadequate and horribly patronising. It would later be reproduced and distributed to the press attending the film's preview. By the time of that preview, the Reykjavik arms control summit would have broken down and the Chernobyl accident devastated vast tracts of Eastern Europe, making the issue even more topical.

Despite the book becoming a surprise best-seller, the film was not such an easy sell to possible financiers. They did not at that stage have Reykjavik and Chernobyl to promise newsworthiness: all they had was a studio currently in production on *The Snowman* now wishing to develop something diametrically different, with little family audience potential and at three times the length and thus, they assumed, three times the cost (it would actually run out at even more). Most, including Channel 4, would have been happier with another *Snowman*, but Paul Madden got a copy of *When the Wind Blows* on to Jeremy Isaacs' desk and both Isaacs and Colin Leventhal wanted to support the project. They agreed a development budget of £18,000. This development funding would serve to get the project into a form that might attract other financiers, after which executive producer Iain Harvey would need to put this complex package together.

John Coates' choice of director for the project was interesting. It had to be Jimmy Murakami:
He's very good at black comedy. He's not a romantic. The book plays the comedy right through till the end - it's awful and funny, and Jimmy (maybe it's his Japanese background) has got just the right touch for that kind of thing.[94]
Jimmy's background is indeed crucial to his feel for this subject. Born in California of Japanese parents, as a child he had been separated from his family during the war and sent to an extremely tough internment camp. By the end of a war in which Japanese relatives had been killed - one in a regular bombing raid and one by the A bomb on Nagasaki - he emerged strongly disillusioned by his American homeland and by what he saw as senseless warmongering. After the war he had an illustrious animation career, starting in the mid-1950s in the UPA Burbank studio, but also making notable personal films, some of which revealed his distinctly jaundiced view of the American way of life, notably *The Top* (1964), *Breath* (1967 - Annecy Grand Prix) and *The Good Friend* (1969). He did not, however, restrict himself to animation, and also directed a documentary about democracy as well as the live action feature *Battle Beyond the Stars* in 1980. This live action experience was also crucial to the way *When the Wind Blows* would tell its story.

The first step was for Murakami and Briggs to convert the latter's picture book into a script which would work for a feature-length film. Those pillars of the British acting establishment Sir John Mills and Dame Peggy Ashcroft had agreed - both for the first time voicing animation - to take the two roles. They needed no rehearsal, but fell into the characters naturally and easily.
After the recording there was silence. We, the engineer, John Coates, Raymond Briggs and I had to recover, choking back the tears. I went into the studio to

Hilda makes tea. Objects become drawn animation as she handles them

thank them for the most moving performance. Peggy, with tears in her eyes, told me "Jimmy please don't ask me to do it again, I couldn't bear it." [95]

By now the £1.7 million budget was assembled - most of it from the National Film Finance Corporation and about half a million from Paul Madden's budget at Channel 4, plus an advance from the sales agent, Glinwood, and smaller amounts from other partners, and with a completion guarantee in place (which would indeed be called on as the budget slowly slid up beyond the £1.7 million). The technique Murakami had decided on was complex.

Hilda starts to feel ill

I want to treat the film like it's live action with cuts, camera angles and point-of-view shots. [...] What I want to do is get some excitement happening in the house without having to hold on to the same background for ages. I like the idea of using two people indoors for an hour and a half and trying to sustain interest. [96]

By 'fast', he meant a constantly moving camera and active protagonists. This was all planned in the storyboard, which incorporated the kinds of camera moves which traditional animation simply could not manage - changing camera angles would require far too much redrawing of backgrounds. Now, of course, a computer would make light work of animating those moving backgrounds. But back in the 1980s it was decided to solve the problem by shooting a scale model of the Bloggs' house as the background and animating only the characters via traditional drawn animation. The scale model was set on a turntable and the backgrounds to each scene then shot in a series of tracks and pans within it using a 35mm camera converted to single-frame operation. Each frame of these background shots was then blown up into a paper print which was placed behind the cel animation and shot conventionally, frame by frame using a rostrum camera.

Cooking after the bomb. Cups are models, the pan is drawn

Several precautions had to be taken to ensure that the model set and the cel animation would be compatible. Firstly, the models were given a kind of painted texture: 'If they had been made to look like real rooms, which modelmaker Errol Bryant was quite capable of doing, the animators would not have been able to blend in the characters the way they did'[97]. Secondly, puppet versions of Jim and Hilda had to be photographed in a scene before the background was shot and the cel animation undertaken, in order to check scale, lighting and camera angle. There were, of course, complex moments when the drawn characters and items from the model set had to interact, if for instance a character had to lift a cup. The sack that the couple climb into at the end was another such prop, and was photographed single-frame as a guide for rendering the sacks in the drawn animation. But the production was by that time running out of time and budget and those photos had to be used instead, and animated by cross-dissolves. Cock-up and compromise, but it gives the death scene a very special atmosphere.

Shock wave sequence animated by
Stephen Weston

Jim surveys the damage

Images © Meltdown Ltd

Alongside the model shoot and the cel animation of the characters to go with it, Jimmy had decided to add a long sequence of entirely drawn animation, for Hilda's dream. He says in *Stills* magazine[98] that this section - not a part of Briggs' original - was added to give Hilda more prominence: she had seemed to him, in the book and even at the voice recording, to be the lesser character and he wanted to give her equal presence. Yet I as a viewer always felt this section stood out like a sore thumb. I had wondered at the time whether it had been inserted to make the duration up to a proper feature length to give it a cinema career. It turns out that the prime motivation was far less practical - and very typical of the way TVC was run. *Esprit de corps* seemed to demand that Jimmy bring Dianne (Jackson, with whom he had worked so successfully on *The Snowman*) into the production, so she was asked to produce this dream. In the end, Jimmy, Raymond and Paul Madden all agreed that the style did not fit with the rest of the film, but they realised too late: there was no time or money to do anything about it.

The film premiered in Germany, simultaneously in Berlin and two other cities, and was hugely successful. In Japan too (where noted director Nagisa Oshima had directed the voice track) it was a triumph. It was released in about 25 territories in all, but had only a limited release in the USA and none at all in France - despite its winning the Peace Prize at the Chicago Film Festival and taking the best feature prize at Annecy. Executive producer Iain Harvey always suspected the lack of French interest related to that country's dependence on nuclear power.[99] In the UK it did well, with a run at several West End cinemas and going national with at least 50 prints. It garnered some extremely favourable reviews from publications as varied as the *Daily Mail* and *The Face*, all united in praise of the film's timely message. Derek Malcolm in *The Guardian* felt that:

The film achieves the extraordinary feat of allowing us much gentle amusement on the way to its icy conclusion, and it does this without seeming to patronise its characters unduly. [...] Its complete simplicity is its chief recommendation, and one doesn't often write that nowadays.[100]

After a three-year theatrical holdback, the film had its TV premiere in an excellent 10pm slot in April 1990 as centre-piece to an animation season. When the film was repeated three years later, in a midnight slot, *The Sunday Times*[101] and *The Observer*[101] both included it in their selections of the day, while the *Telegraph* made it Movie of the Week, calling it 'brilliant', 'chilling' and 'dazzling'.[102]

Yet, despite these enthusiastic reactions, some good theatrical deals and plenty of territories buying the TV rights, the income was not enough, the limited distribution in the US being particularly damaging. The elaborate technique had pushed the film over budget and, sadly, investors did not recoup their very considerable investment.

Street of Crocodiles

1986/20½mins

Animation/mise-en-scène/
puppets/camera/decors/
montage
Quay Brothers
Original story
Bruno Schulz
Sound montage
Larry Sider
Music composition
Leszek Jankowski
Producer
Keith Griffiths
Production company
Koninck Studios for
British Film Institute
Production Board
and Channel 4

An old Kinetoscope, on display in a deserted museum, contains the Street of Crocodiles. An attendant spits into the workings of the machine, activating the performance. An interloper begins a futile pursuit.

The Quay brothers are American, but they had been captivated by Polish poster design when they first saw it, as students in Philadelphia. This first contact with central Europe also stimulated an interest in its literature - starting from a chance encounter with the then unfamiliar word 'kafkaesque' in an article on Polish poster art.[103] They subsequently came to London to study illustration at the RCA, but were already, inspired by poster-artists-turned-animators Lenica and Borowczyk, making animated films at the weekends. It was at the RCA that they met their producer, Keith Griffiths, who would help them get commissioned by the BFI and then by Channel 4.

He first took the proposal for *Street of Crocodiles* to the C4 drama department, which had earlier commissioned the Quays to make films on Janáček and Stravinsky, when the Channel was just starting up. Now, however, the department had been remodelled and was making feature films only.

But the Channel had forged a productive relationship with the British Film Institute Production Board, whereby it granted the Board a subvention for the production of films which would be shown on Channel 4. Commissions had to be approved by Jeremy Isaacs and head of drama David Rose, but were overseen by the head of the Board, Peter Sainsbury. So the project was housed at the BFI, with C4 accounting for just over half the modest £80,000 budget.

The BFI had previously funded the Quays' *Nocturna Artificialia*, but Peter Sainsbury had, according to the twins, thought that earlier film 'too errant'[104] and sought to bring them into line by asking for something with a narrative - preferably something from a literary source. The Quays proposed the Polish author who was by now their favourite, Bruno Schulz, and this was accepted, even though Schulz actually eschews narrative. The Schulz story they chose was from the collection *The Cinnamon Shops* and was called 'Street of Crocodiles', but they added in ideas from other Schulz works too, including another story from the *Cinnamon Shops* collection, 'A Treatise on Tailors' Dummies'. This story eulogises mannequins, demands respect for them and professes a desire to create man a second time - in the image of the tailor's dummy. Sentiments which would reverberate throughout this and the Quays' other films. Many have seen the main puppet character in this film as a depiction of Schulz himself in the grimy streets of his home town of Drohobycz. It is certainly Schulz - the brothers would coax him with a gentle 'Bruno, come on, what's going on here?' if his shoulder joint should lock while being animated.[105] And the world Schulz portrayed was indeed the physical world he knew - but it was not only geographical: it was also a realm he had conceived of in an earlier story, that of the 'thirteenth freak month'. It originally implied nothing more than a kind of temporal limbo, but in 'Street of Crocodiles' he went on to describe it as the period when summer refuses to die and instead, like a woman past her prime, continues 'by force of habit' to produce - but these extra days are stunted and useless. Precisely the Quays' own preferred territory.

Peter Sainsbury liked the treatment, which was long and detailed[106], and the film was commissioned. The treatment, having served its purpose, was then put away and forgotten about, and the twins set about making a rather different film, in their characteristically intuitive way. They made it almost entirely alone, designing and shooting the film and making the puppets and sets in their studio in Wapping. The shoot was disrupted by a flood, which caused some losses. However, the Quays consider Schulz's original to be a 'poetic essay about matter' and the flood was seen overall as a benign influence on the film's material appearance: the drenching improved the warped forms and age patina of puppets and props.

Their film is conceived very much as a poem, and thus its musical structure is far more important to them than its dramaturgical structure. Leszek Jankowski is the twins' regular composer and their working method is unusual: he never gets very much information on the film. And in this case he did not need much, being totally familiar with Schulz already. The brothers simply asked him to send something to surprise them. He sent a cassette with three pieces which were 'stunning'.

Once the film gets going, we start building the decors, we re-divide the scenario, we start to really listen to the music. And the film grows, in that way, organically. We shoot the film, and it comes back the next morning. We lay it up against the score, and we see if it's working. If it isn't working, we shoot it again. [...] We much prefer to obey musical laws because it's not logical. You can't print logic on music; it's outside of that. [...] We always felt that with Leszek's music: you hear the images, and you see the music. There's that sort of infiltration. Cinematic music works best when that happens. You sort of know it when you can feel it. The music feels like it is inside the image.[107]

There are several keys to this film, some touched on above, notably its musical structure, its reverence for its puppets and its revelling in matter. Narrative is the last of the Quays' concerns, and they knowingly play with the viewer's inbuilt desire to perceive and comprehend a plot:

Narrative for us is always tangential, it just filters in from the side and creates this climate. In the end you feel this conspiratorial climate that makes you think, "I'm at the centre of something and I don't know what it is." You come out the other end still looking in the rear view mirror and thinking, "I haven't arrived yet".[108]

The viewer's disquiet is heightened by a subjective camera style which, with its sudden changes of focus and fast pans, contrives to simulate point-of-view shots. We, like Bruno, never know quite what, if anything, we have seen.

The brothers accept and perhaps revel in the feelings of disorientation and paranoia their films engender. Yet they are pained when critics take this further and call their films, and especially this one, nightmarish or, as happened in America, 'stuff to keep your kids awake'. When their films were shown at the Academy of Motion Picture Arts and Sciences the auditorium was, unexpectedly (to them), thronged. But, equally unexpectedly, a good proportion of the youngsters present were in gothic gear. They are disappointed to feel their version of Schulz should be so misunderstood. 'The animation isn't ghoulish. There's definitely a malaise, but it's not ghoulish. [...] It was like a pop concert. Very disturbing.' They are also anxious to point out how different their work is from the Czech 'militant surrealist', Jan Švankmajer. They feel very much closer to Russian animator Yuri Norstein. Unlike Švankmajer, Norstein is concerned with poetry and memory. The structure of his *Tale of Tales* 'makes the film infinite'. This is what they hope to have emulated in *Street of Crocodiles*.

The film created a stir worldwide. It took three prizes at the 1986 Zagreb Animation Festival and the Grand Prix at Odense, Sitges, Brussels and San Francisco (for best short film). Critics in France and the US (but not, as far as I can see, in the UK) used the word 'masterpiece'. Most films look better on a big screen than a small one, but in the case of Quay films, with their emphasis on texture, this is even more the case. They also love the disorientation produced by the sight of a giant-sized puppet, and they play on this disorientation by various striking juxtapositions in their films (eg actual, full-size dandelion heads casually mixed in among the puppet props). So it was especially good news that *Street of Crocodiles*, unusually, did get theatrical exposure in the UK. By an enormous stroke of good fortune, at about the time this film was completed Artificial Eye film distributors were looking for a short to go out with their new release, *The Legend of the Suram Fortress* by the Armenian poet of the cinema Sergei Paradzhanov, which at 70 minutes was rather short to go out alone. It was the perfect marriage. The television premiere the following year was at 1.00am on Christmas Day, so it did not attract large viewing figures. (Not that this has ever worried the twins. 'Beggars can't be choosers,' they told me. They were just happy when their work could be funded.) *Crocodiles* fared better in America, where it aired, at 10.30pm, as season opener for the PBS arts anthology show *Alive from Off Center*. Further, it was introduced on that show by the revered performance artist and musician Laurie Anderson: 'she led an unsuspecting public into how to view it'.

It was this film which launched the brothers into their parallel career in commercials and music videos. The day after *Crocodiles*' BAFTA premiere they were offered work on the Peter Gabriel 'Sledgehammer' promo (Aardman also participated) and shortly thereafter on a Honeywell ad, which used their 'cranky old style' to represent mechanisation before Honeywell brought it into the new age. This was an idyllic period, when animated commercials were thriving and there was also rather more funding for personal work. The Quays and their producer Keith Griffiths were able to develop a healthy mix of money-making activities alongside their own more avant-garde projects.

Images © Koninck Studios Ltd

The Black Dog

1987/18½mins

*Director/script/design/
animation*
Alison de Vere
Creative help
Karl Weschke
Art assistance
Ann Kotch
Film in Club Fata
Thalma Goldman
Rostrum camera
Ted Gerald
Music composed by
Peter Shade
Editing/post-production
Sean Lenihan
Producer
Lee Stork
Production company
The Black Dog Ltd for
Channel 4

Woman enters restaurant of the Fate Gaya

A woman wakes to find a black dog on her bed. As everything around her crumbles, the dog leads her into a wilderness and on to a strange journey of self-discovery.

In her youth Alison de Vere[109] studied fine art at the Royal Academy but did not complete the course, instead marrying fellow artist Karl Weschke and having a baby. The marriage was short-lived and de Vere had to take a succession of low-paid and not very artistic jobs: working for a dressmaker, in clubs and as a cleaner and washer-up in a restaurant. When she finally got into animation, it was hardly more creative - in the paint and trace department of Halas & Batchelor. Gradually, however, her design skills brought her more responsible work: she headed up the background department on *Yellow Submarine* and, mostly, directed commercials. She had a life-long interest in world religions and mythologies and belonged to the Theosophical Society, spending hours in their library. She would collect and note her ideas and the snippets gleaned from research, and was constantly experimenting with ways of combining her creativity with the animation skills she had acquired. Her 1975 short film, *Café*

Anubis rescues her after the ordeal

Storyboard images

Bar, was a wordless, perceptive and witty look at sexual politics, in which the characters are based on real people and much of the content on de Vere's personal experience, dreams and fantasies. This was the recipe she would develop for *The Black Dog*, a project suggested to her by a dream in which she saw 'a guy with a dog's head, Anubis the Egyptian deity. He was very real. That's why the film started to happen.'[110]

She had already worked with commissioning editor Paul Madden on the film *Silas Marner*, which the Channel had coproduced, so it was to Paul that Alison and her producer Lee Stork took the proposal for *The Black Dog*, which consisted of a handwritten, half-page synopsis and three minutes of film which she had completed on her own initiative.[111] The project was agreed very quickly, but it took a while for the finance people and producer Stork to thrash out the final deal. They received £80,000, which would have been totally inadequate had a standard team been making the film in a standard London studio. However, de Vere was largely working alone, with only occasional help. She was at the time looking after her elderly mother, finally moving down to Cornwall to be with her full-time. This also lowered her overheads, as well as bringing her closer to ex-husband Weschke, with whom she had always remained friendly, and to her son, who had moved there a few years previously. Both would collaborate on the film.

The first stage was the production of a detailed storyboard, confirmed by a two-page, typed, detailed synopsis. Despite the impression given by the film's structure of a stream-of-consciousness, spontaneous concatenation of events, in fact everything was worked out at the very beginning and very few changes occurred during the animation. Only the events in the pyramid were left vague in the synopsis. They were to be 'of a dreamlike kind, and their duration depends on the length finally decided for the film.' Thus all the film's ideas and motifs, from a multiplicity of sources, were already locked in. These include de Vere's dreams - the black dog, the boat with eyes and the wheel that becomes a child - as well as Egyptian mythology in the character of the dog, a reference to Anubis, the god of death who embalms and purifies bodies in preparation for their rebirth. And, given de Vere's assertion in the original proposal that no mythological references are accidental, Sandra Law's paper 'Putting Themselves in the Pictures'[112] is probably not mistaken in reading biblical stories too into the time in the wilderness and the temptations faced there, as well as the woman's rescue, Moses-like, from the water. There are also references to de Vere's early, low-paid jobs in dressmaking and catering; and to the lack of confidence which she never managed to overcome and which, according to her editor Sean Lenihan[113], is represented in the image of the terrified woman scuttling over a bridge which crumbles beneath her. And there are also references to her family, with son Ben appearing as the baby and husband Karl Weschke seen as the artist on scaffolding painting a mural inside the pyramid, just as he had once painted sets for the Ballet Nègre troupe. The strong Egyptian influence seen in Weschke's later work also finds its way into the film, in the pyramid and the landscape and colour scheme of that section.

Storyboard images

But above all the film's ideas relate to a woman's need to escape from the constraints of a world where her image is regulated, into one where she herself dictates her identity and, ultimately, her destiny - note the scene in a doctor's waiting room where all the waiting patients are different versions of the same woman, which she seems to want to sample. In this she draws on philosopher Martin Buber's distinction between destiny and fate, the latter comprising a set of pre-ordained trials and pitfalls and the former being within our own power to shape. De Vere: 'Unlike fate, destiny is your own as long as you are faithful to it.'[114] Ironically, fate as manifested in *The Black Dog* is not personified by males - whose desires are, after all, predominantly catered for in the Fata complex - but by three grotesque females who place temptations in the woman's path, Fraya (the dressmaker), whom Alison saw as relating to success, Gaya (the restaurateur) relating to greed and Maya (the night club proprietor) relating to illusion. These Fates do not correspond to those of Greek mythology and it seems likely that they were de Vere's own creation, synthesised from various mythologies from around the world.

All of these motifs survived from the original storyboard and treatment, and there was only one major change. At one time she planned an epilogue (it was undecided whether this was to be written or spoken), a poem she had written clarifying that the dog is the harbinger of death, but that death, after the journey taken with him, holds no fears. The idea was, however, abandoned, Alison presumably recognising that much of the strength of the film lay in its enigmatic presentation and the multiplicity of ideas and emotions which a viewer was left to conjure with: words would have destroyed this.

The film was delivered in April 1987 to a delighted Paul Madden ('It's still one of my favourite films'[115]) and went on to win two major prizes at that year's Annecy festival, the FIPRESCI (critics') prize and that for best TV film, and to cause a stir at the (non-competitive) 1987 Bristol Animation Festival. In 1989 it received the Grand Prix at Odense in Denmark, from a jury including celebrated British director Lindsey Anderson and that same year de Vere was the subject of a retrospective at the Bristol Festival.

In March 1988 the film was premiered on Channel 4 in a 9.30pm slot, in an imaginative double bill with Joanna Quinn's *Girls Night Out*, which had also won a major prize at Annecy and which presents an intriguing alternative take on woman's position in a man's world. *The Black Dog* did not get a theatrical release - very few shorts did, even in 1988, and the length and subject matter of this particular film would have rendered it fairly intractable in the eyes of distributors and exhibitors. (The far shorter *Café Bar* had had a cinema release.) Likewise, a trawl through the Channel 4 archives located no substantial reviews

Character design

And another temptation

from the TV transmission: like much innovative animation, it made little impact outside the animation community.

Only after de Vere's death was this wrong righted to some small extent in Richard Taylor's obituary to her in *The Guardian*[116], in which he suggests that '*The Black Dog* represents the same sort of advance in animation that *The Marriage of Figaro* was in opera'. Just as the characters in *The Marriage of Figaro* were portrayed as more rounded, more subtle, more real than those in operas up to that time, so, he feels *The Black Dog* represented 'the most complete rendering of a human being ever seen in animation.'[117]

Alice

(Něco z Alenky) 1987/84mins or 6 x 14mins

Director/script/design
Jan Švankmajer
Inspired by
Lewis Carroll's
Alice in Wonderland
Alice
Kristýna Kohoutová
Art direction
Eva Švankmajerová
Jiří Bláha
Sound
Ivo Špalj
Robert Jansa
Editor
Marie Zemanová
Animation
Bedřich Glaser
Director of photography
Svatopluk Malý
Production manager
Jaromir Kallista
Producer
Peter-Christian Fueter
Executive producers
Keith Griffiths
Michael Havas
Production company
Condor Features in
association with Film
Four International and
Hessischer Rundfunk

At the Mad Hatter's

Alice dozes off to sleep by a stream. Indoors the stuffed white rabbit escapes from his display case and sets off, followed by Alice, on a strange journey.

All Jan Švankmajer's films reflect aspects of his very specific background but *Alice*, his first feature, displays the complete compendium. Born and brought up in Prague, he is, he says, 'steeped in it'[118]. He has a particular interest in the Prague of 16th-century Habsburg Emperor Rudolf II, who ruled from that city, presided over a glittering court and commissioned an array of highly idiosyncratic Mannerist art works, of which the best-known exponent was Rudolf's court painter, Giuseppe Arcimboldo. The fact that the totalitarian regimes running Czechoslovakia in later times strongly disapproved of this work probably made it all the more attractive to Švankmajer. Another passion of Rudolf II was collecting objects for his 'cabinets of curiosities' - strange

Hybrids arrive with the carriage

More hybrids organising transport.
Part of Švankmajer's storyboard

pieces, man-made and natural, animal, vegetable and mineral. Rudolf's original cabinets were dismantled in the 1930s but Švankmajer has been trying to recreate them in his work for many years, and not only in his films. As early as the 1970s he made a series of sculptures entitled *Cabinets of Natural History*, glass cases containing strange beings assembled from incongruous elements of a variety of creatures - and bearing an uncanny resemblance to the hybrids which, for example, will arrive to transport Alice off to the palace.

Likewise, puppets entered Švankmajer's life early on - and transformed it. Like all Czech families, his had a little puppet theatre at home, where he would give performances from the age of 9. He would later study stage design and then puppetry and eventually work at the Laterna Magika, putting on puppet shows for adults as well as children. The acceptance of puppets as an adult form is crucial to his work and one of many elements which make it somewhat exotic for us. Only the Mad Hatter among the *Alice* characters is designed as a traditional Czech theatre puppet, but all are puppets in the sense in which Švankmajer fell in love with them as a child, as magical vehicles for generating life from the inanimate. As an adult, he sees them as the embodiment of a philosophical truth about manipulation.[119] But the Laterna Magika did not only produce straight puppet shows: it also staged mixed-media events incorporating film, and it was the discovery of the cut as a way of changing scene - all those scene changes in puppet shows were so laborious - that inspired him to try the cinema.[120] He began making films in the early 1960s, concurrently with the Czech New Wave of Forman, Menzel and co, but to him they were an irrelevance. His inspiration came largely from art and from the theatre - he cites Ernst and Meyerhold - though he did admire Fellini and Méliès, and would later come to sense a kindred spirit in David Lynch.[121]

The third and perhaps most influential current to enter Švankmajer's life was Surrealism: he joined the Prague branch - which was then, as for most of its existence, forbidden - in 1970, just after the Prague Spring, when the Soviet authorities were becoming ever stricter. Probably because of its underground nature, Czech Surrealism retained a bite which had latterly dissipated in the Western variety, when it found its way into popular culture. In the Soviet bloc the combination of a realistic surface texture appended to an utterly fantastic object, creature or event struck the authorities as in itself dangerous. Švankmajer feels they considered the very exercise of imagination to be a threat. One of the Surrealists' major interests was that of dreams: their concept of 'communicating vessels' maintained that dreaming and waking are two, equally important, sides of our existence. *Alice*, the quintessential Surrealist dream film, would demonstrate this realistic surface detail applied to the logic of the dream world, sprinkled liberally with dark, Surrealist humour.

We have to assume that Jan's late wife Eva was also influential in his work, given that both artists ranged across all the arts and often collaborated on specific projects. Now he is hard to pin down on the actual nature of her contribution:

She was primarily a poet and a painter and had her own programme. I would just ask her for advice in areas where I knew her solution would be more authentic than mine. She would never compromise: when she had created something, she'd say "Here it is. Take it or leave it."

Judging from her other art works, we can perhaps assume that some of the more playful design ideas in *Alice*, on which she was co-art director, might have been hers. She certainly designed the playing-card courtiers and, as a typically sly joke, gave the wicked Queen her own face.

Several of Švankmajer's films were banned - usually without any reason being given. From 1973 to 1980 he was prevented[122] from making films entirely. Two years later, as a result of *Dimensions of Dialogue* (1982) - which, to give the authorities their due, does appear to contain some fairly explicit political criticism - he had to stop production for a further three years. He was not, however, inactive during this time, beginning preparations and scriptwriting for his first feature film, to be based on *Alice in Wonderland*.

The choice could hardly have been more appropriate, given the mysterious workings of the state-run film industry of the period. The *Alice* script would, it seems, certainly not have been accepted as a Czech production, due both to its Surrealist content and to its heroine's habit of challenging authority. Yet, as an official co-production, it might have been accepted, because official co-productions brought in considerable wealth. Czechoslovak Filmexport would work out a budget which was high-ish by Western European standards, then collect all the overseas cash into a central government pot and commission one of the Central Committee-sanctioned Czech companies to make the film. They would of course pay the crew at Czech rates, whereas the overseas co-producers would be paying something like twenty times that amount.[123] Understandably, Western co-producers were not keen on this arrangement. There was, however, a loophole which Švankmajer and his producer Jaromir Kallista would endeavour to exploit, should overseas funding be found.

This latter job was entrusted to two intrepid executive producers. Michael Havas, Czech-born but raised in New Zealand, returned to Prague to study at the FAMU film school and remained there making films for Western clients. He was also a trusted ally of Jan Švankmajer. Keith Griffiths, London-based, had by that time produced several films for the Quays and directed a documentary on Švankmajer[124] for Channel 4. Keith remembers bumping into Jeremy Isaacs in a Channel 4 toilet shortly after this documentary had gone out[125]. Isaacs had liked the programme and was intrigued by Švankmajer. Griffiths told him about the proposed feature, and that thanks to Michael Havas a Swiss producer and a German TV station were already interested. European co-productions were unusual in those days and this also impressed Isaacs, who instantly agreed, in

Eva Švankmajerová gave the Queen her own face

The White Rabbit arrives at the palace

principle, to the project. Paul Madden, who would commission the film, also needed little persuasion, having commissioned the Švankmajer documentary. Channel 4 boldly signed the deal, contributing £70,000, ie 43 per cent of the budget, in the full knowledge that that this production was not sanctioned by the Czech authorities and that the film might not even get made.

The next problem was that of getting the money to Prague without the majority of it going to the government. The loophole offered was a little company specialising in audiovisual displays for exhibitions which, as a major foreign currency earner, had various privileges, such as authorisation to get film processed at the state-owned Barrandov labs. The contract Švankmajer signed with them was for a 'film and slide show, with cartoons' entitled *The Demystification of Time and Space*.[126] Funds for the production were thus transferred to Prague with a proportion left in Western currency, which was extremely valuable on the black market.[127] The rest was handed to the audiovisual displays people, for legal conversion into Czech crowns. It is unclear how much commission they charged for this service and, presumably, for their discretion - but their usual rate was 40 per cent. Given the modest sums which left the UK, Switzerland and Germany, this did not leave much to produce a feature film.

But Švankmajer's team did not need a great deal. They had their own studio in what had been a bakery, in the old town, with an adjoining flat which housed a production office and editing room. Today the studio is a pizza restaurant. It was, as Kallista points out[128], a good thing that Alice and therefore the set was small, because the bakery ceiling was only 2.3 metres high. Likewise, because the majority of the film was shot in interiors, they only needed a crew of five. These were the same trusted colleagues whose names appear on the credits of all Švankmajer's films and they worked together well, even in such close proximity. And because Švankmajer owned his camera and lighting equipment they were able to work at their own pace, long hours if need be.[129] This small team would toil away, invisibly, for a year, processing the film in minute rolls via the 'front' company. Keith would visit periodically to see 'tiny fragments on a shaky editing machine'. The first screening of the fragments joined together was notable. The co-producers were brought out to Prague and the film was projected in a screening room at Barrandov. The projectionist must have shopped them because a black, ministry car was already waiting as they left the screening room. There was an almighty row: 'You can't do that, you can't make a feature film', ranted the ministry people. 'Well I'm sorry, we've done it', said the Swiss producer Peter-Christian Fueter, and indeed they had. Or perhaps they had not. A print was already en route for Brussels, where Surrealist friends of Švankmajer had mounted some kind of commercial exhibition featuring truncated sections of the film, which clearly demonstrated that it was not a feature but short scenes for an audiovisual exhibition.[130] The reconstituted print then made its way to the Berlin festival, where it had been

Alice after the shrinking potion

invited for a special, out-of-competition 'guest' slot. The Czech delegation was decidedly discomfited by the buzz around this Swiss feature they knew nothing about, made in Prague by Jan Švankmajer.

Švankmajer never intended the film as an adaptation of Carroll - it was his interpretation and as such he entitled it, in Czech, not *Alice* but *Something of Alice*. He is happy to agree that the whole thing is far more Prague than Oxfordshire. And in terms of plot incident, it is not that faithful. Carroll did not feature an underground larder, but the cellar is a recurring theme in Švankmajer and relates to a particular childhood fear of his own. And much of Carroll is missing - including the Mock Turtle, the Dodo and the Cheshire Cat. However, what remains packs such an authentic punch that, according to Philip Strick, 'one has the unsettling sense of watching an old and well-remembered dream in a new and disturbing state of hallucination'.[131] Švankmajer is confident that his own take on the book - his understanding of the story as a metaphor for the traumas of childhood and adolescent growth, of dreams as a totally amoral phenomenon - is far closer to Carroll's than that of the majority of adapters, who have seen *Alice* as a fairy tale and imbued it with all sorts of moral messages. Perhaps Švankmajer's particular style of filmmaking, with its alarmingly magnified sound effects and disorienting editing technique, has brought it even closer.

A mouse prepares his camp fire on Alice's head

Alice took the best feature prize at Annecy and enjoyed successful theatrical distribution in the USA, France and the UK, where it ran at the Institute of Contemporary Arts. Some critics did not get it. Philip French called it a 'humourless Mittel-European nightmare'.[132] Others were extremely enthusiastic. Marina Vaizey: 'This is a surreal film of elegiac melancholy [...] an astonishing feat of visual imagination. The whole has a weird, compelling beauty.'[133] For Geoff Andrew:

... no other filmmaker - and I include David Lynch - is so consistently inventive in his ability to marry pure, startling nonsense with rigorous logic, black wit with piercing psychological insights. [...] Švankmajer's brilliance lies in his ability to imagine the unimaginable, and to invest his impossible universe with a wealth of subtle, sinister meanings of nightmarish familiarity. [...] He is clearly in touch with dark, subconscious forces of which other directors are barely aware.[134]

Once the film had finished its theatrical career, it was to be aired on Channel 4 over the New Year period 1989-1990, by which time I was in post. Scheduling was not easy. The German co-producer, from Hessischer Rundfunk, had used funds from that channel's children's programming budget, so the film had been delivered in series as well as feature-length format. At the beginning of the film, Alice says: 'Now you will see a film for children - perhaps,' and Channel 4 shared her doubts. While we were convinced that children are by and large considerably more robust than their parents and usually seem to enjoy a bit of spookiness, even a few children complaining of nightmares would have looked bad on the duty log of phone calls into the Channel. But I was very anxious for the series to be shown - I actually prefer it to the feature. For me Carroll's episodic format works well in a novel, which is not usually read in one go, but a feature film needs a more differentiated form to carry at least this viewer through. We finally scheduled the series as far away from bedtime as possible, at lunchtime - 1.40pm - stripped across a holiday week when adults might also be around. We took the precaution of asking the ITC regulators to screen it beforehand and they demanded some cuts for the pre-watershed transmissions. The nails in a pot of jam had to be removed, for example. As far as I remember there were no problems from parents - though Švankmajer remembers hearing that Swiss parents were up in arms. The feature-length version aired several times, but never before midnight.

After *Alice*, Švankmajer made a few more short films (including *Food*, also co-funded by C4) but since 1994 he has made only features. This is not, he says, because he does not want to make any more shorts, but because he has a large backlog of feature film ideas 'in the drawer', written during the period when he was not allowed to make them. The production of features, and their funding by overseas co-producers, has brought him up against Western capitalism:

I am under no illusions that the monies people are willing to give me now for my films don't come with their own type of demands. The capital creates its own form of censorship, which we'll have to struggle against. One has to struggle just as one had to struggle with ideological censorship.[135]

He has in fact, so insiders say, encountered amazingly little 'interference' from Western co-producers. Yet the struggle must, of course, continue. For conflict is the very source of Švankmajer's creation.

Images © Athanor

Girls Night Out

1985-88/6mins

Director/animation
Joanna Quinn
Script
Angela Hughes
Joanna Quinn
Voices
Myfanwy Talog
Gillian Elisa Thomas
Catrin Llwyd
Sian Jones
Stephen Lyons
Sound
Les Mills
Cast Director
Pat Griffiths
Colouring
Antonio Leslie
Simon Josebury
Neg Cut
Steve West
Production company
Chapter Film Workshop
Cardiff and Middlesex
Polytechnic with
financial assistance from
S4C and Channel 4

Beryl, a buxom factory-worker, is taken out on a surprise treat by a crowd of women friends from work. Leaving her husband in front of the television, she makes her way to The Bull, where the cabaret is a male stripper.

At the age of 14, Joanna Quinn liked drawing and liked *The Beano* comic, so she decided to put together a portfolio of her drawings and apply for a job there.[136] They suggested she should first go to art school, a totally novel idea to the young Quinn, but one which seemed to make sense. So after an art foundation course at Goldsmiths College, she enrolled to study graphic design at Middlesex Polytechnic. Among the various disciplines embraced by the graphic design department, she was most enthusiastic about life drawing and photography - the latter being the career she most wanted to pursue. Both require a talent for observation and a curiosity about people which have been noticeable in all her work. (And in the street: 'I'm always getting shouted at for staring at people'.) Animation was another of the skills she was encouraged to try, though that very small option in the department seems to have been managed somewhat chaotically. The head had just left and it was being run, by default, by administrator-cum-technician Phil Davies. Later to become one of the country's most successful animation producers, he knew very little about the subject at that time. But occasional visiting lecturers, access to a bit of equipment and a general benign neglect appeared to be all Joanna needed. Early efforts include a traditional cartoon entitled *Superdog* ('really terrible' - but actually extraordinarily accomplished for a beginner) and an experiment in animating life drawing which definitively established her future style.

Joanna's life drawing classes paid off

While she was acquiring these skills, she cannot have escaped the generally feminist climate of Britain in the early 1980s, but at that stage it was not of particular interest to her: at her college interview she had been naïve enough to cite Helmut Newton as her favourite photographer. If her films have a certain feminist tone it far more probably derives from her upbringing by a single parent, her very gutsy mother. 'She was always struggling to pay the bills, but always laughing. She never told anyone her problems.' Her mother was, in fact, one of two women who would coalesce to become Beryl, the star of *Girls Night Out*. The other was a motherly woman with a great personality who worked in the canteen at the Poly, a place where Joanna would frequently seek refuge from the general trendiness of her fellow-students. Another influence was a spell of holiday work in a pharmaceutical factory, where she had been greatly impressed by the female camaraderie on display, the determination to make the best of the most tedious jobs. As for the incident which was to trigger the tale: well, male strippers were just coming in at the time and a research trip to one such performance convinced Joanna that this would be the perfect vehicle for her story of women turning the tables on male superiority.

Image from the original comic strip

The original plan was not an animated film at all, but a comic strip version of Beryl's adventures. This was not very sophisticated, with Beryl, having torn off the g-string, taking a snap of what is revealed and leaving us with a view of the stripper's behind but robbing us of his reaction. Various storyboard versions and character studies sharpened up the humour and the message and made Beryl less of an elderly frump and more of a personality. The style Joanna evolved showed evidence of her penchant for life-drawing (especially in the character of the stripper), but the film was predominantly cartoony. The life-drawing influence would become more marked in her later career. The technique she used was, appropriately, a mixture of drawing and animation techniques, with everything originally drawn on paper and thereafter a mix of paper and cel.

It was very ambitious for a student film, and Joanna had not managed to colour the whole film by the time she had to submit it for evaluation. Partly because the film was unfinished and partly because of restricted budgets, there was no question of a professional voice track at that time. So Joanna, Phil, Les Mills (who had taught and encouraged her at sixth form college and is now her producer and writer) and the canteen lady herself were all enlisted, the latter suffering horribly from stage fright and conveying nothing like the gutsy extrovert character of her fictional incarnation. Phil, as the stripper, was encouraged to ad lib as he flirted with Beryl: 'Let me take you away from all this' was his big line. This 1985 version, though incomplete, was nevertheless an astonishingly good student film, but deemed by faculty insufficient to win Joanna a first class degree. Phil surmises that this was unrelated to the quality of the film - it was just that the course leaders did not consider animation a serious option.[137]

Britannia (1993). Less cartoon, more life drawing
©S4C/Channel Four Television Corp

On graduation, Joanna moved to Wales. There was a lot of animation activity there at the time and S4C was sponsoring locally-based filmmakers. Now working with Les, Joanna approached S4C for funding, since she would now produce a Welsh as well as a new English language version. She was also encouraged to approach Channel 4, and Paul Madden managed to persuade her to increase her extremely modest funding request to the princely sum of £4,500. This, together with S4C's input, was enough to cover the film's original £2,394.58 budget, some extra colouring work, new, professional, English and Welsh soundtracks and a new optical print.

The new English soundtrack, Joanna's first experience with professional voice actors, nearly came to grief. In an attempt to simulate the pub atmosphere and elicit some appropriately ribald improvisation, she put three bottles of Spanish champagne in the booth with the actors. They just finished recording as one of the actresses collapsed on the floor. As it was, the voices were just right. All were provided by Joanna's preferred category: radio actors or voice professionals rather than well-known faces, people whose only tool is their voice and who have therefore cultivated a richness and versatility often lacking in TV or cinema stars.

Early character designs: a frumpier Beryl

The film was accepted for the 1987 Annecy festival, which was quite an eye-opener for Joanna. Brought up in a Britain in which feminism had already affected basic assumptions, she was amazed by the sexist humour on display in what was still at that time a male-dominated area. 'In the French films most of the women were naked. And the audience loved it. I was really shocked. They'd have had eggs thrown at the screen over here.' After this revelation, she did come to feel that perhaps she had a duty to her sisters to continue the rather feminist trend of her work - though her anti-masculine jibes are at the most gently mischievous.

In that Annecy milieu the film must have stood out as something totally fresh, for it won three prizes including the prestigious Special Jury Prize. The combined print had not been ready in time, so a separate magnetic track of the new, professional soundtrack had been synchronised to the original film, which ran faultlessly for the competition screening. Sadly, when it came to the end-of-festival prize-giving ceremony and screening of the winning films, flustered technicians somehow ran, instead, the original version with its amateur and very embarrassed voices. But at least it was too late to take the prizes away.

The film was premiered on Channel 4 in March 1988, in an enterprising double bill with *The Black Dog*, both having won major prizes at Annecy and both challenging preconceptions about the role of women. These were the days when odd slots could be found for animation in peaktime (9.30 in this case) and the press responded: 'Good to see M Grade scheduling animations at mainstream time, especially when they're as original as *The Black Dog* and *Girls Night Out*' (*The Independent*)[138]. *The Daily Mail*, making this double bill its Pick of the Day, called the films 'revelations' and *Girls Night Out* 'best laugh of the night'.[139] Likewise, *Time Out* gave the programme broad and enthusiastic coverage, ending with 'The film is clearly feminist in intent but it doesn't smash you over the head with its message. Instead you are drawn along by the fabulous graphic style of Quinn's work as well as the irresistible, cackling Welsh voices that leave you clutching your sides. Quite brilliant.'[140] (So perhaps the Spanish champagne was a good investment after all.)

Joanna would go on to make a further Beryl film for Channel 4 and S4C, *Body Beautiful*. By 1990 Beryl has matured, while the latest thing to make its mark on Welsh society is now Japanese companies setting up in the valleys. *Body Beautiful* is set in such a factory, with a surreal clash of cultures going on in the background, while the *coup de grâce* Beryl visits on Vince, the factory's resident male chauvinist - brilliantly, leeringly voiced by Rob Brydon - is no spur-of-the-moment, booze-inspired urge, but a cleverly thought-out and long-rehearsed strategy. Understanding that shorts were an uncomfortable fit in the TV schedules - and more so as the years went on - and that being a comedy director her ideas would work equally well in series format, Joanna then brought us, in 1999, a proposal which had again moved with the times. By now Beryl had become a little more introspective. She had also acquired a video camera with which to record her activities as well as her musings on life - and she had taken a course in film studies. The proposal was for a series of 3-minute segments in the slot following the news, each reporting an incident - a friend's wedding, a visit to her sister in California, etc. It did not find favour at Channel 4, so Joanna and Les funded the first episode themselves, with generous input from S4C. It has taken an unprecedented haul of prizes, including four Grands Prix, various critics' prizes and audience prizes and the Cartoon d'Or for best European film. Yet, sadly, there are still no prospects of a series. The combination of that fluid, labour-intensive and hence quite pricey draughtsman's style, and the female gender, age and lack of glamour of its protagonist appears to have done for the project. Joanna and Les, however, are not quitters and are working on the next episode as this book goes to press.

Body Beautiful. Beryl and Vince
© S4C/Channel Four Television Corp

Girls Night Out images © Joanna Quinn

Feet of Song

1988/5½mins

Director/design/animation
Erica Russell
Assisted by
Adam Parker-Rhodes
Liz Spencer
Michelle Salamon
Chris Jones
Music
Charlie Hart
And featuring
Gasper Lawal
Alfred Bannerman
Camera
Begonia Tamarit
Ted Gerald
Editor
Picturehead Productions
Producer
Lee Stork
Production company
Malinka Films for Channel 4

Artwork figures © Erica Russell

A stylised figure appears and slowly stretches, to a simple melody played on a pipe. Gradually other figures appear and explode into a combination of graphics, sound and animation.

Born in New Zealand, Erica Russell grew up in South Africa, in an environment which is clearly visible in her work. There was no television and she rarely saw any animation. As a child her passions were dance (she went to ballet classes) and art. She was also exposed to African music from an early age, thanks to a mother with broad cultural interests and a black nanny. But when, as a rebellious teenager ('I was completely out of control'[141]) she left home and settled in the now notorious Hillbrow district of Johannesburg, her artistic interests became more focused. She joined dance workshops and mixed with dancers and choreographers. However, these were mostly gay and/or black, which - given that homosexual activity was then illegal in South Africa and that under apartheid blacks and whites were not supposed to fraternise, not to mention the ubiquitous drug culture of the time - made life quite dangerous for the young Erica. Her mother bribed her to attend an art school, but this only lasted four months. In the end, she was dispatched to London, on a one-way ticket, to get her out of harm's way.

Abstract image from a close-up

Artwork figures
© Erica Russell

Arriving here at the age of 19, after a chance meeting she ended up in the paint-and-trace department at Richard Williams' studio. This was the early 1970s, when commercials were plentiful and Williams was also working on a feature film. A combination of luck and talent brought her to the attention of Disney veteran Art Babbitt, who was there for six months teaching classic animation skills to the Richard Williams staff. He liked her drawings so much that he asked for her as his assistant, and trained her to produce work that was 'wild and free. And if I drew too much he'd fight me.' A viewing of Len Lye's *Free Radicals* a little while later confirmed her in the desire to make her own wild and free film.

Via a succession of free-lance jobs - animating, notably, her first dance for Paul Vester's *Sunbeam* - she developed her style: short, sharp, punchy and visually innovative. Having set up her own studio in partnership with John Challis in 1985, she directed a 60-second commercial which launched Virgin Megastore. This generously paid commission enabled her to buy the line tester which would change her life. Playing on it - feeding into it some already-completed drawings and manipulating them in various ways - suggested the idea of *Feet of Song* to her. She would make a film consisting of a series of the 'accidents' which arose via such manipulations.
[I'd] get a nice chunk of animation that kind of worked and then take it to the line-tester and start to play with it, flip it and flop it, underlight it, make patterns based on dances, and set them to music. This machine was like my baby.

Starting to put together a pilot to attract funding, she discovered that the line-tester also presented one major problem: 'Because it enabled me to do anything at all, I really needed to create a box that I had to fit myself into.' The 'box' she decided on was 'a film that celebrates the influence of Africa on 20th-century modernist art, using music and movement from Africa. A celebration of that combination.' The images would suggest Braque, Picasso, Matisse, Léger. Len Lye would also be recognisable. A second criterion was that the film needed to be flat, like a painting. This was a time when computer animation was the new big thing and the trend was into volume - all the more reason for Erica to shun the third dimension. A further consideration related to an article in the 'Mission Statement' section of her cv: 'The human body is inexhaustibly interesting.' Even when the dancing bodies in *Feet of Song* were stylised to the point of abstraction they would remain anatomically correct, with none of the 'squash and stretch' found in classical cartoon animation: they would retain muscle strength and human dynamics and they would be sexy. (Erica is fond of quoting a choreographer who once said that dance is generated neither in your brain nor in your feet, but 'somewhere in between'.) A mutual friend put her in touch with Lee Stork, a producer who had worked with Alison de Vere at Wyatt Cattaneo, had just finished de Vere's Channel 4 film *The Black Dog* and now decided to retire. But the *Feet of Song* pilot changed his mind. He rushed it over to Channel 4 and Paul Madden's response was immediate. The film was in production a couple of months later.

The production process was unusual in several ways, perhaps the most unusual being that music and visuals were created in parallel, rather than one following and depending on the other. Charlie Hart (who has since worked with Erica on all her films) is a musician with broad interests, encompassing classical, jazz and soul, who had spent his 'gap' year before university in Ghana and then would occasionally return there to brush up on highlife music and marimba-playing and play alto sax with local bands. Erica was able to bring him up to date on the most recent developments in African music, and on what inspired her: the emotional impact, mood and energy of the music. In the absence of a storyboard, the film's structure - initially very loose - would be provided by a breakdown of the music tracks. Charlie would send tapes of tunes and Erica would decide which ones to use and at what length - 'we'd squash it and cut it and manipulate the sound a lot'. This very rough guide track was broken down and transferred to a chart and the animation was done to the music, with each piece dictating a specific look.

Artwork figures
© Erica Russell

Abstract image from a close-up

Erica worked with a South African dance troupe, Shikisha, and the Nigerian choreographer George Dzukunu, to construct the dances. The original animation was just as loose as the guide track. Then, somehow, in collaboration 'we forced the two together.' Charlie was, according to Erica, 'not precious... very receptive and great at socialising and getting the right people together.' Thus the music was African-inspired, composed and produced by Charlie and performed by both Africans and Europeans, with Charlie playing flute, rhythm guitar, bass, keyboards and some percussion and Les Morgan on drums underpinning some sections. Charlie explains the final structure thus:
Intro: played on a small wooden flute by me.
Part 1: rhythm guitar riff (again played by me) is inspired by Mbira/Chimurenga music from Zimbabwe. There is a flute theme which is repeated at end of part 4.
Part 2: Erica and I were looking for something very tropical and sensuous sounding, possibly Congolese-influenced. The lead guitar is Alfred Bannerman making a gorgeous entry which Erica capitalised on brilliantly.
Part 3: percussion section. Definite mood change. Gasper Lawal had a major input. However, I played a few parts (on a western drum kit!), notably the gelede section (Nigerian inspiration) - red and black dancers using their elbows.
Part 4: abstract section: the mood is almost intoxicated, inspired by Malian kora music. I played the lead lines on a synthesizer in my own flat. At the end there is a restatement of original flute theme.
Coda: similar to intro.[142]

Both the dance and the music consisted of cycles of about 30 seconds, with the six different dance sequences being achieved by a variety of techniques - cel, cut-out, airbrush - and then being manipulated in a variety of ways in the

Storyboard panel for Levi's Jeans for Women ad - usually Erica eschews storyboards
Courtesy Erica Russell

line-tester. So, for example, limbs are multiplied, lines of dancers extended and close-ups reduce already-stylised dancers to dancing lines and shapes. Additionally, a very expensive and rather rough kind of paper was used so that the ink would sink in to produce more vibrant colours, and camera person Begonia Tamarit could light it in such a way as to bring out the texture. The visuals were 'more or less together' by the time the musicians came in to do the final recording. Charlie had socialised well and recruited London-based star drummer Gasper Lawal, who was initially a bit sniffy at the prospect of working on an animated film, but as soon as he saw Erica's line test for the stamping sequence (based on the gelede) he became an enthusiastic member of the project.

The production took about ten months and the budget (around £60,000) was not, of course, as generous as those for commercials. But it was enough to enable Erica to stop doing ads for the whole period and devote herself to the animation, employing others to come in to do stencils and various bits of artwork, as well as Begonia Tamarit to shoot the film. Towards the end of the production, the film finally received its title. Adam Parker-Rhodes, Erica's partner, discovered that the word for dance in the language of the Dan people of the Ivory Coast translates, literally, as 'feet of song'.

The film premiered at 6pm, in a double bill with a repeat of *The Black Dog* as part of Channel 4's 1989 Animation Festival season. Responses were good - 'A riot of pure line and colour, exhilarating in its grace and beauty' (Geoff Andrew, *Time Out*) - and it turned out to be a film which worked well, not only for viewers but also for the schedulers, so it benefited from several repeats over the following years. It also took the BFI's Mari Kuttna Award for best British animation of 1989 and was seen at various overseas festivals, which led to three commissions from Levi's for women's jeans commercials based on the ideas and look of *Feet of Song*. One of these would win a prestigious Clio award.

Producer Lee Stork, however, warned Erica against getting typecast as a decorative animator of 'moving wallpaper' and both he and her partner Adam urged her to add a narrative element into her next film. This next, also for Channel 4, would be *Triangle* (1993), Oscar®-nominated and honoured with the British Animation Award for best film under 15 minutes. It would also lead to a third dance film, *Soma*.

Lip Synch: War Story

1989/5mins

Director
Peter Lord
Animation
Peter Lord
Janet Sanger
Nick Park
*Art direction/
assistant director*
Janet Sanger
Photography
Andy MacCormack
David Sproxton
Tristan Oliver
Model makers
Janet Sanger
Debbie Smith
Roger Jones
Elizabeth Hadley
*Interview/
sound recording*
Peter Lawrence
Narrator
Bill Perry
Editor
Helen Garrard
Production
Melanie Cole
Alan Gardner
Sara Mullock
Production company
Aardman Animations
for Channel 4

A Bristol man is interviewed about life during the war: shift work at the Bristol Aircraft Company, a noisy dustman and much more, all brought to life in plasticine.

The key role of Peter Lord, co-founder of Aardman, in the rise of British animation is well documented. But it is not widely known that plasticine was not always his medium. Or rather, he did sculpt in clay from a young age, but in his and David Sproxton's earliest animation efforts they tried out everything else first, dabbling in Terry Gilliam-style cut-outs, chalk drawings animated under the camera and then cel animation.[143] Their first big break, while still at school, was the result of good timing and a bit of nepotism. David's father, an ordained vicar and producer in the BBC's religious affairs department, happened to encounter there the producer of *Vision On* - a programme originally designed for hearing-impaired children but also watched by hearing children - and persuaded him to look at the schoolboys' work. This eventually resulted in a commission for thirteen 1-minute cel animation pieces featuring a rather feeble Superman-style character called Aardman. They completed these during a gap year and then went off to university, continuing to animate during their holidays. But, by now finding cel animation rather tedious for a two-man team, they started experimenting with plasticine, in the form of bas-reliefs. But the reliefs gradually grew higher.

It was perhaps lucky that the pair had seen very little puppet animation and had of course never been to an animation festival. They had seen photos of the Czech master, Trnka's, puppets but otherwise their diet had been restricted to *The Wombles* and other standard children's TV fare. Puppet animation of that period had used models made of latex and fabric built round an animatable skeleton. Because heads tended to be solid, any changes of facial expression were rudimentary. When, in 1976, *Vision On* came to an end, they were asked to develop the Morph character for its successor programme *Take Hart*, and this was when they started some limited experimentation with facial mobility. This was something most children's series did not attempt, for reasons of economy, and something which Trnka and the other East European schools of traditional puppet animation considered rather poor taste. But luckily none of this would affect Peter and David.

Early characterisation of Bill from Peter's sketchbook

The real breakthrough came with *Down and Out*, part of the BBC's 1979 *Animated Conversations* and their first foray into real-life dialogue. As already recounted, this led to the pair's first Channel 4 commission thanks to a meeting with Jeremy Isaacs at the 1981 Cambridge Animation Festival. The *Conversation Pieces* for C4 would mark Aardman's transition from that early flirtation with journalism to its real vocation, comedy. Like the *Animated Conversations*, this series was also based on recordings of ordinary people in specific situations, but by now it was apparent that subjects for eavesdropping were becoming ever harder to find and to record audibly. The animators had been dreadfully disappointed with a couple of the original recordings and had discovered that the only possible way to salvage reasonable films from them was to play the visuals for laughs. This trend would be pursued in the *Lip Synch* series.

The commission for *Lip Synch*, which would feature Peter's *War Story* and *Going Equipped* as well as Nick Park's *Creature Comforts*, Barry Purves' *Next* and Richard Goleszowski's *Ident*, finally went through four years later. By this time Aardman had matured as a studio, largely because the *Conversation Pieces* had led to a great deal of commercial work, so they now had cash, and were pleased to contribute almost 50 per cent of the *Lip Synch* budget, thereby retaining rights.

The other three directors would diverge wildly from the vox pops concept, but Peter's two contributions, *Going Equipped* and *War Story*, did remain faithful to the original concept. Both used interviews, with the interviewer entirely or almost entirely excised so as to leave a monologue. *Going Equipped* - the

Delivering coal in a house on the slant

reflections of a young man who has spent most of his life in various penal institutions - was shot first. Like *Down and Out*, it was done as serious journalism, based on an interview which extracted considerable emotion from its subject. Peter then turned his mind to *War Story*. In order to generate stories for *Lip Synch*, the studio had contacted various radio journalists for recommendations as to good interviewees. Peter Lawrence of Radio Bristol had done a documentary on Bristol in the Blitz, and recommended the elderly Bill Perry as a great raconteur. As had become the norm for the Aardman vox pop films, Peter Lord decided not to meet Bill 'because we preferred to work in a state of innocence'[144], but instead commissioned Peter Lawrence to do the interview - for there was already a rapport between the two. Bill had obviously told these old stories many times, and when, after the interview, it transpired that due to a technical problem it would have to be done again, he reproduced them once more - pretty well word for word.

The two and a half hours of interview which were produced actually ran a broad gamut of emotions. Bill had suffered from shell-shock when his factory had been blitzed, and there had been other sad moments among the reminiscences. The first cut, intended as the basis of the film, was nostalgic, imbued with regrets. But at about this time *Going Equipped* had been completed and shown. It was plain that audiences felt unsure how to react to animation - normally seen as a comedy medium - without gags.[145] So Peter changed tack on *War Story* completely and 'decided to go for cheap laughs'. This involved a different selection of material and also left in some of the exchanges between interviewee and interviewer, notably one where the latter is reduced to helpless laughter.

Because of Bill's style of story-telling - which seemed to move from one tale to another via some pretty nebulous connections - most anecdotes had no clear start point or punch-line, making it particularly difficult to find start and end points for the whole film. Peter decided to begin the film, *cinéma-vérité* style, with Bill in the present time having a slight altercation with the interviewer, before diving into the past. The end was rather harder and Peter had to make the best of the existing material. He ended on the story about Bill sheltering from bombs in the coal cupboard, with his mother-in-law and pregnant wife both on his lap. 'It was agony, Ivy, I was tattooed all over', Bill had said - 'It was agony, Ivy' being a catch-phrase from the 1950s radio show *Ray's a Laugh*. Peter uses this as an illustration to aspiring animators in his book *Cracking Animation*:
Then I had him clamp his pipe firmly between his teeth with a loud click, rather like Eric Morecambe used to do, waggle his eyebrows - and that was it. That was our ending. Not the world's best, perhaps, but it is quite a good example of how to bring your film to a pleasing end when the action or dialogue does not provide you with an obvious choice.[146]

Sketchbook page with gag possibilities

These were the days before digital technology could solve the many production problems it can today. On the most basic level, there is the issue of the nylon threads used to support puppets when their position is not balanced or, indeed, when they leave the ground. Nowadays digital post-production will remove these threads or whatever structures are used for this purpose. In 1989 the thread would have to be painstakingly coloured so as to merge into the background and above all the light had to be prevented from reflecting off it. In *War Story* the threads are still occasionally visible. In the absence of digital technology and of a budget for whatever optical post-production tricks were then available, they decided to do as much as possible in the camera. They also felt that these in-camera processes seemed to generate a certain energy: 'The energy that goes into the making of it somehow comes out on screen.' [147]

But sometimes these efforts did not come off. The transitions between the present-day Bill telling the story and the wartime Bill acting it out were particularly complicated. One transitional scene had present-day Bill talking in front of a very fine net. They were planning to fade down the lights on Bill and bring up the lights on the scene behind the net, as is done in the theatre, and the camera would track through to a scene from the past. But for some reason - now lost in the mists of time - this scheme came to nothing, the transition did not work and Bill is left talking in front of a dull net screen instead of the set he had previously inhabited, for no obvious reason. Another really tricky transition - but this time more successful - was where wartime Bill comes to the front door to see lights falling from the sky and the camera pans off him away from the sky over to another set, in darkness, with present-day Bill in front telling the story. As the light comes up we move forward over his shoulder into the wartime living room set. Doing this physically, with a complicated camera move between two sets, accompanied by changing light settings and shifting focus was extremely complex. Peter recalls shooting long into the night, praying that nothing would go wrong to require a re-shoot. Mercifully, on this occasion nothing did.

Another complication resulted from his design decision to abandon for this film the simple and elegant solution to the 'dead eyes' problem which he and David had pioneered, the use of beads moved by a pin. He decided the irises in these characters' eyes must be upright plasticine ovals, which of course could not rotate in sockets as round beads could. So to bring Bill to life his irises had to be moved, manually, across the whites of the eyes. Far more time consuming.

With Peter animating alone and so many complex shots, and with commercials work coming in to interrupt it, the film was taking for ever. Finally producer Sara Mullock brought in an extra cameraman and two animators to help Peter with the final touches. (Nick Park was one of the animators, and he did the scene where Bill runs down the corridor to the coal-hole holding the dog.[148]) The film represented a steep learning curve for Peter:

The bad joke, to me, was that it was meant to be an economical shoot. "I'll write in lots of visual gags. I won't have to spend long on the animation. It'll be easy to shoot." But all the different sets and rigs demanded otherwise… [149]

But the most important attribute of *War Story* is its handling of the humour. Peter's taste in comedy was largely formed in his teenage years, the late 1960s and early 1970s, when *Monty Python* and other zany TV comedies were running. 'There was a lot of physicality in their humour. It was based on surreal situations. I loved absurd physical juxtapositions of costumes, characters and locations.' Jacques Tati was also a hero, as was Tony Hancock, for character-based comedy. *War Story* embodies all these tendencies, with Peter's skills in comedy acting and timing most perfectly demonstrated in the two invented characters, the cat and the dog, which he decided to add in once he had committed the film to its comedy genre. The dog's routine, particularly - breathing a sigh of relief after a narrow escape from being mown down by Bill, only to be clobbered while off guard - is a very old slapstick gag, but achieved to perfection. Colleagues at the studio say that you can always recognise Peter's animation because he puts his own expressions and gestures in. Peter claims to be unaware of this - 'Moi? No, I'm totally idiosyncrasy-free' - but he does acknowledge the general truth of this, the fact that puppet animators *do seem to end up performing self-portraits. It's things they're totally unaware of - the way you hold your shoulders, the tilt of your head. I know, because people have told me that Morph moved like me, and when Nick animated Morph he's always sort of turned into Nick.*

War Story took a BAFTA nomination and major prizes at Ottawa and Chicago and led to a commercial in similar vein for the Britannia Building Society. The *Lip Synch* series in general led to a growth in the studio's prosperity and launched Peter on a journey towards longer-form animation, executive producing the two Wallace and Gromit half-hours, *The Wrong Trousers* and *A Close Shave*, co-directing *Chicken Run*, producing *The Curse of the Were-Rabbit* and also being closely involved with *Flushed Away*. These activities would, sadly, take him and the studio away from Channel 4, with the exception of some short film projects, which they would still bring our way. Most of these were by the studio's younger protégés, though Peter brought us his *Wat's Pig* (1996), which earned an Oscar® nomination.

The studio is now in partnership with an American major, and Peter is currently involved in five or six developments with them, some stop-frame and some CG (a technology which Peter characterises as 'an adventure holiday, exciting and slightly scary'). 'Our pitch', he says, 'is to produce British films. British films which will play all round the world, of course, but fundamentally… well, just doing what we instinctively do.'

Images © Aardman Animations Ltd 1989

Bill ending the film

Lip Synch: Creature Comforts

1989/5mins

Director/animation/
art direction
Nick Park
Models/sets
Michael Wright
Greg Boulton
John Parsons
Cliff Thorne
Animal sculptures
Debbie Smith
Photography
David Sproxton
David Alex Riddett
Andy MacCormack
Fred Reed
Editor
William Ennals
Producer
Sara Mullock
Production company
Aardman Animations
for Channel 4

A series of interviews with plasticine-animated animals in a zoo. Some feel well looked after. Others complain of cramped accommodation, bad food and bad English weather.

Ask a member of the public to name an animation studio and Aardman Animations will certainly be up there, along with Disney and Pixar. The studio's four Oscars® and a large proportion of its other awards, along with massive co-production investment by American major studios in its feature films, are a direct result of Aardman co-founders Peter Lord and David Sproxton coming across Nick Park at the National Film School. Nick was born and brought up in Preston, Lancashire, in a large family where people were making things all the time, from clothes (his mother) to an elaborate caravan for family holidays (his father). He had begun experimenting with traditional, drawn animation as a schoolboy and then, emulating his hero Ray Harryhausen, moved on to puppets. After a BA at Sheffield Polytechnic, he gained a place at the National Film School in 1980, and started work on *A Grand Day Out*. By 1985 the film was still not finished, so David and Peter invited Nick to join the studio to complete it.

As it happened, David and Peter had at that time just been commissioned by Channel 4 to make the follow-up series to the successful 1983 *Conversation*

Pieces, and they decided to assign some of these segments to newcomers in the studio Richard Goleszowski, Barry Purves and Nick Park. That earlier series had marked a transition from mostly journalism to mostly entertainment. But the new series, ultimately titled *Lip Synch*, was still intended to have a basis in real life situations and real conversations - yet somehow the interpretation of this brief varied widely from film to film.

It was fortunate that the Channel's attitude was so very hands-off because Aardman included in this new batch of supposed vox pops one film which had no dialogue at all (Barry Purves' *Next*) and one which had mostly grunts (Richard Goleszowski's *Ident*). Peter Lord's two contributions, *Going Equipped* and *War Story*, did remain faithful to the original concept, however, and Nick's *Creature Comforts* made a valiant effort.

By the time it was delivered to C4, I had replaced Paul Madden, and I have to confess that I was a bit sniffy about it on first viewing. I loved the gags and the characters but was slightly irritated by the way it seemed to change horses - not once but twice. It started as vox pops about zoos, then became (mostly) vox pops about people's own housing conditions and finally committed the cardinal sin of presenting as a vox pop the comments of a Brazilian student who had, I was sure, been let in on the secret and therefore peppered his comments with references more appropriate to his jaguar persona: 'carnivores', 'wild animals', etc. Posterity must be grateful that I was not in the commissioning job at the time or I would probably have tried to get Nick to sort out a more consistent soundtrack before starting to animate, possibly ruining it in the process.

Nick had decided - unlike Peter and David - to do the interviews himself and David acknowledges that they were 'not that rigorous about it. [He] came up with bits and if they were funny enough they got included'[150]. It was originally supposed to be about zoos, so Nick went to a zoo with his recording equipment, to eavesdrop on people's comments. However, neither the zoo authorities nor the people he was trying to record were particularly happy about this and the sound quality was abysmal. He then went to the friendly shopkeeper round the corner from the studio and asked whether he and his family would be good enough to discuss zoos for him. They obliged, with the wonderful series of non sequiturs that was subsequently put into the mouths of the polar bear family. But after a couple more such felicitous sound-bites, that vein was exhausted, so he moved on to interviewing people about their own accommodation. To me these interviews - such as the elderly bush baby who feels 'secure' as the bough she clings to lurches violently: 'They'll look after me, put me where I ought to be...' - offer the most touching insights into human beings, what they will put up with and how they try to put on a brave face. And I cannot but agree that the Brazilian student talking about his cramped hostel accommodation is wonderfully expressive - which made this by far the easiest character for Nick to animate. The voices do seem perfectly suited to the animals they represent, though the matches were not always obvious to the filmmakers. The Brazilian, for example, originally voiced a penguin rather than a jaguar.[151]

The character design was fairly traditional for most of the characters - only the birds were the result of a flight of imagination. Whatever bird design was adopted, they figured, they would in any case need detachable beaks to synch with the dialogue - so they decided to make a virtue of this and make a gag of the detachable beaks, with the gaudy colour scheme following on from that. As the two cameramen, Dave Riddett and Andy MacCormack, point out on the DVD commentary to the film[152], the characters in *Chicken Run* owe a considerable debt to these birds. The gorilla and the polar bear bodies feature large expanses of smooth, single-colour plasticine which reveal a changing pattern of finger prints as the characters are moved by the animator. Nick, apparently, used to assure his crew that 'we should never be ashamed of our medium', and indeed this low-tech insouciance even adds to the film's charm.

The shoot proceeded without incident. Video assist is now the norm when shooting, to provide instant evidence of what has been recorded and how it looks, and to check the timing. At the time of *Creature Comforts*, the studio did not have this safety net and most animators tended to send their footage off to the lab frequently. But Nick is a supremely confident animator and would refuse to send material off to the labs until the whole shot was finished. He simply trusted his instincts.

The humour has two main sources. One is Nick's extraordinary powers of observation. Although these are obviously animals - with the birds not even resembling anything in nature - their mannerisms are totally and very recognisably human, from the turtle drumming his fingers, perhaps out of embarrassment at the personal nature of the questioning, to the gestures of the infant multicoloured bird as she struggles to articulate her views about animals' lives in zoos as compared to circuses. This acute observation is accompanied by an impeccable sense of timing.

The other major source of humour is the whole other layer of narrative taking place in the background or intruding from outside the frame: faeces being delivered from the back end of a hippopotamus, while a young hippo tells us that some zoo cages are a bit 'grotty'; a resigned turtle walking round a treadmill while his cage-mate concedes that 'I've been in more comfortable rooms, yes…'. It turns out, as Paul Wells discovered while interviewing Nick[153], that these extraneous events were largely inspired by one of his favourite TV shows as a youngster, *It'll Be Alright on the Night*, a compilation of out-takes from programmes where serious recording is spoiled, more often than not by something beyond anyone's control happening in the background, unknown to the actor or presenter blithely carrying on in front of the mayhem.

Loved both by the public and by specialised animation audiences at home and abroad, the film propelled Nick, Aardman and, for a while, British animation to stardom. It was not only the brilliant observation and the very special humour. In the animation world the Aardman approach to puppet animation - fairly rough plasticine figures with mobile, expressive faces - suddenly hit the headlines. The innovation was noted with a special sense of shock in Czechoslovakia, home of the puppet theatre and of puppet animation:
To us Creature Comforts was almost like the explosion of a small atom bomb. [...] Trnka always insisted on puppets with an immobile face and he had to use a great deal of artifice to find a genuine cinematic solution... [...] Something like lip synch was unthinkable in Trnka's films. It smacked of Disney and that was something this great revolutionary who had declared war on superficial prettiness and on bad taste would never admit.[154]

Festival audiences, too, far more accustomed to the Eastern European style of puppets, were bowled over by the Aardman characters and the film went on to take top prizes at Hiroshima, Ottawa, Stuttgart, Annecy and many others. It took the Cartoon d'Or for best European film and the Oscar® for best short animation. In the UK it took the Mari Kuttna award for best British animated film and, at the British Animation Awards, both the best film under 15 minutes and the best use of humour. Its impact is still not forgotten. Naresh Ramchandani recently wrote in the MediaGuardian that:
When Creature Comforts was released in 1989, every creative person I knew was jealous. Like Harold Pinter, Gary Larson and Video Diaries all whizzed up in one big cultural blender.[155]

In the spring of 1991 Prime Minister John Major invited Nick to a cocktail party at 10 Downing Street, the BFI launched The Connoisseur Animation Collection[156] on video, a superb programme entitled The Best of British Animation ran at the Institute of Contemporary Arts and City Limits was able to write about 'a burgeoning and fertile area of current British filmmaking which is the envy of Europe'[157]. Advertisers wanted to cash in on this success and it seemed that the future of British animation was secure. In the event, though, many British animators would find that advertisers were asking only for Aardman imitations.

The effect of Creature Comforts on the studio itself was dramatic. Its first screening, at the British Animation Awards, unleashed an avalanche of proposals for commercials which really set the studio on a firm footing. Most advertisers, however, were suggesting carefully-scripted dialogue to simulate vox pops while still selling their product, whereas the Electricity Association's agency was willing to give real vox pops a try. Peter and Nick, the two directors

on the campaign, were even able to bring back some of the interviewees from *Creature Comforts*: the Brazilian student as Pablo the Parrot and the local shopkeeper and family as penguins. The resulting campaign won all the advertising awards of that year and gained a tremendous public following. Sadly, however, subsequent research revealed that a large number of viewers thought the ads were for gas, so the vox pops later had to be manipulated a bit to ensure more frequent use of the word 'electricity'.[158]

The speed of commercials production being what it is, the HeatElectric campaign was well under way before we had taken delivery of the whole *Lip Synch* series. If we held back *Creature Comforts* until the whole series was ready, the campaign would already be on air and it would look as if the film copied the ads rather than vice versa, so we rushed it out alone in a 10pm slot in April 1990 - though even that did not stop significant proportions of the press, especially in the US, reporting that the ads came first. We repeated the film later in the year with the whole series stripped across a week in peak time and, after the Oscar® in 1991, devoted a whole hour at 7pm on a bank holiday Monday to a celebration of Aardman. Channel 4 realised what a gem it had. On its website there is a potted history of the Channel, giving key moments, special honours, major controversies and so on. The only mention of animation in the whole history is the screening of *Creature Comforts*, the 'key moment' of 1990.

The film later did what I had hoped our most entertaining shorts would do - it became a high profile series. But not, sadly, on Channel 4. Immediately after the original short, the studio did not feel able to consolidate on this success with a series. They had no pool of animators - just Peter, Nick, Barry and Richard Goleszowski - and their thriving commercials business was keeping them far too busy for such ambitious new initiatives. The series idea only came to them many years later, when they had a studio-full of animators waiting to go on a feature project with DreamWorks. When that failed to get the go-ahead, they desperately needed something that could be developed fast.[159] And so it was that the first *Creature Comforts* series, directed by Richard Goleszowski, became one of the hits of 2003 for C4's erstwhile senior partner, ITV.

Images © Aardman Animations Ltd 1989

Deadtime Stories for Big Folk:

Deadsy / Door

1990/2 x 5mins

Director/ design/
performed by
David Anderson
Script/narration
Russell Hoban
Music
Dirk Campbell
Editor
Patrick Moore
Model camera operator
Fred Reed
Producers
James Bradley
Barnaby Spurrier
Production company
The Redwing Film Company
for Channel 4

Deadsy
Rendering/2D animation
Keith Rogerson
Angus Oliphant

Door
Animation
David Anderson
Fred Reed
Location camera unit
Fred Reed
Dave Alex Riddett
Andy MacCormack
Art direction/model making
Tim Farrington
Model makers
Louise Pratt
Fenella Hemus
Mark Gunning
Sound editor
James Mather

Deadsy as Mizz Youniverss
Photo David Anderson

Deadsy knows he is already a megaguy, but decides he will be even sexier, and will have even more people wanting to make it with him, if he changes sex. The Grim Reaper will become Mizz Youniverss.

On a planet consisting only of doors, he and she discuss going to 'sum uther playss' to search for a key. But they open the door that 'you berr not mess with', the one leading to the 'end of snivvelyzashuns we knowit'.

After completing his first Channel 4 project, *Dreamless Sleep*, in the absence of any immediate commissions David Anderson took a variety of jobs, mainly as a cameraman (which is what he trained as at the National Film School). He did some work for Aardman, who by this time were doing commercials, until being offered his own commercial, for 3i, which was to be based on *Dreamless Sleep*. By this time, David had gone into partnership, firstly with producer James Bradley, and 'I had to start letting go of total ownership, which was quite difficult for me - I'm an only child. It was good, a big breakthrough!'[160]

Deadsy's David Anderson mask

Deadsy

Subsequently the company was expanded to include a further three partners and named The Redwing Film Company.

This had solved David's production problems but he felt he also had a writing problem - in this area he had been 'tying myself in knots'. And he was indeed having trouble pinning down his initial idea for the project which would become *Deadtime Stories for Big Folk*. David's 'thing of the moment' in 1987 was transpersonal psychology, a discipline which combines elements of spirituality into the practice of modern psychology in the pursuit of personal development. He saw it as an aid to deciphering the complexities of childhood, upbringing and heredity; had himself benefited from such therapy and subsequently done some training as a practitioner. 'I thought it was the best thing since sliced bread.' He was now hoping to explore relationships, the pitfalls and the challenges, in this light. David now remembers no apocalyptic element in his original musings - still less any nuclear weapons - save for the tendency for us to self-destruct in our relationships with others. Yet the writer he approached to partner him on the films was Russell Hoban, someone he greatly admired and whose corrupted, post-apocalyptic language narrating the novel *Riddley Walker* interested him particularly. David feels that it was the fact that he mentioned *Riddley Walker* in his initial contact with Hoban, and that he had enclosed a copy of his own apocalyptic *Dreamless Sleep*, which sent the scripts down the nuclear track (as well as the fact that Hoban declined to read the books on transpersonal psychology that David had lent him[161]).

One characteristic of the language Hoban created for the films was certainly, in his mind, post-nuclear:
Between two to three thousand years from now, after the destruction of civilisation and after a long dark age and vicious reaction against science and technology and even all learning [...] people certainly wouldn't be talking received BBC English.[162]
It would be, in his words, 'a corrupted, degraded, survivor kind of speech.' The second characteristic was its embodiment of Hoban's ideas of the way the human mind works. It is not linear and does not just travel from A to B:
While you're thinking about whatever's the business at hand, all kinds of words and pictures leap in unbidden and they're part of the experience of the present moment. [...] I think all of us have a number of voices speaking inside us and we mostly give utterance only to the socially acceptable ones. [...] We have a lot of crazy voices in us, a lot of strange ones, and I'm always listening for those strange ones.[163]

A major problem in the collaboration could have been Hoban's matter-of-fact view of Death as a middle-man simply doing his job, which was certainly at odds with David's spiritual concept of death as a renewal of life. Yet the latter would finally see even this as liberating him from the parameters which had previously confined him. It was a classic example of a creative collaboration taking on a mind of its own. David was 'blown off course, but happy to be.' *Although the form was not in the direction I intended, there was something in his writing, particularly in* Door, *which was everything that I was thinking about… in other words. […] I ended up with a poem rather than a script!*[164]

This 'poem' was sent to commissioning editor Paul Madden, who deemed Anderson and Hoban a 'killer combination'[165] and enthusiastically backed the two films with 100 per cent funding. So then David simply had to find the right images to match Hoban's words. At first he felt paralysed, unable to add anything: 'It was such a good radio play already'[166]. He would pace round his garden, wearing headphones, listening over and over again and trying to summon up interesting visual ideas. Finally he went into production on *Deadsy*, in a studio in Clifton (Bristol) which had once been a coalman's store and was caked in coal dust. 'And I had this team of slaves, kids colouring in bits of paper. It was very basic and quite cold in the winter.'

Deadsy. A distorting mirror

Deadsy. Print-outs were photocopied and coloured

Like *Dreamless Sleep*, the *Deadtime Stories* production methods were highly experimental. *Deadsy* started off as a live action performance. David was the actor - for all sorts of reasons, ranging from the economical and practical benefits via his enjoyment of (and previous experience in) acting to an acknowledgement that his films 'are all bits of self-exploration. My mask shows my own face and I'm willing to accept those darker sides in me'[167]. A friend was shooting his performance in the Bristol coal store-cum-studio and they were trying to make the lighting look more interesting by bouncing it off a piece of bendy mirror foil which was being flexed randomly. When they noticed what an interesting image was being produced on the foil, they turned the camera round and re-shot the whole thing as seen in the foil. The frames of video thus produced were printed out by a video graphic printer, then photocopied and enlarged in order to increase the contrast, and the live action performance divided into sections, each being treated slightly differently - some in oil pastels, some in dry chalk pastels, some in felt-tip - before being re-filmed under the rostrum camera. David found the advance planning needed for this technique and the consequent loss of spontaneity particularly gruelling and a bit depressing: 'You don't see it coming together for a very long time.'[168]

For the 3D element, it was decided that the stark subject matter here demanded the starkest of puppets and no set at all. Armatures with sophisticated joint mechanisms had been developed and improved throughout the 1980s by Mackinnon and Saunders in Manchester and featured in productions such as Cosgrove Hall's *The Wind in the Willows*, embedded within elaborate character constructions. The Deadsy character was also based on such an armature, but he consisted of little more than the skeleton. (When the same armature was later recycled to provide our Four-Mations ident, he would sport a fluorescent, tribal costume).
But there was a point in there - quite a lot of points - when I had no idea,

or no firm idea, what the end result was going to be. Half-way through the process, when I finally knew what the images were doing, I went back and re-storyboarded. It was the look of it that decided how the whole thing was put together. Then it would change again in the editing process at the end. Then there were a very few optical effects, marrying things up, but no use of computers, contrary to what people often think.

After the uncertainties of *Deadsy*, David found the production process for *Door* far more relaxing, despite the more complicated techniques used. It was invigorating to work with a larger team (the crew for the exterior shoot and the model-makers), although 'it still ended up with me alone in the studio late at night, animating. But when the team were there they were great'. He enjoyed the more theatrical element, creating weird performances both in his model animation set and in the open spaces he used for his pixilation, both techniques more welcoming of spontaneous inspiration than minutely-planned 2D work. And of course the very fact of shooting a great deal of the film out of doors was liberating after a year incarcerated in the coal store. It also gave this film a greater connection with real life, rather than being contained in a 'cartoon' world. His location shooting, all done very close to his home, would be sumptuous, partly because he insisted on shooting on 35mm but also because, he felt, natural images are bound to be stronger - the real elements being sure to work better than any imitations we can mock up on a film set. Parallel to his longing for open spaces after the confinement of *Deadsy*, he was also keen to make *Door* rather looser than its predecessor could be - shot in a more relaxed way, and shot over-length like live action so as to be able to shape it in the edit.[169]

Again the choice of techniques was born of an urge to extend his palette. He liked pixilation, admired McLaren's *Neighbours* and so wanted to try his hand at it. His choice of motifs was intuitive. Taking his cue from Hoban's urging that we should open up to the unbidden voices inside us all, David tried to tune his personal antenna to pick up the images rising from his subconscious as a response to the Hoban text. He would know if it was going to work, because it would 'feel right'. *Door* is the film where David feels that Hoban's text and his own sub-text complement each other almost exactly. While Hoban sees the door and the key on a cosmic level, David sees them as a part of our humanity, for we are all searching for our one particular door and the right key for it. But: *It's often not keys that unlock doors, but bits of understanding that open doors in our consciousness. Curiosity can reach through walls but sometimes also cause disaster. Some doors should not be opened perhaps.*

Channel 4 did the films proud, and they were premiered within an excellent *State of the Art* documentary, transmitted at 9.30pm on a Sunday as part of a Four-Mations season. Prizes abounded, including a BAFTA nomination, a Zagreb category prize and a Los Angeles special jury prize for *Deadsy* and

Deadsy

Door. A world of nothing but doors

Door. Location shooting plus pixilation

the critics' prize at Annecy, the McLaren award for best British animation at Edinburgh and several other top prizes for *Door*. Reactions were stunned, but enthusiastic, this review by Peter Castaldi in the *Sydney Cinema Journal* on the occasion of an Anderson retrospective in 1990 or 1991 being perhaps extreme, but not atypical in sentiment:

Door, *by David Anderson, rolls Cocteau into* Psycho, *over Dalí, up Freud's nose, along Kerouac's fuel line, through the spark of a Burroughs drugged synapse and on… essential viewing.*

Nearer home there were some less enthusiastic reactions. A few elderly friends of David's mother's found the films (especially *Deadsy*) terribly offensive and decided her son must be 'completely deranged'. David himself, of course, had been 'fairly appalled' when he first received Hoban's *Deadsy* script. Previously he had been 'a sort of romantic spiritualist'. His world view had been determinedly positive. 'I didn't figure violence and sex in that kind of landscape.' But he was surprised to note, while working with these unsavoury elements, that he was finding them liberating. 'It loosened me up a bit. […] I'm not squeaky clean any more.'

After *Door* was seen, it elicited a commission for a McEwans lager commercial. It was based on the *Door* universe and in fact recycled the set used in that film (just as *Door* itself had re-used various figures from previous commercials). But David's thinking was beginning to change. His roots were in live action and he slowly began to migrate back to it, and away from animation. In the case of commercials it was pure rebellion against 'that amount of work - sixteen hours a day for six weeks - to sell products'. But in the case of his personal films he was beginning to doubt himself. '*Deadsy* and *Door* were a bit convoluted and rambling - it's hard to get a grip on them. The world I was operating in was a bit convoluted.' He found himself longing for clarity, wanting to make clearer statements, with 'more spaces and stillness instead of stuffing my films with all sorts of things.'[170] But he still has his doubts, and articulated in our recent interview what must be the constant concern of any artist:

The fear was that it could all fall apart and become very banal. If you unpack the film and are left with a very clear statement, that's not art any more. So I'm trying to find a balance, saying something that's understandable but is still in a package so that it remains interesting and stimulating. And I'm still in that process.

His next film for Channel 4, *In the Time of Angels*, was an attempt to reconcile these two imperatives. Shot in live action, using many of the animation effects

Door

Door. The end of snivvelyzashuns we knowit

now regularly seen in fantasy features, it tells the story of a heroine wanting to reverse time and undo what has already been done. Festivals in Europe obviously preferred David's old, cluttered, allusive style, for *In the Time of Angels* was cold-shouldered by most juries (except Zagreb). In the US, however, it won every prize going. Now he appears to have reconciled himself to the conflict and, polymath that he is, he has recently shot an Animate project and a CG commercial for a US client and makes occasional dance films in live action - as well as running a conference centre and being chair of trustees at the school he co-founded.

When I tried to sort out what seemed to me to be an inconsistency between something he told me in our interview and something I had read in the Edwin Carels interview, David cheerfully suggested that he was 'probably talking bollocks'. But he summed the situation up a bit more elegantly in that same Carels interview: 'I'm full of contradictions.'

Secret Joy of Falling Angels
1991/11mins

Director/animation
Simon Pummell
Skeleton armatures
Ian Nicholas
Cinematography
Curtis Radclyffe
Isabelle Perrichon
Music composed by
Annabelle Pangborn
Sound editing
Larry Sider
Producer
Keith Griffiths
Production company
Koninck Projects for Channel 4

An Annunciation

A variety of animation and optical techniques are marshalled to evoke the confrontation - at first nervous and then increasingly erotic - between a woman and a winged creature.

Simon Pummell's background is unusual in the animation world. Perhaps his childhood attachment to *Snow White* is not that unusual, though the way he has continued throughout his career to mull over 'its innovation, its pop culture perfection, its sentimentality and violence'[171] is quite special. It would later lead to a learned essay comparing Disney and Francis Bacon, to an interactive 'sculpture' of the *Snow White* story structure on his website, and to much of his philosophy as an animator. Yet his first degree, at Oxford University, was in English literature, and it was only after this that he developed an interest in drawing and spent a year studying life-drawing[172] and anatomy. He then took a job as art director in an advertising agency, finally enrolling for a post-graduate degree in film at the Royal College of Art, where he made his first film, *Surface Tension* (1986). The virtuoso animation in this work brought him to the attention of Oscar Grillo, who hired Simon to produce his commercials, thus adding to the latter's toolbox a mastery of various new technologies. This unusual journey very much defined the kind of filmmaker he would become:
My training was first in literary critical analysis. [...] I find the labyrinthine quality of modernist literature with its layers of accumulated meanings very seductive.

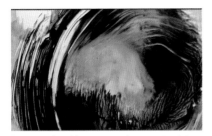

The opening title emerges from wet paint

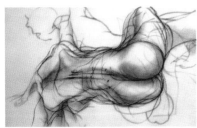

Bodily movement

I then trained as a filmmaker, not an animator; so for me animation is a technique I use rather than a defining calling.[173]

Via Oscar he met the Quays, who were extremely supportive and introduced him to their own producer, Keith Griffiths. Working with Keith proved to be a helpful reality check for Simon. He had an ambitious live-action feature film project, a tragic story about a transsexual, intercut with animated sequences of the twelve stations of the cross. Keith's proposal was that he should instead plan to make a short Annunciation scene and offer the project to Channel 4.

Simon has said that film ideas suggest themselves to him as 'a cluster of images which, despite no obvious context, persist as if looking for a home in some sort of narrative.'[174] In the case of *Secret Joy* these original images were, one assumes, of the human body in some kind of violent flux (a research project he had initiated with *Surface Tension*) and were perhaps indirectly inspired by two artists he admired and on whom he had written a dissertation while at the RCA: Francis Bacon and Walt Disney. The dissertation took art historian John Berger's essay on the subject in *Ways of Seeing* and disputed Berger's somewhat dismissive attitude to Bacon. Whereas Berger saw in his work unnecessary violence done to human forms, Simon feels that *the profound transformation Bacon seeks is to introduce obsession with time and change into the single image of traditional oil painting. To Bacon, appearance is inextricable from time and change and so, memory and mortality.*[175]

The Disney artists, on the other hand, would 'pour most creative effort into the animation stage leading to pencil tests. Animation directly drawn; rough, shimmering pencil lines defining form and movement'. Their studies of the human form in movement would lead them to extreme distortions (eg squash and stretch), with the flow of line running 'in overlapping patterns from one drawing to another'. Thus, in the line tests, the process was visible, as was a potential for change. But in the clean-up and paint and trace stages 'a potentially disruptive and problematic dynamism of form [was] then laid over with the sickly colours of rigid sentimentality.' Pummell admires in Bacon his courage in confronting this flux head-on and laments in Disney what was destroyed while concealing it, in the interests of 'realism' and clarity. One particular aspect of the 'squash and stretch' idea that Simon wanted to explore was the challenge of giving the squashy musculature a skeleton to hang off: 'Bodily movement is a clash of the rigid and the squashy with the skeleton as the pivot - the axis around which the muscles cluster.'[176]

The film would emphasise sometimes the skeleton and sometimes the distortion of the fleshy body.

But another drawing style also seemed to have something to offer:

Both Disney and the great Renaissance artists built up figures in the same way: out of simple ovoids. Michelangelo would use two hundred to build the muscles on a back: Disney would use seven to create a whole character. [Secret Joy's] character animation was an attempt to fall somewhere in the middle - using the principle of squash and stretch with relatively complex bodies.[177]

The potential narrative in which the 'cluster of images' in his mind might find a home was also provided by Renaissance art, by an Annunciation by Filippo Lippi, which he had seen in the National Gallery.

The commissioning of the film by Channel 4 was a long drawn-out process, since Paul Madden, who liked the project, was unable to give a firm commitment as he was soon to leave. By the time I had arrived at the Channel and Simon came in to try for a second time, he had been working on the project for about eighteen months. Strangely, given the seeming spontaneity of the final film, the storyboard was extraordinarily detailed, and produced in a large and beautifully-bound book. I wondered at the time whether Simon felt such elaboration was needed to impress Channel 4, but it transpires that it was more a way to keep the project alive during the hiatus in C4 commissioning. 'An expression of faith that it would happen'. This has now become a part of his work habit and all his development materials are equally beautifully produced.

He outlines the film's technical processes thus:

Technically I restricted myself to very simple tools for the drawn animation in the film. Graphite pencils and 90 micron 15 field animation paper. The drawings were heavily worked over and stacked on a lightbox for the shooting. I shot the footage to reflect the way an animator looks at their work in progress, leaving varying numbers of sheets of paper on the lightbox at any one time, adding a sheet to the top, losing one from the back of the pile. It is this that gives the diffusion and softness to the lines.

Other sections of the film were created with an initial shadow puppet, the shadow shot through translucent paper to give the grain and texture of paper. The shadows were shot on an old Nikon with a zoom lens and a motor drive, and printed up and pegged. The shadow puppet was a real bird skeleton with tiny flexible brass joints inset into each bone. [...]

The whole film was prepared as artwork, with each shadow being printed on photographic paper and treated as drawing, with similar stacking and backlighting to create depth and texture.

The whole film was shot on a traditional 35mm rostrum camera with a simple multiplane set-up. Developing a multiplane you could shoot backlit was quite tricky. The whole film is backlit and there are always multiple layers of drawings. There is never a clear toplit surface the drawing sits "on".[178]

The sound in Simon's films is as distinctive as the images. Without dialogue and therefore not needing synch sound, the sound was added at the end.

The shadow puppet
Photo Curtis Radclyffe

The shadow
Photo Curtis Radclyffe

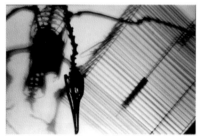

The final image

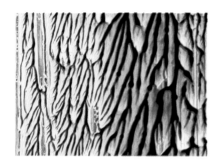

It was Larry Sider, who also works with the Quay brothers, who created the haunting effects here:

Particularly with more fantastical animation, Larry believes that sound is your live-action track. Because sound is so specific, it creates the space in which the film is taking place. Whether it is huge or tiny, arid or watery has enormous impact on the audience, even if they are not consciously aware of it. Larry builds very dense sound composites. The wings in Secret Joy of Falling Angels *were combinations of many sounds, ranging from pigeons' wing flaps to the rustling of shaken silk scarves. Sound is 50 per cent of the film, as it brings scale and scope to a short.*[179]

The music was by Annabelle Pangborn, who trained as an opera singer and therefore used a singing voice to represent Mary's state of mind.

It is ethereal and distant when she is inside the cage, whereas when she's transforming into more cartoony shapes scat singing has been recorded and sung closely into the microphone with a breathy, jazzy sound. Finally, when the Angel and Mary have sex at the end of the film the ethereal vocal is recorded in a similar way and as such the two styles merge.[180]

The animation department at Channel 4 graciously ceded the film's premiere, (in June 1992) to the independent film and video department for their *Dazzling Image* programme (this episode presented by Spike Milligan) and we screened it two weeks later in a Four-Mations UK season, in a double bill with the Quays' *The Comb*, thereby offering the film to two different viewing constituencies. Critics were not slow to note the erotic element: 'Delicately perched on the fine line between pure abstraction and implied narrative, it also has a disturbing erotic edge' (Jonathan Romney)[181]. Ruth Lingford saw it as an 'embodiment of emotion rather than a depiction of behaviour', its subjective if grotesque body representations allowing

far more identification than the objective portrayal of the body seen in much pornography and erotica. [...] The visceral impact of his film is achieved partly by the use of music to build expectation, apprehension, anxiety and then climax, but mostly through use of somatic rhythms and movements, of pulsing, oozing, flailing, pumping and falling.[182]

Science fiction novelist Simon Ings (who would later collaborate with Simon on *Butchers Hook* and *Rose Red*) saw that

Beneath a very cold and precise employment of special effects and images that bordered certainly on the grotesque and at times on the horrific there was a romance trying to get out.[183]

The film also did well at festivals, with a shared Grand Prix from Oberhausen and a prize for best experimental film from Stuttgart.

Though the technologies on show in *Secret Joy* were not very new, Simon's ingenious contriving of '2½D', by projecting his shadow-play against a tilted screen, and other low-tech but inventive methods foreshadowed an extraordinary future range of new styles and technologies - though always

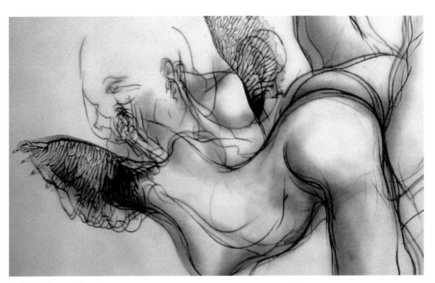

A disturbing erotic edge

as a means to an end rather than as an end in themselves. Most of Simon's subsequent films would be backed partially or entirely by Channel 4: *The Temptation of Sainthood* (1993), *Digital Baby* (1995), *Butchers Hook* (1996), *Ray Gun Fun* (1998) and *Bodysong* (2003). The tendency has been towards narrative and towards live action, though he consistently takes time out for the next experiment, such as gallery installations, film sequences as backgrounds for an English National Opera production and work for the web. As Edwin Carels wrote in the catalogue for a British animation exhibition in Brussels[184]: *With the healthy curiosity of a child Pummell goes from one technique to the other and takes up challenge after challenge, which only goes to strengthen his personal style and identity.*

Stills © Koninck Projects Ltd

A Is for Autism

1992/11 mins

Director
Tim Webb
Based on drawings by
Nicky Braithwaite
Stephen Quinn
Daniel Sellers
Christine Taylor
Darren White
Animation
Ron MacRae
Daniel Sellers
Tim Webb
Narration spoken and contributed by
Temple Grandin
Luke Hemstock
Stewart Hogg
Daniel Sellers
Justin Sutton
Darren White
Matthew and Sheila Baguley
and others
Lighting camera
Dave Affleck-Green
Colin Hawkins
Rostrum camera
Heather Reader
Music performed by
Alan Carter
Thomas Wickens
Editor
Matthew Dennis
Consultant
Professor Elizabeth Newson
Produced by
Dick Arnall
Production company
Finetake for Channel 4

From an original drawing by Darren White

People talk about their problems growing up with autism. We see drawings by autistic people brought to life in animation and a youngster's animation of trains accompanied by his own commentary.

In his youth, Tim Webb was not considered artistically gifted and left school at 16 to become a dental technician, a career he pursued for six years. Animation was nowhere near his radar. However, while making teeth Tim was also doing a lot of photography and studied for an art A Level at night school, followed by a one-year art foundation course. This is where he discovered animation and experimented with a variety of techniques. He identified good reasons to reject fine art, graphics, sculpture and textiles - so by a process of elimination animation became his career choice. He moved on to do a BA at the West Surrey College of Art and Design at Farnham.

After constant technical experimentation on his foundation course, Farnham would make him *think*. The course was about ideas and film language at least as much as technique and style. Even at the interview he was taken to task for thoughtlessness about images of women in the work he had shown there. On the way back his 'brain was awash with all these ideas I'd never thought about before.'[185] This difficult lesson for Tim paid off in his degree film, *Smoke Rings* (1986), a reasoned critique of cigarette companies sponsoring sport and high art and government hypocrisy over health issues in this context.

After graduating, he could find only very occasional bits of animation work. The rest of the time he was a cycle courier, with a few spells on the dole. When Channel 4 and the Arts Council initiated the Animation Awards scheme, he applied. He had seen a programme on the BBC's *QED* series about the autistic artist Stephen Wiltshire, then a mere 12 or 13 years old, but drawing with a masterly grasp of perspective and amazing spontaneity. Tim did some research and decided that some traits of autism - such as the steps we take in order to avoid communication, avoiding eye contact on public transport - could be used as a metaphor for alienation in the city. His proposal, based on a hoped-for collaboration with Stephen Wiltshire, was shortlisted but ultimately rejected. The awards committee (of which I was a member) very much approved of the collaboration idea but not the overall thrust of the proposal. We felt there was a more interesting film to be made in collaboration with autistic artists, one which would shed light on autism itself rather than using the condition to shed light on something else.

Programmes relating to disability were central to C4's remit, and shortly after Tim's application arrived it transpired that the Channel was planning a season on disability for February-March 1992. Called Disabling World, it would focus on the relationship between disabled and able-bodied people and how each group viewed the other. The season would be supported by the kind of back-up material which is so crucial to such endeavours, an accompanying publication and factual resource/contacts data on 4-Tel/Oracle. Sensing that the support of a good and sensitive producer would be vital in the case of a filmmaker as inexperienced as Tim and a film project as delicate as this one, I asked Dick Arnall whether he would be willing to work with Tim for a period of development and research to identify the real subject of the film, locate helpful autism professionals and autistic artists and potential contributors, and produce a treatment and storyboard. Tim and Dick agreed, they were allocated a bit of development funding and the results were to be delivered in six weeks.

The development period was extremely trying for all concerned. A combination of the psychologists' desire to protect their patients from exploitation and a sudden surge in media interest in autism meant that Tim was presented with a succession of brick walls. But I was willing to wait (and the development period in fact doubled) and at the last minute doors began to open, the key contact being Elizabeth Newson, professor of child development at Nottingham University. She was more receptive to the idea of her patients taking part, and put Tim in touch with two of them, Darren White and Daniel Sellers, the latter a 9 year-old, very prolific artist. The other important contact was Temple Grandin,

From an original drawing by Christine Taylor

an autistic woman, now fully functioning, who had worked as a consultant on *Rain Man*.

The treatment and storyboard finally arrived at the end of January. The film's centrepiece, Daniel Sellers' magnificent animation of trains, was not yet included, since it had yet to be established whether this was feasible. At this stage the storyboard featured comments by experts and parents, as well as the autistic people themselves. Later on, it would become clear that the comments of the autistic people were far more poignant and equally informative in their way, so they would constitute the whole soundtrack. Animation is expensive and time-consuming, so it is normal for films to follow the storyboard closely and for editing to be minimal. On the other hand, many filmmakers see the editing stage of the film as key to shaping it. In Tim's treatment, which accompanied the storyboard, he acknowledged that the structure was still vague and requested a free rein to incorporate ideas which might later arise during the editing.

Nowadays Tim talks about how brave Channel 4 and indeed I myself were in accepting this fluid state of affairs and putting the film into production. But the fact was that, being a very inexperienced commissioning editor at the time, I probably did not realise how risky the project was - and I did sympathise with his point about creative editing. Anyway, by this time Disabling World was only a year away and a year is not long for an 11-minute animated film of the complexity of this one, so they needed to move into production quickly. Had I known how tempestuous that production would be, I might have insisted that the storyboard stay locked in as it was, so it was fortunate that I did not know. But we did have Dick, who had agreed to continue as producer on the film.

The late Dick Arnall is acknowledged in the animation world to be a strong candidate for canonisation. His patience and his capacity to nurture, coax and cajole the directors he worked with were seemingly endless. Yet five months after the development work was delivered, with Sue Shephard (the C4 commissioning editor responsible for Disabling World) and me haranguing them for a finalised storyboard, his production notes for Tim begin:
WHAT IS THE FILM THAT YOU WANT TO MAKE? [...] The deadline for the re-defined 'working storyboard' was last Tuesday; it MUST be completed by Monday 29 July, with a deadline of Monday 5 August for the final definition of all film elements and format. After that date, all other conceptual ideas and possibilities [...] are GONE! After that date there is NO time to consider setting up other collaborations, and NO time for ANY more detailed research. NO exceptions...
... And so it went on. Tim was very hard to work with. Paradoxically, it was his perfectionism and what Dick would later call his 'staggering integrity'[186], along with his willingness to work himself into the ground in order to get things right which generated the problems. He would worry endlessly about new theories

From an original drawing by Stephen Quinn

Set used for pixilation scene
Courtesy Tim Webb

From an original drawing by Darren White

and contrasting points of view and was loath to bring his research to an end while there were still any stones left unturned.

Some elements in the production did gel, however. Professor Newson came on board as a consultant and her proposal for the animation collaboration, 9 year-old Daniel, turned out to be a natural. The initial idea had been for the autistic collaborator to do only the repetitive drawings, the 'inbetweens'. As it turned out, after minimal tuition in the principles of animation, Daniel was able to produce key drawings, leaving Tim and animator Ron MacRae to fill in the inbetweens. Daniel's passion was trains and one of his favourite spots for watching them was the Tesco car park in Worksop, overlooking a railway siding, so this was where Tim took him. Tim based the exercise he was planning on one which Dr Neil O'Connor (an expert in the field, who had headed the Medical Research Council's Developmental Psychology Unit) had practised with Daniel, whereby having first drawn an object from the viewpoint where he was sitting he was to remain in the same position but try to draw the same object from various different points of view. From his base in the car park, Daniel produced twenty or thirty drawings from different angles, with trains passing through. Tim noted that:

Every train that passed worked as a sequence. So he not only had the ability to draw from all these different viewpoints but there was a record of the time as well, and the perspective. Amazing.

Far from damaging Daniel, the experience had, according to Professor Newson, been a real success for her patient.

An enormous volume of material was shot and Tim would continue animating right up to the deadline. When this moment was reached, there was plenty of surplus footage, enabling him and his editor to produce the kind of creative edit he had been hoping for. Although he, as director, had had overall control of the structure and content, every single design in the film originated from a drawing by an autistic person. All of the narration was spoken by autistic people and the piano and flute music was performed, arranged and some of it composed by autistic performers. It was the first such collaboration in the UK. Another vital contribution was that of Tim's partner, Janice Biggs, who had been a psychiatric nurse and was therefore a great help in the initial stages, encouraging Tim into appropriate directions, and subsequently choosing from a mass of material the most meaningful quotes to use.

The film never quite resolved two problems. Firstly, only about ten per cent of people with autism are able to communicate and express themselves, and so this glimpse of autism from the inside is inevitably extremely partial. (But we felt it was not too presumptuous to hope that this minority's experience mirrored that of the silent majority.) Secondly, the Stephen Wiltshire and *Rain Man* phenomenon of 'special talent' applies to an even tinier percentage of people

Daniel Sellers' train animation

Daniel animating
Courtesy Tim Webb

Another Daniel train

with autism, so highlighting talented, natural-born animator Daniel Sellers might have been thought misleading. There were some grumbles but very few.

The film became a reference work, both for autism studies and for animation studies, being seen as seminal in the animated documentary genre. The autism experts including the National Autistic Society, initially sceptical, finally came round and now it is regularly screened at autism conferences and events. The Channel treasured the film, giving it a good 10.55pm slot in the Disabling World season, and it would be repeated three months later and again on several occasions over the following years (twice during the halcyon days of the 45-minute *Dispatches*, when we were able to squeeze a Best of British Animation season into the 15-minute slot following it). We also treasured the collaborators on the film and all were brought to London, plus carers, for a special preview screening. It garnered a clutch of major awards at animation festivals, as well as the McLaren award for the best British animated film at the Edinburgh festival, the BFI/Mari Kuttna award for the best film by a new animator and the special prize of the UNESCO International Fund for the Promotion of Culture. It was nominated for a BAFTA and for the Cartoon d'Or for best European animated film of 1993, and was also brought out as a VHS/DVD by the BFI, the only short animation to be issued as a single.

A Is for Autism opened doors for Tim. From 1992 he was invited as a visiting tutor to various animation departments around the country and in 1996 was taken on by the Royal College of Art, where he remains as Senior Tutor today, in a part time position enabling him to pursue his own projects. More recently it also brought him a commission to direct two margarine ads using ideas from *A Is for Autism*. The experience was not a good one - he took it 'way too seriously' and got very stressed.

Tim's forte is projects in which he can invest tremendous effort and preferably plenty of time to delve deeply into subjects and tell stories in new and exciting ways. Autism had suited him perfectly. Perhaps, as he had pointed out in his treatment for the film, the repetitive nature of animation and the sometimes isolated existence of animators incline them to some very slight understanding of the condition.

From an original drawing by Nicky Braithwaite

Screen Play

1992/11mins

Director/script/animation
Barry Purves
Music
Nigel Hess
Voice
Michael Maloney
Dialogue
Ernst Loub
Editing
Flix Film Editing
Sets/puppets
Barrow Model Makers
Costumes
Nigel Cornford
Art work
Barbara Biddulph
Lighting camera
Mark Stewart
Production company
Bare Boards for Channel 4

Takako is promised by her father to a powerful samurai, but she loves the gardener, Naoki. They flee to a distant island, but the idyll is not to last.

After Shakespeare (in *Next*, part of Aardman's *Lip Synch* series), Barry Purves was in search of another theatrical mode with different conventions, and for different ways of telling stories - the more artificial and more stylised the better. One day while eating Sunday lunch, he noticed that beneath his very beef and Yorkshire pudding a story was being told. The tale in the willow pattern design is, it seems, an English confection, based on various decorative elements seen on 18th-century Chinese porcelain. As the passion for orientalism grew in the Victorian period, so did the popularity of the story. The plate started Barry thinking along oriental lines. A visit to the Hiroshima festival (where *Next* took best debut prize) confirmed his interest and a later, British Council-sponsored lecture tour to Tokyo, Osaka and Kyoto gave him his first experience of kabuki. *I was absolutely riveted by the whole five-hour experience. It was an event for the audience. I loved the way that a simple raising of an eyebrow or a flash of colour meant something to that audience. [...] I particularly enjoyed the puppet theatre, bunraku, where you could see three operators working a puppet, but by being in black they were as good as invisible. The performance of the puppet was so riveting you did not notice the operators. I adore conventions like that.*[187]

So enthused was Barry by this introduction to such a different way of telling a story that he resolved to use it, and others too, in the film he was preparing. A puppet narrator would tell the tale at stage front, but as well as speaking (in the honeyed tones of Michael Maloney) he would also sign it in British Sign Language, which Barry learned specially for the purpose of this film. His main interest was aesthetic - the puppet's over-sized hands would almost be dancing - but we at Channel 4 were delighted at the prospect of a programme which would appeal to deaf as well as to hearing viewers. The first 9½ minutes of the film would use these means, plus an element of mime, to tell a tightly controlled tale with a conventional happy ending. The need for control would also extend to the challenge Barry would set himself as an animator: to shoot this giant chunk of film as a single take, needing nine weeks to shoot. This was an extremely risky procedure - most animators do not even like to risk leaving a shot over night, in case of accidents. But Barry enjoys the pressure of the long take: 'a form of adrenalin that can be so absent from animation. To try and sustain this shot was like being on stage the whole time, knowing you couldn't go off and start again.' (He had, in fact, made an Edam cheese commercial the year before in a single take, which had elicited a phone call from Disney asking how it was done.[188])

Black-clad bunraku puppeteers in the background

The narrator uses British Sign Language

But this was not all. Having reached the presumed happy ending, with the narrator having revealed that he is in fact that gardener and is recounting his own past, Barry resolved to finish the tale in a determinedly *cinematic* as opposed to theatrical narrative mode. The love story would become revenge tragedy. After 9½ minutes without a cut, the 90 seconds of denouement would comprise 30 takes.

In theatre, where there is generally just one perspective, the director tells the audience where to look through groupings, the use of light, movement, colour, and all manner of obviously artificial means. In cinema, the director has the camera and its close-ups, long shots and camera moves to tell the audience where to look. [...] The two halves of Screen Play *were trying to show these differences. In the first half the blood is red ribbons, and in the second it is real flowing blood. In the first half the make-up is very much kabuki-based and in the second the faces are unpainted. Likewise the music in the first half is part of the story telling, but in the second it is much more incidental, background music.*

The film would end with a zoom out, revealing the miniature set, Barry's hand as he ticks off the last shot of the film and a bit of domestic clutter, betraying the fact that that this production would, in fact, be shot in Barry's living room. The budget was not ungenerous (it ended up at just under £100,000), but Barry wanted the film to be even more lavish than would have been affordable if paying rent on a studio. He would also be able to work longer hours if he did not have to travel. And his system is to prepare thoroughly in advance (five months of pre-production in this case) so that the actual time spent shooting is efficiently used. He would get his living room back after three months.

Gilbert and Sullivan: The Very Models.
D'Oyly Carte acted as narrator
Photo Jean-Marc Ferrière

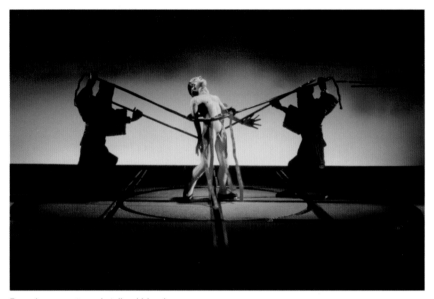

Bunraku puppets and stylised blood

One major element of pre-production was the design. For Barry the design is integral to the story, so a large part is done before he involves other people. (He has designed several stage shows, most of which he has also directed, and here too he aims for the sets to 'become part of the narrative'.) But once the initial work is complete he also enjoys working with other artists, who 'help make sense of my strange imaginings'. Most of these came up through the ranks of Cosgrove Hall, the Manchester studio which was Britain's - and probably Europe's - largest, offering a supportive and nurturing environment to a whole generation of world-class designers and model-makers. Some of the Cosgrove Hall staff lent a hand incognito, with model-maker Peter Saunders thanked in the credits under the near-anagram of Rupert de Sands.

The shoot went well, save for a hiccup at the beginning, when it transpired that the camera which had been bought for the production was not up to waiting for such long periods between frames, and funds had to be found to hire a Bolex. Even Barry's producer, the long-suffering Glenn Holberton, said this production was 'a joy, pretty much'.[189] Barry's determination to make the best film possible and to focus on the tiniest of details sometimes overrides considerations of schedule and budget, and later productions (notably *Achilles*) would not be quite as harmonious. Barry is contrite:

Glenn is without a doubt one of the great producers, and it is rare to have such support, tolerance and creative encouragement from a producer. [...] Directors tend to get the limelight, but really we couldn't do anything without them.

The completed film put Barry on the map in various ways. Academics began to study him and the themes which were beginning to emerge. One aspect was his innovative espousal of what Professor Paul Wells would call the 'operatic nature of emotions', his insistence on the 'high passion and seriousness of sex and sexuality, rather than the more graphic, titillatory, snigger-inducing expression of the erotic depicted in many animated films.'[190] Another aspect was that of the 'outsider'. Paul Wells would note that Peter Hall in *Next*, the narrator in *Screen Play* and later the assassins in *Rigoletto*, Greek chorus in *Achilles* and D'Oyly Carte in *Gilbert and Sullivan: The Very Models* all seem to look in at Barry's films and sit in judgement on them.[191] While making the point that the outsider is a good catalyst to get plots going and give audiences a helpful perspective, Barry does acknowledge that he himself often feels like an outsider, 'watching and observing rather than joining in'. His favourite piece of theatre is Stephen Sondheim's *Sunday in the Park with George*, about the artist Georges Seurat, in which 'the artist has the dilemma of being too busy watching and creating rather than participating. I can understand that.' And, conversely, he admits to being extremely sensitive to judgements of his own work.

He is also quite often amused by the amount of subtext written into this film by students who have it set as a piece of analysis. But I seem to be the only person who was literal-minded enough to worry about the old narrator revealing himself as the gardener, only seconds before we see the young gardener murdered. This, says Barry,
makes him a ghost telling his story, or simply the story living on. The narrator did step out from behind the screen that has a picture of him on, so it could be that we are looking at the screen of the old man and here is his story. It's an old story. Hmmm?
Hmmm indeed.

One might have expected this British take on the orient to go down badly in the East, and indeed Kihachiro Kawamoto - the Japanese master animator of folk tales via severely stylised puppets and minimal movement - did vouchsafe to Paul Wells that he was not taken with Barry's more realistic puppets.[192] Yet the film took the Grand Prix at the Shanghai festival and the prize for best film from 5 to15 minutes at Hiroshima. Internationally, it was an enormous hit, garnering more than twenty prizes, including the audience prize at Brussels, as well as an Oscar® nomination and one for the 1993 Cartoon d'Or for best European animation.

Barry and set, in his living room

At home, the film was premiered in a Four-Mations: Winners season, in the magical 9.45, post-*Dispatches* slot. *The Independent on Sunday* critic Allison Pearson caught it there and declared it her 'programme of the week':
Any description is pedestrian beside this puppetry: a flicked fan changes a face from friend to foe, the set revolves ushering in winter, silent as dots on a disc of snow, the lovers are wrenched apart and wings clatter up through the dark over an egg-yolk moon. Michael Maloney read Ernst Loub's beautiful words with plangent sweetness. And out of balsa came something infinitely weighty, infinitely sad.[193]
(She probably did not know that Ernst Loub was another anagram - the beautiful words were actually penned by the less exotic-sounding Les Burton.) Other papers, from *Time Out* to the *Los Angeles Times*, were equally enthusiastic. *Televisual* devoted a two-page spread to the film and put it on the cover of its August 1992 edition.

Barry was by now in constant demand from festivals, schools and studios all over the world to lead stop-motion workshops. Interestingly, several Hollywood studios, and even Hollywood studios already specialising in CG (such as Pixar, PDI and DreamWorks) were among his customers. Unusually, for Barry felt his classical proclivities might be a deterrent to advertisers, *Screen Play* did attract a commission for a commercial. Ironically, his romantic and dramatic talents were now deployed selling Toilet Duck lavatory cleaner. His subsequent career has included more shorts for C4, *Rigoletto* for S4C and the BBC, a couple of brushes with the world of animated features, several stage productions and *Rupert Bear*, back with Cosgrove Hall. He also claims to have hosted the Chinese version of *Pop Idol* in Beijing. But that's another story…

Screen Play photos Mark Stewart

The Mill

1992/7mins

Script/animation
Petra Freeman
Editor
Mark Farrington
Music
Sofia Gubaidulina
Camera
G & M Productions
Producer
Richard Taylor
Production company
Richard Taylor Cartoon Films
for Channel 4

A girl introduces a thread into a mill-wheel and it guides us through a bizarre train of thought, through metamorphosing scenes centring on bees and a beekeeper.

When Petra Freeman graduated from Wimbledon School of Art, she went to the Royal College of Art to study for an MA in illustration, though in fact spent much of her time in the print-making department. She would constantly produce lithographs in narrative sequences and seemed to want to tell more elaborate stories than could be expressed in a single image. Finally, her tutor suggested she should visit Professor Richard Taylor, who ran the animation department, to find out whether he could help bring her stories to life. Petra was a complete newcomer to animation. She had not even seen any, apart from Disney as a child (which she had not been keen on). However, some of her RCA works did suggest a specific animation technique. She had developed a way of drawing figures in soot on glass with her finger, and then photographing them in front of actual landscapes, and had loved this tactile experience. So Richard Taylor gave her a bit of advice about animating paint on glass under the camera, frame by frame, and found her a room in the basement with a camera.

There she was able to improvise and, finally, make her own animated film using this technique.

When Petra graduated, her tutors were concerned for her future. Her penchant for serial works and her attraction to dark, mystical themes did not seem to fit her for the commercial world in which illustration graduates would have to make their way. So it was lucky that Channel 4 and the Museum of the Moving Image launched their Animator in Residence scheme for new graduates right on cue. Petra applied, with a proposal for a film using this same paint-on-glass method, the theme a development from a series of lithographs she had made for a book while at the RCA. It would take as its central idea that of a mill, in constant motion - an image which related to Petra's Cornish childhood and the string of mills along a valley close to her home, where she would often play - and it would weave memories from this childhood into a dreamlike narrative. When the selection committee looked through the proposals submitted, this one really stood out: her sample designs and student film, *Felt, Lifted and Weighed*, which also formed a part of the submission, were of high quality and the approach was totally original. It was accepted and, at the allotted time, Petra moved into the tiny animation booth in the Museum of the Moving Image to begin three months of development work on the film, after which Channel 4 would consider putting it into full production.

People reacted in different ways to life in that booth. There were no windows or, it seemed, other ventilation. The animator in residence was one of the Museum's exhibits, and so would be stared at by school parties through the glass wall. Some animators found it all rather trying. In Petra's case, life was especially uncomfortable, because of the technique she was using: oil paint thinned with white spirit. It was 'pretty smelly'[194] in the booth and the poor girl developed spots. What made it worse was that this technique of wet oil paint on glass demanded seven days a week attendance, otherwise the paint would dry and the work would be ruined. But she was a trooper. And 'I wasn't self-conscious in the booth because I was too busy, and generally in a slightly confused state because of the fumes.' In fact she enjoyed three very happy months. The Museum of the Moving Image was staffed by enthusiasts, always ready to help, and the scheme's production adviser, Lisa Beattie, was extraordinarily nurturing. 'I could talk to her about anything.'

Petra loved the film-making process, becoming seduced by the tactile experience of manipulating the paint. Some images - notably the red curtains - were included partly for the 'sensual quality and graininess of the paint', though all derived from her childhood memories, some from an extremely early age. The overarching theme of the film is bees, a constant presence for the young Petra, since her father was a beekeeper. He rented a field near home for his hives and she spent a lot of time helping him with his work. Bees have always fascinated her. Sadly, while Petra was in production on this film her father was

Millwheels and thread

becoming progressively more ill with Alzheimer's. Though not consciously at the time, she now feels that 'making the film was an attempt to hang on to something I was losing.' Every single image relates to something in her childhood - from the purple methylated spirit that her father, a keen amateur magician, would pour on his hands and set alight as part of his show, to the red blanket thrown over a chair in a game of 'trains', to the magnifying glass she would use to magnify the sun's rays and try to ignite things. But all would be couched in terms of magic and mystery, giving the viewer endless opportunities for interpretation. Petra herself confesses that 'I see new things in it all the time'.

Petra's father was a beekeeper

A red blanket in a game of trains

Girl faces bee

All of this was not, however, visible in the development piece which was delivered to me after the three months at MOMI. This consisted of about two minutes of 16mm film, samples from various scenes - the fruit of constant experimentation without the pressure of deadlines. It did not purport to be even part of a finished film. However, it was plenty to establish that this original piece should certainly be put into production. Petra chose as her producer that same Richard Taylor who had guided her first steps in animation back at the Royal College. His production credentials were impeccable, having run Richard Taylor Cartoon Films since the 1960s as well as latterly heading up the RCA animation department. He hired studio space with a camera, and Petra set to work making the final film. Of course, it meant starting again from scratch, this time on 35mm. But in fact, even though it meant spending seven days a week for a further six months or so in a dark, smelly room, she was looking forward to it. ('Animation is,' she comments, 'for weirdos.') There were many things she now did differently from the development piece. One was a more abundant use of colour - her RCA work had tended towards the monochrome, and her development work had been decidedly muted, but she found herself gradually embracing a wider palette. And then there were the sudden flashes of inspiration which had been waking her in the night and for which she had scribbled drawings in a notebook, for later incorporation. The production did go over schedule, and Channel 4 had to shell out a bit extra for the studio rental. But even so, the total of £33,000 seemed moderate.

Petra's editor, Mark Farrington, helped her to structure the piece and was particularly creative at assembling the soundtrack. The crowning touch was the distinctive Sofia Gubaidulina music track. While working in the stinky MOMI booth, Petra would often get away during the evening to a concert at one of the South Bank auditoria, and one evening she heard this piece, *Offertorium*, performed. But its acquisition was not straightforward. After lengthy enquiries, it transpired that there was no route to it within the UK. However, Petra's Russian landlady had musical connections and managed to reach a colleague of Gubaidulina, who put Richard Taylor in touch with a radio station which had recorded the piece. Now, in the period of perestroika, they were more than happy to talk to Western producers and indeed to sell to this production a tape

Playmates

and the rights to use it. But, in that period when no simple structures existed for trade with the West, how to implement the transaction? As it happened, I was about to leave for a business trip to Moscow, so I was furnished with the appropriate quantity of US dollars, secreted in a money belt. The exchange was not entirely satisfactory. I received a large spool of magnetic tape, which I just had to hope contained *Offertorium*. But when I handed over the cash, no receipt was forthcoming. Russian state radio, like all the other state monopolies, had just ceased to exist in its previous form and no one knew quite what would replace it. Not only were there no receipt forms - neither was there any headed notepaper. The receipt was finally scribbled in a page of my notebook and signed, and this had to suffice as evidence of the exchange.

The film was finally completed and a test print produced. Then Petra received a phone message to the effect that the negative had accidentally been destroyed in Technicolor's cleaning machine. As it was April 1, she thought it was a joke - but was soon disabused. Had a test print not already been struck, the film and a year's labour would have been lost. The job of producing an internegative from the test print was long and fiddly, and Mark Farrington returned print after print to the lab until a version appeared which was close to the original - though some detail was inevitably lost in the process.

The film had its Channel 4 premiere in July 1992 in the first of the *Secret Passions* series made for us by Paul Madden (who was now operating as an independent producer). The programme brought together new films by young British women animators - *The Mill* was grouped with another AIR film, Marie-Cécile Pattison's *Prayer to Viracocha*, and Karen Kelly's outstanding student film *Egoli* - and each was interviewed briefly about her work. *The Mill* even took the debut prize at the 1992 Hiroshima Festival, which got the AIR scheme off to a resoundingly good start.

Petra went on to make an equally evocative and mysterious film for the Animate scheme, *Jumping Joan*, which also related to her childhood. She then disappeared into motherhood for some years and is now starting to re-emerge. The current project is a children's book; dark, mysterious, and with illustrations which cry out to be brought to life in animation...

Bob's Birthday

1993/12½mins

Directors/script
Alison Snowden
David Fine
Voices
Andy Hamilton
Harry Enfield
Alison Snowden
Andrew MacLachlan
Tessa Wojiczak
Sally Grace
Animation
Alison Snowden
David Fine
Janet Perlman
Animation camera
Pierre Landry
Lynda Pelley
Raymond Dumas
Robin Bain
Music
Patrick Godfrey
NFB producer
David Verrall
Production company
Snowden Fine Animation for
Channel 4, co-produced in
association with the National
Film Board of Canada

Bob's 40th birthday provokes a mid-life crisis and much soul-searching. He gets home from work in a foul mood and unaware that his friends are hidden behind the furniture as a birthday surprise.

Alison Snowden and David Fine met in 1980 at the National Film School, where they were studying film direction. Both had previously dabbled in animation but had decided live action was a more mature way to express their ideas. However, as the two youngest on the course they felt somewhat intimidated, so when it transpired that Alison had a bit of money left over from her live action diploma film, they decided to spend four months in the animation department making a film and 'developing our technique as we went along.'[195]
The result, *Second Class Mail*, about an elderly woman who sends off for an inflatable companion, was nominated for an Oscar®. It also highlighted their real interest:
We try to write about real people in stressful, normal situations who are having trouble coping with life. People who feel out of place, like we did at film school.[196]

Second Class Mail
© National Film and Television School

Graduating in 1984, they moved to Canada for a few years, working at the National Film Board before returning to the UK in 1989, looking for congenial work. The proposal they brought me at Channel 4 was outstanding. It was truthful, touching, thought-provoking and hilarious. There was however one problem. Since, unlike almost all the shorts we commissioned, it was a candidate for possible co-production, we were obliged to seek a co-production partner in order to reduce C4's input. It was a candidate for co-production partly because it was less challenging than much of our output and partly because Alison and David were well known to the National Film Board of Canada and much liked, having recently made for them the couple's second Oscar®-nominated film, *George and Rosemary*. So we approached the Film Board. The negotiations were extremely lengthy but ultimately successful.

The production would start in Snowden Fine's Carnaby Street studio (above a dental surgery) and migrate to Montreal after the animation stage, for shooting and post-production. But pre-production began with the scriptwriting. The writing, like the design and animation the couple do together, is such a close collaboration that they cannot remember afterwards who did what. They gave these characters their own insecurities - which seemed to loom large at that time, though Alison and David have gradually come to see that they are not the only ones to suffer in this way. In fact most people recognise their own foibles all too clearly in those of Bob and Margaret.

The next, crucial, stage was the voice recording. As often happens with animation, it was thought that a famous voice might be a good investment - and famous voices tend to be relatively inexpensive for a voice-only recording session, which needs very little rehearsal and no time-consuming make-up and costumes. So they hired Harry Enfield, a comedian whose skills seemed perfect for the role, for Bob as well as all the other male roles. The session went badly. Enfield simply could not 'get' the Bob they wanted, depressive but still endearing. His frustration turned to anger. He would later recall this in a rueful piece in *The Independent on Sunday* which congratulated Alison and David on their Oscar® win and marvelled at the fact that they had thanked him in their acceptance speech,
… especially as I did my best to ruin their film. […] I started thrashing round the tiny studio ranting and raving like a mad King George, and yelling at the producer and director as if it was their fault. […] My role was reduced to doing all the minor characters who say 'hello Bob' and things like that.[197]

In fact his minor characters said a lot more than that - the dentally-oriented cocktail party chit-chat before Bob's stormy entrance is hilarious, and Alison and David were genuinely grateful. But it did leave them with a rather large gap in the casting. They were looking for someone who could read the lines naturally, leaving the humour to crystallise out of the words and situations - but an intrinsically funny voice would help. Finally, listening to the radio one day,

they heard the perfect voice. It was that of Andy Hamilton, humorist, raconteur and writer, being interviewed about his comedy series *Drop the Dead Donkey*, which had just hit our screens and started winning awards. He was no actor. His utterly human tone and naturalistic delivery would make him a kind of Everyman that audiences could identify with, and there is no doubt that his slightly nasal quality did - for reasons I cannot entirely pin down - make one laugh when appended to a potato-nosed cartoon character.

The search for the equivalent female voice for Margaret was equally problematic. They originally recorded an actress who had left a phone message when the team were casting for Margaret. On the phone she was, according to David:

… nervous and vulnerable and so very Margaret, full of gulps and umms and ahs. But she sounded too polished when she read. It was Derek Lamb who suggested Alison and I liked the idea, but felt like it was the lazy option so resisted at first. I was wrong![198]
Alison's voice would be sped up a tiny bit to make it a little higher and, perhaps, more vulnerable.

The animation process was long and complex. It would be the couple's last film before the software became available which could automate the laborious process of painting and tracing each individual cel. (David compares the old-fashioned, manual paint and trace system to 'a writer having to chop down trees and make his own paper as part of the writing process.'[199]) Now Alison and David would also spend time in Montreal, overseeing the music and notably the sound, which is key in any Snowden Fine film, is written into the storyboard and influences story decisions. Indeed it was one of the reasons for making Bob a dentist, drills and so on possessing strongly evocative powers. The lengthy animation stage plus the co-production arrangement would ultimately mean a production schedule of two and a half years.

The long wait was even longer drawn out in the event, since an early transmission would have rendered the film ineligible for an Oscar®, so though it was delivered in 1993 it did not get seen on TV until the eve of the Oscar® ceremony in March 1995, when we were able to show off the two C4 commissions nominated that year (the other one was Erica Russell's *Triangle*) plus the third British nominee, Tim Watts and David Stoten's *The Big Story*.

The hiatus due to Oscar® eligibility was worth the wait. Bob had already started picking up top festival prizes including Annecy, Ottawa, Toronto and Espinho, which would later be complemented by nominations for the BAFTA and the Cartoon d'Or, the Canadian Academy Award for best short animation - and it would be third time lucky at the Oscars®. (Any doubts we had as to the film's chances were dispelled when I bumped into Chuck Jones in the foyer: he told me *Bob* was 'a shoo-in', *le tout* Hollywood having voted for it.) Unusually for a short these days, the film also had a limited theatrical run in the UK, playing at some London cinemas with the Australian comedy *Muriel's Wedding*. *The Evening Standard* and *The Independent* both made it plain they far preferred *Bob* to *Muriel*. The *Standard*'s Alexander Walker thought it 'A hilarious squib of a film... As soon as it was over - far too soon - I wanted to see it again.'[200]

Encouraged by all this enthusiasm, the Channel had already financed six scripts towards a series. The big issue after the Oscar® was whether we could convert this success into substantial co-finance. Alison and David returned from Hollywood to find a large bouquet from Warner Bros awaiting them - though Warners were actually more interested in a feature. Universal appeared serious about partnering us on a series, but months went by and the enthusiasm failed to translate into a firm offer. And they really wanted the whole series to be set in America. But Alison and David 'were very steadfast about sticking to the exact formula that won the Oscar® IN AMERICA, by the way...'[201] Eventually, enthusiasm was succeeded by silence: it seemed there had been a change of staff at the top. Finally another Canadian organisation came forward (the Film Board's remit being exclusively shorts) and Nelvana became our partner, offering an excellent deal from Channel 4's point of view. We were to put in only a minority of the budget but the writing, actors and creative control would remain British. *Bob and Margaret* would look for all the world like a hundred per cent Channel 4 commission.

Not only were Alison and David themselves talented scriptwriters but they also recognised that the strength of writing in US series was due to teamwork in this area, and they gradually set about recruiting compatible writing partners. The pair wrote most of the scripts in the first series, with Peter Baynham also doing two. Subsequent series would be written by a steadily growing team with, initially, Alison and David story editing. The process was hard, but in many cases the scripts were outstanding, featuring as they did some big names in British comedy, including Baynham, Jeremy Hardy, Sally Phillips, Kevin Cecil and Andy Riley, along with Snowden and Fine themselves. Andy Hamilton and Alison would continue to voice Bob and Margaret, to be joined by a supporting cast which included another pillar of British comedy, Steve Coogan. By the time the first series went into production, technology had moved on apace. Nelvana was responsible for layout, design and storyboarding and they were using the Animo system for digital paint and trace and compositing. They had the actual animation done in the Philippines.

The series had good reviews in the UK, USA and Canada, though it had a far longer life in North America than in its homeland, probably due to more congenial scheduling. On Comedy Central, where it aired at 10.30pm between *Dr Katz* and *South Park*, its ratings were second only to that latter show. In Canada, on Global TV, it was the highest rated Canadian show, though in truth it did not sound very Canadian. It was subsequently seen in the US on

Bob and Margaret™: Burglary Series 1 1998
© Nelvana Ltd/Channel Four Television Corp

Bob's Birthday

Showtime and in the UK on the Paramount Comedy Network and sold in many other territories. It garnered a clutch of script prizes and viewers' choice awards, as well as the best prime time animation award at the Los Angeles Animation Celebration 2002 - which was specially gratifying given that second prize went to Matt Groening's *Simpsons* follow-up *Futurama*.

Finally, despite Alison and David's initial reluctance to move their characters across the Atlantic, they had to give in. In the absence of British funding and given continued support from Canada, Bob and Margaret emigrated to Toronto for seasons 3 and 4. By this time, Alison and David themselves had bowed out of directing and story editing, simply acting as overall consultants. Sadly, without funding possibilities in the UK, they themselves decided to follow their protagonists westwards and are now happily settled in Vancouver, where they are enjoying considerable success getting new projects off the ground.

Bob's Birthday stills used with permission of Channel Four Television Corp and The National Film Board of Canada

Eldorado
1993/11mins

A film by
Phil Mulloy
Music composed by
Alex Balanescu
Played by
The Balanescu Quartet
Voice
Beñat Achiary
Saxophone
Michel Doneda
Drums
Steve Argüelles
Production company
Spectre Films for Channel 4

Wolf cleans the city's windows by day and plays saxophone at a charity dinner by night, seeing poverty followed by over-indulgence. When food at the dinner runs out, the cooks go to extreme lengths to get more.

Critic Richard Meltzer poses the question: 'Who on the fat bloody planet makes hotter anti-war, anti-state, anti-church, anti-crummy-ideas, screw-the-rich, pro-'diversity' films - hitting the nail on so many goddam heads - than Phil Mulloy?'[202] Well said, sir. No one does, obviously. And he hits a good few of those nail-heads in *Eldorado*, the film Professor Paul Wells has called Mulloy's masterpiece[203]. He hits them directly, violently, viscerally. Ryan Gilbey, reviewing the film from a screening at the ICA likened it to 'a blow-torch in the face'.[204]

What, you may wonder, was the origin of this violence, the anti-clerical passion, the strong morality, the fascination with death and mutilation? And, indeed, with what Richard Meltzer delicately refers to as 'shitpissdoodooweewee - not to mention pustules, scuzz and scum,' in which areas, he suggests, 'PM is a beacon in the night'? Yet given Phil's background - brought up by the Mersey (then 'an open sewer'[205]), where he would happily swim among the used condoms, convinced that the whole of Britain bathed in water of this colour and quality, and educated by the Christian Brothers, a particularly strict Roman

Catholic order ('they felt they had to beat knowledge into you') - perhaps it would have been more surprising if some form of violent rebellion had not ensued. Fear and violence were constants at the school - the only exception being the art classes - and the tales of the martyrs influenced the young Mulloy massively at this period when adolescent hormones were active.

My mind was filled with fantasies of my own lingering death and redemption. Of course much of the iconography of the Catholic church, the naked tortured bodies, reinforced these feelings. The ecstasy of eternal love alongside the blood and iron of the cross is a pretty powerful mix.

He even considered, at one stage, taking the cloth himself.

But instead he went to Ravensbourne College of Art in south London to study painting. As part of his course he made a short animated film ('it was terrible') which was sufficient to get him into the Royal College of Art film and television department. By that stage he had gone off animation and pursued mainly experimental filmmaking for a couple of years, approaching it 'pretty much in the same way that I had approached painting'. In other words, his ambition was to produce work for his own satisfaction, and that put him at odds with the college, which seemed a lot more industry-oriented. It was some years later, and especially after Margaret Thatcher came to power in 1979, that his political concerns along with the inspiration of left-wing European directors such as Godard and Bresson led him to switch from formalist abstraction to films with scripts and actors. From the late 1970s to the late 1980s he made a succession of committed films, mainly documentaries with an experimental approach and mainly for the Arts Council and, latterly, the independent film and video department of Channel 4.

In 1988, almost by accident, he started drawing - something he had not done since art school - while awaiting funding for one of his live action projects. The drawings were loosely based on a series of photographs he had seen as a child, of Russian peasants being hanged by their German captors, which had affected him profoundly. 'It was a moment in which I lost a certain aspect of my own innocence. The images I created were a poetic meditation upon this moment.' The drawings were turned into an animated film for the Arts Council, *The Eye of the Storm* (1989). So satisfying was this activity, this 'reawakening in me of the sheer physical joy of drawing', that he changed course there and then, and *Possession* (1991), the next proposal he submitted to Channel 4, was also animation. Apart from the pleasure of drawing, and the recognition that his political anger could just as well be expressed in this medium as in live action, he saw that without actors or crew to pay it would also be cheaper to produce and therefore perhaps more attractive to funding bodies.

The die was finally cast when he and his family moved out into the Welsh countryside. The family included his partner, Vera Neubauer, who had been making her own unconventional animated films for a decade by this time and could well have been an influence on Phil's evolving technique. They converted a cowshed into a studio, set up an old rostrum and 35mm camera and began making films. Coincidentally, the Animate scheme started up at this time, hoping to attract unconventional artists with low-budget techniques. Phil's *Cowboys* series was the first work completed under the scheme and it set the parameters for his future films:

I developed a way of working that was simple and fast. I tried not to bother about making aesthetic judgements. Black ink painted on paper at speed. Paper cut and ripped out. The image was to be purely functional and nothing else. Mistakes were made and left unedited. The films were to have a strong sense of their own materiality. The language the films spoke was to be that of the street rather than the dining room. They were to be moral tales told with an eye and ear for the immoral.

To Phil's surprise, he found his animation beginning to relate back to the iconography which had accompanied his youth, and all the half-forgotten feelings began to pour out, 'the violence, the blood, the moral viewpoint. Only now the pleasure of eternal life had been replaced by the pleasure in the act of creation and the manipulation of the image'.

Cowboys: Outrage. Iconography of a religious education
© Phil Mulloy

Eldorado original storyboard image. The poverty-stricken saxophonist with window-cleaners outside

Eldorado - which would also be known for a time as *The Sound of Music* - was to be a development from the *Cowboys* strategy, but with a more poetic approach to the film's structure: the narrative was to be minimal, with the emphasis on 'the physicality of the editing, its rhythmical dynamic and the shock value of the individual images.' The film was originally to be punctuated by live action inserts, montaged to near-abstraction, of food being prepared, partly to introduce some colour but also adding rhythm. In the end they were not needed: the music and the narrative editing provided a dynamic which is breathtaking when you see it in action. It is epitomised by a magisterial sequence where the window-cleaner, in a hoist which inches up the side of a high-rise block, sickened by the scenes of degradation that he witnesses through the windows, turns away and throws up over the edge of the hoist. The vomit fells a passing bird, which splatters to the ground and is pounced on by a cat which is flattened by a car. Eight seconds and as many cuts. Richard Meltzer also rhapsodises over the Mulloy sense of rhythm, the way an animated film of all things - with all the pre-planning and storyboarding that implies - can seem so 'ongoingly ad hoc [...] The simulation of real time and the go-go-go of hot synthetic time. Some things feel inevitable yet gratuitous; others are total surprises that seem totally reasonable and totally, well, silly.'[206]

In fact, though the film was, like most of Phil's films, closely storyboarded, he does nevertheless leave some room for spontaneity and is liable to change things while he is animating. In this case, there was one major change: the film was to begin from the point of view of the window-cleaner, then moving through the window to that of the saxophone player, one of the poverty-stricken inhabitants of the high-rise. It became far neater when these two characters

merged into one, with a day job and a night job. Otherwise, there were only minor additions and deletions in the course of production. The ad hoc dynamic was mostly pre-planned.

The final stage was the music, and Phil went back to Alex Balanescu, who had written the score for *Possession*. His music has the intensity of feeling that Phil was aiming for in this film and his approach is very personal and very free. Phil gave Balanescu the finished film and very little briefing - the score simply needed to move from the sophisticated and restrained music accompanying the charity dinner to a free jazz evocation of the anger and chaos of the final scenes.

The production was a good experience for Channel 4 (this time it was the animation department rather than independent film and video). It was quick, cheap (£44,000, a real bargain) and problem-free. The TV premiere - and indeed only transmission - passed without event, though that was not for want of trying on our part. The film was scheduled in a late slot in the context of one of our Four-Mations series. On the basis that any publicity is better than the stony silence usually encountered by our animation seasons, and knowing the press was not averse to throwing up its hands in horror at the excesses of Channel 4, our press officer phoned around to alert TV critics to the treat they had in

store - and discreetly suggesting the nature of some of the film's delights. This cannot have been easy, as these highlights were almost certainly outside her usual vocabulary. Nevertheless she met with some success. One of the tabloids asked for a copy as soon as possible. But they returned it just as quickly: 'too artistic', they said.

The film was more successful on the festival circuit. It was premiered at the Stuttgart animation festival. The preselection committee had announced that they considered *Eldorado* the best film of all they'd viewed and the organisers, wanting to create a bit of a splash, opened the festival with it. The opening night, of course, is the (only) one when the local dignitaries and sponsors turn up, and they all walked out when the full horror of the narrative hit them, some of the latter threatening to withdraw their sponsorship. The film was projected in the wrong format and Phil also felt like walking out - but decided he was probably safer inside. However, it went down a storm elsewhere, winning several awards including the McLaren prize for best British animation at Edinburgh and the critics' award and best music award at Zagreb and, top in my book, the first of our two Dick awards[207] for 'the most innovative, subversive and controversial short film of the year' (the second one going to Tim Webb's *15th February* two years later). The actual award was a bronze penis, which caused quite a few raised eyebrows when Phil took it home (he was by now living in Brixton) on the 59 bus.

Sadly, even a good-value filmmaker like Phil is finding it ever harder to get funding for short films. 'It's a pity. It's easier to take risks in a short film. The cost of producing a feature and the emphasis on the target audience tends to force the writing into fairly narrow guidelines.' But he is nevertheless joining the general migration towards features (though he still manages to find funding for occasional shorts as well). These are not, however, standard animated features. *The Christies* took best feature prize at both Espinho and Ottawa, with the latter jury citing its 'uncompromisingly experimental approach and anarchistic dialogue and humour, never before seen in an animation feature.' But he has also written a script for an international consortium which has had to correspond to rather more standard specifications.

Phil is modest about his achievements:
I just take little bits of crap and try to turn them into something grand. [...] Not everyone likes my work. I've been at screenings where half the audience are booing and the other half are cheering. I generally go and sit with the half that are cheering.[208]

The Village

1993/14mins

Director/script
Mark Baker
Animation
Mark Baker
Pete Western
Neville Astley
Paul Stone
Gaston Marzio
Sound
Danny Hambrook
Camera
Jim Davey
Editor
Annie Kocur
Music
Julian Nott
Backgrounds
Rachael Stedman
Producer
Pam Dennis
Production company
Pizazz Pictures for Channel 4

Starting with the ants outside, the villagers demonstrate some unattractive attributes, escalating from fruit surreptitiously pinched to robbery and murder.

Mark Baker came to animation via an interest in the technical aspects of the craft[209]. In his youth, family holidays were long, and spent in rural France. Mark and his sister would be kept busy with 'projects'. One summer it was a comic strip diary of the holiday. The following year the plan was more ambitious: a home-made optical toy, which appeared to make their drawings move. Back home, Mark had a stab at animation with an 8mm camera, but encountered a few technical problems. In 1974 his problems were solved by an inspiring BBC TV series, *The DIY Film Animation Show*, in which Bob Godfrey and Stan Hayward demonstrated to amateur animators some low-tech tricks to enable their home movie camera to function as an animation rostrum camera, to keep their successive sheets of drawings in register, etc. The die was now cast. When the time came Mark would go into animation.

A foundation year at St Martin's School of Art confirmed him in his plan. It was here that he first came across animation which would really inspire him: the work of Paul Driessen, Richard Condie, Geoff Dunbar, Bruno Bozzetto and above all Jiři Trnka, and it was in this period that he saw a student film with a

delicious sense of timing by Michael Dudok de Wit. So Mark decided to follow Michael to the West Surrey College of Art and Design, where most of his efforts would go into developing a professional-looking, cartoony style. On graduating with an outstanding diploma film, *The Three Knights*, he was immediately employed as an assistant animator on commercials at Richard Purdum Productions.

But what Mark really wanted to do was to make his own film, so in 1983 he returned to college, to the (then recently re-named) National Film and Television School, where the animation course which Derek Hayes and Phil Austin had pioneered nine years previously was 'still only half-official'. Students had a budget for their film, which they could spend as they liked on bringing in professionals to teach for a day whatever aspect they felt weak on. Asked what was the most useful thing the Film School gave him, Mark decided that it was probably the confidence to abandon the more commercial drawing style he had finally managed to acquire at Farnham and revert to his own, natural, somewhat naive style. But there were other good things too: this was a film school, not an art college, so the animation students also had to attend other parts of the course, learning about sound, editing, scriptwriting, cinematography, etc and working with students in those other disciplines. This was particularly helpful in Mark's case, as he would continue after graduating to work with specialists he had encountered there, his editor Annie Kocur, composer Julian Nott and sound man Danny Hambrook. His completed film, *The Hill Farm*, took a clutch of top prizes (including the Annecy Grand Prix, a BAFTA award and an Oscar® nomination) and seemed to guarantee him plenty of work. After a while he found himself at Pizazz, working on commercials.

But Mark was anxious to make another short, and Pizazz was extremely supportive of this. Mario Cavalli, who headed the studio, had recently taken time out for an Animate short, *Soho Square*, and he and producer Pam Dennis were keen to help Mark get his idea into a fit state to propose to Channel 4. The origins of *The Village* lay in *The Hill Farm*. Mark recognised that the latter had been a rather one-sided view of country life, as an ideal world where things only seem to go wrong thanks to intrusions from the outside. But he had actually observed that rural life can get very oppressive, and he wanted to bring out this other dimension in his new film. To underline this oppressiveness, he resolved to have no interventions from the outside world, but to contrive a plot in which all motivations would derive from the villagers' own, largely unpleasant, character traits.

He had also encountered - again on a rural French holiday - the germ of a story idea. He had met a British widow who had inherited her husband's farm. The locals, sure that a woman could not cope, were desperately trying to find a man to look after her, and did indeed introduce her to a man who was more than acceptable. But, rather than admit this, she would embark on the walk

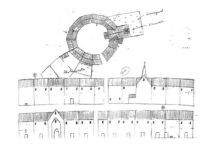

Plan of the village

Character sheet for the priest

to his farm by setting out in the opposite direction before coming round in a giant loop to reach her beau, in order to foil the nosey villagers. Mark was as interested in the visual implications of this situation as he was in the emotional dilemma. The design of certain French villages also fed into the idea: totally circular, inward-looking, they lent themselves to spying on one's neighbours' activities from windows facing both into and out of the village. This design idea was further refined by an engraving he had seen of Shakespeare's Globe Theatre (London's replica had at the time not yet been built).

The proposal Mark brought to me at Channel 4 was for a 5-minute film without dialogue, based on these concepts, but it did not yet have a definite plot line. However, it was plain that this was a proposal to be encouraged and that the impeccable timing and understated humour of *The Hill Farm* proclaimed an enormous talent, so I gave him a small amount of money to fashion it into a workable story. His original idea depended on each character having a secret, some of which were quite complex and impossible to work into a 5-minute plot, especially without dialogue. It went through several versions before Mark decided that those particular secrets would be too ambitious and decided instead on some simple vices - greed, nosiness, a taste for the booze, etc - to move the story on. The running time was now to be 11 minutes, which would fit into the post-*Dispatches* slot, where we were from time to time able to run our most popular films.

Animation proceeded in the normal way, in pencil, on paper over a light-box. The backgrounds were also drawn initially in pencil on thin animation paper, so as to be visible when the animators placed them beneath the scene they were animating on the light-box. But technically, too, Mark wanted to move on from *The Hill Farm*, and this time the characters were being coloured in cel paint - which meant that pencil-rendered backgrounds would no longer be appropriate. He would need the more vibrant qualities of paint. The background process he chose was fairly complex, and all the more so given that there were so many different backgrounds needed - for although the film is set in a single location there are a great many different points of view. Background artist Rachael Stedman had to produce just over 80 backgrounds in her cottage in Scotland. The first step was to xerox the pencil backgrounds on to cartridge paper and then, to introduce more texture into the paper, each sheet was painted with a thin coat of white emulsion and stretched on a wooden board for days while drying. Finally, the backgrounds were painted on, using very thin layers of oil-paint.[210]

At Mark's insistence (in order to keep the expense down) and against the advice of his sound man Danny Hambrook, they embarked on recording the individual sound effects themselves, as they had as students, for later incorporation into the film. Things progressed very slowly, and Mark finally bowed to Danny's expertise and brought in two foley artists. These are real

specialists, who know their trade back to front and are able to record while watching the film, which both makes for better effects and also enables a director to see immediately if something is not working. Composer Julian Nott had, it seems, initially been sceptical about writing for animation. He feared directors would expect a bland, traditional Hollywood cartoon-style track, filling up all the gaps which quirky pacing actually required. However, he misjudged Mark, who was quirkiness personified. In both *The Hill Farm* and *The Village* music is sparse but revealing of character. Nott would later specialise in music for animation, continuing to work with Mark and another Film School alumnus, Nick Park.

During the production Mark came to me with a problem: the film would have to exceed the 11 minutes. The narrative would be compromised if it did not. Although this was not an unusual request from filmmakers, and although I was absolutely sure in 99 per cent of cases that the original estimate was more likely to be correct than a later conviction born out of the director's love affair with certain scenes, in this case I agreed to the extension (and the extended budget, which ended up a whopping £114,000). It did seem to me that Mark's magisterial pacing would suffer from being rushed and, besides, he was an extremely determined negotiator so I acquiesced, only sad that we would thereby exceed the 9.45 post-*Dispatches* slot.

However, the decision seemed vindicated and the prizes rolled in again. Another Oscar® nomination, a BAFTA nomination and the Cartoon d'Or for the best European animated film, among many others. The Cartoon d'Or event that year was something of a triumph for the UK, as all five nominees were British, and especially for Channel 4, which had commissioned four of the five. The event circulates around Europe, but in 1993 it took place in Inverness and for some reason Prince Edward was attending. Mark and I were to meet him, and looked forward to this opportunity to get news of British animation's great achievements out into the echelons of power and influence. However, we were a bit thrown by HRH's questions: 'How did you two meet?' and 'What is foley?', after which he moved on. But C4 did manage to spread the word in a small way, via a documentary about that year's Cartoon d'Or, shown in a *Secret Passions* series of November 1993, in which we also housed the TV premiere of *The Village*.

The Village led on to a further Channel 4 commission, *Jolly Roger* (1999), which took advantage of the advances in computer technology, and led on to *The Big Knights*, a series for the BBC, and thence to the creation of Astley Baker Davies Ltd with partners Neville Astley and Phil Davies and to the pre-school series *Peppa Pig*. This, again, has scooped all the major awards and been sold to 120 overseas territories as this book goes to press. Commentators often note a freshness of approach which marks this company's series out from the normal run of children's entertainment, and Mark agrees that his pre-history with C4

Character sheet for the eloping lovers

shorts counts for something here: he and Neville approach each episode as though it were an individual short film. There are no standard formulas in sight.

Series work has been a rewarding experience, and the constraints of budgets, delivery dates and slot lengths - initially seen as tough challenges - now feel more like a helpful discipline. When I recently asked Mark whether his increased running time on *The Village* had been due to a change of intention or emphasis during production he confessed that it was not really either. It was his first film after the freedom of college. 'I wasn't too worried about the length. I thought we could sort it out later.' Not only that: 'Now I could probably take *The Village* and cut it to fit the slot. You just need to make certain scenes go faster. Actually, varying the pace like that usually improves the end result.'

Abductees

1995/11mins

A film by
Paul Vester
From an idea by
Michael Buhler
*Based on interviews, hypnotic
regression tapes and original
drawings from*
Linda Cortile
Rusty Hudson
Alain Kendirgi
Rosemary Osnato
Helen Wheels
Artists
Ron MacRae
John Parry
Anna Saunders
Mark Shepherd
John Tynan
Duncan Varley
Tim Webb
Brian Wood
Alan Andrews
Barry Baker
Luc Chamberland
Jane Colling
Damian Gascoigne
Jonathan Hodgson
Karen Kelly
Susan Loughlin
Ravindranath Narayanswami
Colourists
Ann Goodall
Sandra Hill
Consultant
Budd Hopkins
Music
Steve Parsons
Francis Haines
Producer
Irene Kotlarz
Production company
Speedy Films for Channel 4

Sequence designed and animated by Ravindranath Narayanswami and based on contemporary comic book art

People who believe they have been abducted by aliens speak of these experiences. As they describe and draw the aliens and their actions, the story is taken up by animators.

Paul Vester's films all have a dark side, a hint of paranoia, some of which reflects elements of his past. His father had - through an accident of birth and a peripatetic lifestyle - found himself on several occasions stateless and adrift. Paul himself was born during the war and brought up in London, with its aftermath of bomb-sites and rationing. Thanks to his father's strong Middle Eastern connections, he spent time in Israel, witnessing at first hand the treatment meted out to the Palestinians. At the age of 25 he lost an eye as the result of a stabbing. 'I have a real fear of things - I know it's possible to get killed, displaced, bullied…'[211]

Another formative influence was his animation training, at a time when animation students were still often outsiders, shoe-horned into film and television courses, given a rostrum camera and left to work out for themselves what to do with it. Having somehow managed to make two animated films off his own bat (and funded by compensation money for the stabbing) at the Central School of Arts and Crafts, Paul was allowed to take a one-year film and television course at the Royal College of Art because he already knew what he was doing technically. As well as improvising his way towards a distinctive animation style, he had to study live action, which would also mark his future films. Many of the traits later visible in *Abductees* would be seen in his first personal film, *Football Freaks* (1971) and, especially, *Picnic* (1987) - notably a mixture of different styles and techniques, including documentary still photographs, and a sense of urban paranoia.

It was an old friend, Michael Buhler, who suggested the abductees phenomenon as a subject. In the late 1980s we were just beginning to hear about these people who believed they had been abducted by aliens, and Michael had been collecting their drawings of these experiences, which had been published in various UFO magazines. Paul was very interested at the time in 'outsider art', untutored drawing, technically bad but in another way 'these were beautiful'.[212] In 1990 he sent me a stack of these drawings, together with a proposal for a half-hour documentary on the phenomenon. I did not feel able to 100 per cent fund such a programme, but did agree to put in some money for the animation part if Paul was able to come up with co-funding, maybe from a factual programming source. So in 1991 he set about developing the project himself prior to seeking further funding. Since he was, anyway, working on commercials in New York quite frequently at the time, he took a Hi-8 camera with him on one trip, and UFO researcher and author Budd Hopkins put Paul and Michael in touch with members of his abductee support group. They interviewed the group members in their homes, asking them to draw for the camera. Armed with this video footage and a new proposal Paul started doing the rounds of the European TV companies.

This was problematic. The encounter with French broadcaster La Sept was typical: they demanded to know whether or not Paul believed the abductees' stories, because his opinion would have to inform the documentary - which, as they saw it, had to be about whether or not the abductions actually happened. Professor Paul Wells would feel the same way, when later writing about this film: 'the idea of "documentary" is compromised [...] by the implausible nature of the subjective voice'[213]. But when, in 1992, I was finally able to commission the film (albeit at a running time of only 11 minutes), I did not ask Paul whether he believed the stories - partly because I assumed he did not (though he is now teasing me with suggestions that perhaps to some extent he did) but also because it was not relevant. To me the film did have a strong documentary aspect, but its subject was not the abductions themselves but these people's psyches. For Paul:

it was about what the abductees thought they'd seen, what they thought had happened, what they thought the aliens looked like, how they moved. [...] The animation was about the drawings, about the attempt to describe something imperfectly understood in often clumsy ways. The abductees, if they did see something, didn't understand what they were seeing, or thought they were seeing, so they described it in terms of things that they did understand and

Sequence originating in one of the abductee drawings found by Michael Buhler and animated by Ron MacRae

When Speedy was doing Babycham commercials, Paul Stone had been the best designer and animator for the character. Now he only had time to contribute a few drawings, which were worked up by Luc Chamberland

Original drawing by abductee Rusty Hudson

Paul's original treatment for Rusty's semen extraction sequence

Jonathan Hodgson was chosen to animate this scene as his style came closest to Rusty's

recognise. [...] The film is in a sense about limits: limits of understanding, limits of imagination, limits of drawing ability, limits of vision...

Paul was proposing to use different animators' distinctive styles to characterise the different abductees' accounts. Where a particular look was indicated in the original drawings, or a specific area of popular culture in either the drawings or the spoken testimony, he chose an animator who could tap into that same area. Whether because of the consequently large crew and the varying techniques, or because of Paul's acknowledged perfectionism or for some other reason, the budget was high - it ended up at £131,000 - and I had to dash his hopes of returning to New York for a proper live action shoot. He would have to make do with the test footage he had already shot.

Paul's method was to categorise on index cards all the information he had in the video footage: firstly how the aliens looked, how they moved, whether they had feet, what kind of eyes they had, etc, and secondly what they did to the abductees. With the index cards as a guide he put together a complete 11-minute cut of the video footage. He then worked up versions of the abductees' drawings and made a style reference sheet for each sequence and started assigning animators, based on how well the animators' individual 'handwriting' matched the style sheets and the way he wanted the sequence to move. The project meshed with his philosophy of treating his animators as individuals, each with a unique voice.
Speedy was always a small outfit, a relatively tight group, a group that functioned (I hoped) more like a band (eg Duke Ellington's) where each person contributed his or her voice to the mix and was capable of improvising a solo. I wanted the animators to have a hand in designing their own sequences and I customised the sequences with specific artists in mind.

One of the 'soloists', Jonathan Hodgson, explained how this had worked:
Paul saw a stylistic link between my drawings and one of the abductees he interviewed, Rusty [the young man whose semen had been extracted by the aliens], who drew quite loose sketches in pencil. Paul liked the way I draw: mainly the messy, sketchy drawings. While working out the animated sequences I probably used an eraser quite a bit and he saw that the traces of the drawings that I'd revised somehow fitted in with the whole idea of the abductees recalling vague memories under hypnosis. The idea that a memory is not a solid thing but something that changes over time could be visualised with subtle multilayering of slightly differing versions of the same information. I've seen the same idea used in live action but never before or since in animation.[214]
Paul also, helpfully, brought in some S & M equipment - shiny black rubber and metal - to inspire Jonathan as regards the mechanics of the semen extraction.

The original idea was that each artist would develop his or her sequence design from an original concept, sometimes but not always storyboarding too, and then see it through animation. But it did not always work out like that. British animation was hit by a recession in the early 1990s. While it meant that there were a lot of good artists who would normally be engaged in commercials work now available for this job, we all knew that broadcast TV work was not paid at the high rates of commercials. So the deal was that any animator who managed to find a better paid job was free to drop out.

Paul managed to turn the necessity of using the original Hi-8 footage to his advantage. He was looking for a low-tech way of transferring it to 35mm film, but also wanted the live action to look more graphic, so as to fit better with the animation. The solution was to video-print every other frame, which were then photocopied and re-registered and pegged, and shot on doubles (as animation is) under the 35mm rostrum camera. With the technology then available - a U-Matic, on which production co-ordinator Chris Shepherd would have to adjust the tracking for each frame, and an old thermal printer - the job was a nightmare. But it did give the live action a more graphic look and the method would inspire others to incorporate treated live action into their animation. Jonathan Hodgson would later use a development from this system for *Feeling My Way*. The treatment also enhanced the documentary aspect of *Abductees*. As pointed out by Sylvie Bringas and mentioned elsewhere in this book, live action filming can become voyeuristic where the subject is of a sensitive or traumatic nature. Few animated documentaries have, therefore, used any live action, but where they have it is often somehow processed, either by rotoscoping or, as here, by photocopying, to create a healthy distance.[215]

Image taken directly from abductee Alain Kendirgi's drawing and worked up by Paul with Mark Shepherd

Original owl drawing by Jane Colling, worked up by Duncan Varley and Paul

The final touch was the music. One of the abductees gave Paul some music that she had received from an alien and had notated by a musician. But sadly the alien music was not very good and Paul's music team, Steve Parsons and Francis Haines, could do nothing with it. They all knew they wanted to avoid the cliché of spooky UFO music and finally came round to the idea of the equivalent in music to the somewhat limited cultural models evoked in the abductees' sketches. They decided the 'elevator music' genre would be appropriate.

The completed film encountered hostility among some of the more traditional animators, who were still at that time prejudiced against the use of live action in animation and some of whom also denied Paul's authorship of the film because they could not perceive in it his personal drawing style. Both these schools of thought appear to be less prevalent these days, as animation has expanded to become the 'manipulated moving image' and can happily encompass any number of different techniques and personal inputs.

But the film has been extremely popular in other quarters, taking top prizes at San Francisco, Sitges and the Everyman Animation Festival in London. It had an extended run at Film Forum, New York, and the BFI toured it around the UK,

Sequence designed and animated by Karen Kelly. Paul heard she was available and invited her to do this sequence in her own style

premiering at the ICA, in a package entitled Live Wires and Raw Drawings. Of this latter, *The Independent* felt that

the most affecting thing here is Paul Vester's 11-minute Abductees, *which utilises the confessions of people who have been kidnapped by aliens, as well as bringing to life the drawings that were wrung out by their therapy. Five years in the making, the film's compassion and generosity negate scepticism.*[216]

Paul was unhappy that he could not make the full half-hour version he originally planned, but at least it meant that - unlike much of the animation output - the film enjoyed a good TV career. For its premiere, *Abductees* was packaged into a lengthy interview with Paul and shown in a *Secret Passions* series in June 1995. The following year it opened the Four-Mations: UK series in that fabled 9.45pm slot and has enjoyed a good few transmissions on both C4 and FilmFour since then. It is a film which speaks to audiences in a most direct way. To complete that *Independent* quote: 'It has a quiet profundity about it, painfully communicating our crippling fear of loneliness in a stark universe.'

Crapston Villas

Series 1 1995/10 x 11mins

Director/script
Sarah Ann Kennedy
Voices
Jane Horrocks
Alistair McGowan
Lesley Sharp
Alison Steadman
Steve Steen
John Thomson
Liz Smith
Animators
Timon Dowdeswell
Tobias Fouracre
Mark Waring
Sets/props/costumes
Cod Steaks
Barbara Cowdery
Einstein's Octopus
Jane Whittaker
Puppet/character designs
David Stoten
The Puppet Factory
David Pedley
Spitting Image Workshop
Titles
Steve Bendelack
Sound
Rob Butler Biggs
Original music
Rowland Lee
Lighting camera
Adrian Chaldecott
Gray Pettit
Executive producers
Joanna Beresford
Andy de Emmony
Producer
Jonathan Bairstow
Series producer
Richard Bennett
Production company
Spitting Image for Channel 4

Marge, Sophie and Fatso

In a seedy London suburb the various inhabitants of a converted Victorian house interact - to often disastrous effect.

Sarah Kennedy studied fine art at Newcastle Polytechnic in the mid-1980s, but soon discovered that her burning interest was in telling stories - stories about real people, stories which would be hilarious, but would be based on serious concerns. Her models were Mike Leigh and Alan Bennett. So it had to be filmmaking. She gave live action a try but at this stage in her life it seemed a terrible hassle, recruiting and dealing with a crew, so she started experimenting with various kinds of animation, eventually deciding on puppets as the easiest medium. 'I could write them, voice them, film them, edit them all myself.'[217] She would have more control. Sarah's Newcastle film, *As It Happens*, was about her disillusionment with feminism at the time - she felt it oppressive. Women were

Character designs for Flossie and Sophie

supposed to talk like feminists and dress like feminists (no make-up!), while in fact many self-styled feminists were restricting themselves to these outward appearances and not truly asserting themselves in the way they lived their lives. The film illustrates this, in a story that is 'much ruder' even than the unbuttoned Sarah we are accustomed to from her later films. But it was that kind of time. 'They were doing naked performance art in the fine art department.'

She started to hone her various skills, doing an animation MA at the Royal College of Art, where she developed her rather primitive style of puppet making and outrageous humour, which would later result in two commissions from C4's editor for youth programmes, Stephen Garrett. She then spent some time as a researcher on the C4 series *Sex Talk*, also for the youth department. 'For a whole year I went round the country, talking to an incredible range of people I'd never normally have come across, asking all sorts of questions about their sex lives… and getting paid for it!'[218] She also had a spell researching *EastEnders* for the BBC. Her dialogue became almost painfully real. The combination of funny and authentic dialogue with simple technique is a precondition for series work, and Sarah's mind was indeed moving in that direction. She is also, unlike many animators, happy working in a team: 'getting the right people together, letting them go for it… and come up with great ideas'[219]. Ideal for series.

By 1992, when I was beginning to nurture ambitions to develop some adult animation series for Channel 4, Sarah had already made the one-off 11-minute short *First Night*, for Stephen Garrett's *He-Play, She-Play* series of films by first-time filmmakers. I commissioned her to write and co-direct a further four episodes, following the same romance through to the bitter end in the same mix of live action and animation. Stripped across the week leading up to Valentine's Day 1993, *Nights* was well received, more than justifying the next step, a pilot for a longer, fully-animated series. Sarah was not short of ideas, and one seemed ideal for an animated comedy soap: a house based on the one she had lived in when she first moved to London from the calmer waters of her home town, Stratford-upon-Avon, and student life in Newcastle. She had already started developing the idea with one potential studio, but the relationship had soured. However, she had rented a studio at Spitting Image to shoot *Nights*, and Roger Law liked Sarah and liked the idea, especially as his company was looking for a new role since the demise of its national treasure of a satire show, and was keen to get into animation. Roger and colleagues took Sarah to their heart and invested their know-how and some development money in a proposal that I could not refuse.

I did not initially realise quite how rude it was going to be - we were, after all, aiming for the relatively respectable slot after *Dispatches* at 9.45pm. But I did know that it would be fairly vulgar and pretty 'childish' (Sarah's description of herself and the series) and I liked the way that quality promised to combine with the skilled soap plotting acquired from her experience on *EastEnders* and,

Character designs for Marge, Larry and Robbie

as far as I could judge from the proposal, with a far more interesting range of characters and situations than were usually found in live soaps. It also had a ghastly ring of truth, mainly, it transpires, because most of the characters were based on real people: I seemed to sense a real sympathy in the authorial point of view.

Sarah herself provided the model for two - diametrically different - characters; both aspiring actress Flossie, who mirrors Sarah's own sense of wonderment at even the most unappealing manifestations of London life, and sensible Sophie who has bought a dreadful flat and has a dreadful partner:
That happened to me. We had this absolute dump and couldn't afford to do it up and I just hated it. And he wasn't working and pottering around at home and doing nothing. But it's exaggerated of course.
Marge was loosely based on Sarah's mother. 'Obviously my mum's not an old slapper like that', but she did struggle to bring up three children alone and was indeed on the look-out for romance. (She eventually found it and is now happily married.) Marge's daughter, Sam, is - again - based on Sarah herself:
When I was young I was really naughty. But you know, when I look now, those things I got Sam and [her friend] Betty to do… some of them were based on things I did but some were really exaggerated. But now, that's actually what kids are like! It's really shocking.

I was also taken by the relationship between the gay couple - Robbie, young, uncultured and absolutely charming, and Larry, far older, terribly highbrow and a bit pretentious. Sarah had observed this exact same attraction of opposites in a heterosexual couple of her acquaintance. But my favourite house-mate was, sadly, not based on anyone she knew. The character of Enid was probably wishful thinking - I imagine few actual senior citizens are willing or physically able to buck the stereotypes and devote themselves to a life of hedonism, no matter what havoc that may wreak around them. (One of my favourite scenes would have the ancient Enid hijack a motor mower and career about, cigarette dangling from lip, in a Nazi helmet bearing the legend 'Live Fast - Die Young'.) But it is a delicious thought.

Sarah set about writing the pilot script. For all the air of mayhem she creates, scriptwriting is an extremely serious matter to her. It has to sound real.
I'm really perfectionist about it - I like the sound to be really tight. As long as the people doing the voices are on your wavelength all that matters is that they don't try too hard to be funny delivering the lines: it should already be there in the writing.[220]

The starry cast she managed to assemble for this series - headed by Jane Horrocks as Flossie, Lesley Sharp as Sophie, Alistair McGowan as Jonathan, Alison Steadman as Marge, John Thomson as Robbie and Steve Steen as both Larry and Enid - could not have been bettered in this respect.

There were some production problems. Spitting Image - world renowned for their magnificent puppets - of course made the puppets for the pilot in house. But their puppets for the *Spitting Image* series had been enormous, life size, operated by puppeteers, and they had no experience of tiny puppets with small armatures. And they were still using latex for the skin, which tended to crack. The puppet-making function would be farmed out to The Puppet Factory for the actual series.

Enid puppet ready for action. Character created by Sarah Kennedy, designed by David Stoten and made by the Puppet Factory. Lawnmower by John Wright
Photo Clare Kitson

Marge's daughter Sam and her chum Betty

Otherwise the pilot went according to plan, except that it did somehow turn out a bit more shocking in the flesh than I had assumed from the written page. Nevertheless, when it was passed to our head of scheduling he declared it absolutely fine for that 9.45 slot. However, as already mentioned, by this time pilots were frequently subjected to focus groups - groups of viewers in a range of age groups and social classes whose opinions were used to gauge potential popularity and ideal scheduling. *Crapston Villas* hit the jackpot. Hated by the older groups, it was a gigantic hit with the 18-24 year-old men - the Channel's most sought-after demographic, and that which constituted the most avid viewers of the Friday night, post-pub youth gross-out, *The Word*. This was the show in which worms had been eaten, bodily excretions drunk and a colostomy bag used in a stunt. But, sadly for the young men and for C4, it was not on air all year round and a replacement was needed. They had found it in *Crapston Villas,* and it was put into production immediately, with this 11.15 slot in mind.

There were fewer technical problems during this shoot, though even the silicone-skinned, Puppet Factory puppets were problematic. Silicone looks great, but it has a super-smooth surface and nothing will stick to it. In the end, superglue had to be used every time a character picked something up, so the hands were constantly falling apart and needing to be replaced. And by the end of the series the puppets had pretty well melted. But all went well otherwise and the 'childish' delight at each new outrageous thought continued throughout the shoot.

I made one rather half-hearted attempt to raise the tone. I did not feel that 'Crapston Villas' as a title was intrinsically very witty. It did combine 'Clapham' and 'Brixton', it sounded like 'Aston Villa' and it had 'crap' in it, but that did not quite do it for me. My suggestion of 'Valhalla Villas' fell on stony ground. Few of the crew had heard of Valhalla, so it seemed unlikely that our Friday night post-pub boys would have - or would care much how satirical the title was. So 'Crapston' it remained.

Everyone expected a lot of flak when the series went on air - in fact Roger Law declared that he'd be extremely disappointed if there were *not* a lot of flak. But in the event we ourselves removed the one really dubious happening. Good-time gran Enid had wandered into a party Marge's son Woody was holding in his mother's absence and, in the dark, had been mistaken for an eligible young mate. We originally saw Woody snogging his gran - but decided that must go. In the final version it is not clear what did or did not happen.

Of flak there was some, of course, though the audience for that 11.15pm slot, where they were used to finding *The Word*, were unlikely to complain. Some of the more strait-laced papers were a bit stuffy about it. Christopher Dunkley in the *Financial Times* ended a slating of various recent BBC2 and C4 programmes with 'Worst of all is *Crapston Villas*…' though in essence he agreed with Sarah: 'It puts you in mind of a dysfunctional 9 year-old with a spray can and a garage door.'[221] Others got into the spirit of the thing, with the *Telegraph* noting that the characters are well-crafted - 'there is a horribly recognisable kernel of truth behind each of them' - and the actors' portrayals 'a hoot'.[222] Jasper Rees in *The Independent* noted a list of 'firsts', which distinguished *Crapston Villas* from standard soaps:

Woody and Enid the morning after

… the first to let you see a cat vomiting copiously and then licking up the mess, the first to show a woman naked in bed. It's also the first soap in which all the characters are genuinely made out of plasticine but sound real, as opposed to looking real and sounding plasticine.[223]

Well, silicone actually, but who's quibbling? He also noted that the dialogue was spot on:

Flossie the lodger, a magnificent gargoyle who looks and talks like a vanilla cone in a 36DD, is done to a tee by Jane Horrocks. All her previous roles seem to have been but a preparation for this squawking numskull. If the litmus test of a soap is that it offers for your inspection characters you recognise, then Crapston Villas *sails through.*[224]

The apogee of *Crapston*'s success was the awarding of the *Broadcast* magazine award for best new programme of 1995. Given the range of outstanding new work that year across all TV genres - the other two nominees were a much-lauded comedy, *The Mrs Merton Show*, and an innovative documentary, *Russian Wonderland* - it was a stunning success. We learned that it had 'received unanimous approval from the judges for its "wonderful characters and fantastic sophistication" '[225], at which point we did rather wonder whether they were having a laugh. Thanks to the fact that we had the right programme in the right slot and the Channel was behind it with a lively on-air promotion campaign, the series got excellent ratings, even exceeding 2 million for a couple of episodes. It also took off in certain overseas territories, with the US and France really taking it to their hearts - a look on Google reveals any number of fan websites still active. Even now, visitors to YouTube reminisce about it: 'Better than *The Simpsons*, *Family Guy* and even *South Park*! Better than everything!', said one. 'OMG… they made my first bedsit into a show??… COOOOOOL', said another.

Channel 4, delighted with this success, immediately commissioned a second series. But Sarah then went to Kenya for a holiday and had an accident

Larry and Robbie

which damaged her back. She was stretchered back to the UK and was unable to direct series 2, which was scheduled to start immediately. Instead, she would lie nearby, executive producing, while Peter Boyd Maclean and Timon Dowdeswell directed. The second series was good (it won the 1998 Independent Television Award for best animation series) but different. 'Technically better,' Sarah felt, 'but no subtleties. Not that the first series was all that subtle, but I think the timing was better.' At the end of production, she needed a major back operation, which took her out of action for several months. We then commissioned a script for a Larry and Robbie Christmas special, but somehow Sarah's heart was not in it. After four months on her back, the prospect of another time-consuming animation project did not appeal. She had already done some voice-over work for Channel 4, notably playing the lead in Candy Guard's *Pond Life*. Now she embarked on a variety of comedy roles - as a stand-up comedienne, as an actor and with more voice overs. She also began to expand her writing repertoire, including children's TV series.

Since 2004, Sarah finally has a formula which suits her. She is course leader on the animation MA at the University of Central Lancashire, which still allows time for some voice-over work. She spends the long academic holidays writing, developing her own comedy ideas for submission to the large companies which nowadays largely monopolise independent production for television. Her current project is, like *Nights*, basically a live action series with animated flashbacks telling the ghastly truth of a situation. I look forward to another ensemble of 'plasticine characters sounding real', to set against the plasticine dialogue that is still the norm.

Crapston Villas photos courtesy Channel Four Television Corp

Many Happy Returns

1996/8½mins

A film by
Marjut Rimminen
Cast
Kevin O'Donohue
Sarah Strickett
Voices
Anthony May
Melanie Hudson
Camilla Hunsley
Words
Harriett Gilbert
*Live action design/
production*
Daniel Simpson
Adam Cutts
Mark Sewell
Lighting
Layne Comarasawmy
Digital compositing
Timo Dan Arnall
Picture/sound editing
Tony Fish
Dubbing mixer
Nigel Heath
Produced by
Lee Stork
Production company
Tricky Films for
Channel 4

A modern-day young woman has difficulty relating to her partner. The childhood traumas which still inhabit her are glimpsed in puppet animation and various manipulated images.

The Stain (1991) was Marjut Rimminen's first foray into dysfunctional families, seen from the psychoanalytical viewpoint she had come to understand via the therapy she herself had been undergoing since 1989. By 1993 she was ready to confront full-on the problems of her own early life. For one thing, the therapy had brought her out of the depression she had suffered for years; for another, the technology now available offered a perfect vehicle for doing this.

The therapy had brought her 'some kind of understanding of how the psyche works - and how my psyche works. And I just wanted to work on that material.'[226] But until that time she had not had the means to do so. For one thing, none of the traditional techniques of animation would offer an equivalent to the multi-layered nature of memory and how our psyche deals with it. For another, the traditional means were too labour-intensive and too costly for the extensive experimentation she felt she needed to prepare for this very delicate

Storyboard extract from the original, Finnish project
© Marjut Rimminen

project. She did already own an Amiga home computer and was experimenting with 2D animation, which certainly gave her more control than other techniques; but it still required all phases of movement to be drawn in as for traditional 2D. She also had a video camera. The breakthrough came when her young son Timo - now an Oslo-based designer and researcher specialising in all aspects of computing in design - bought her as a birthday present the software which linked the two together. Having filmed the birthday celebrations and instantly put red noses on all those present, she saw both the creative possibilities in this kind of manipulated live action and the total control she could impose on her material for the first time in her life. (She would later say that she 'felt like a god'.)

Fresh from successful psychoanalysis, Marjut's earliest attempts to record her psychological state resulted in a 1993 proposal to a Finnish funding body for a film entitled *Beyond the Blue Horizon*, with a subtitle that translates roughly as 'The things you left behind will return in future'. This fascinating storyboard represents the raw material as dredged up by psychoanalysis. While the main elements which will survive into *Many Happy Returns* are already there - the trauma relating to a disfiguring accident in childhood and the constant background of an abusive relationship between the parents - all sorts of other elements are also in the mix. These include a theme of sibling rivalry which is totally absent from the later work, and various symbols such as a cupboard full of boxes containing each year's memories that the woman is unable to relinquish, as well as various objects, broken and patched up, to represent her attempts to cope with the consequences of the past and get by in an imperfect world. It focuses entirely on the woman's psyche, never looking outwards to suggest ways in which the damage done might continue to affect her right up to the present.

The proposal was not accepted and Marjut revised it somewhat, then coming to Channel 4, where she was offered those most precious commodities, a little bit of development money and the time to get to grips with what the real story was and how best to tell it. She worked closely with both her son Timo and editor Tony Fish to produce a dazzling demonstration reel. The proposal was put into production. The final result was more streamlined than the Finnish storyboard, yet also more poetic. There was a large live action element, telling both the story of the woman's relationship problems in the present day and also, using the same pair of actors, that of the drunken father's abuse of the mother. The child was depicted in puppet animation but shot digitally so as to be capable of layering together with a multiplicity of other, evocative effects suggesting the traumas of family life, of the accident and subsequent surgery, and of the mother leaving. Even the live action - previously such a nerve-racking enterprise with the results invisible until the film was developed - was now a pleasure for Marjut, with the results instantly visible and eminently manipulable, should things need slowing down, speeding up etc. Though everything was shot digitally, and stored on the computer's hard disk, back in 1994 computers were not used for editing as they are now, so the computer-generated material was transferred on to 16mm for this stage.

Therapy had taught Marjut that though she had lost some sight she had 'gained a vision', and this film was her vision. But, she insists, 'the film isn't about me. It's about being able to share sadness. It seems to strike a chord with lots of people.' She received and continues to receive letters from people who recognise their own lives in the film. It also did extremely well on the festival circuit, taking Grand Prix at Tampere and Fantoche, prize for best animated film at Vila do Conde Short Film Festival, the special jury prize at Kraków and a nomination at the British Animation Awards among others. Juries and critics appreciated the originality of approach, 'subverting conventional definitions of story-telling, animation and cinema'[227], 'enhancing the art of animation with a new means of expression'[228], 'like a kick in the kidneys. It was worth the visit to Fantoche, just to watch this film… a masterpiece'[229].

Marjut was disappointed that Channel 4 chose to premiere the film packaged into its Electric Passions computer animation season. After all, 'films are films. Technique doesn't matter. All my films are about something, trying to say something, trying to touch another person with the story or the atmosphere or the poetry.' Slots for individual short films not being on offer in the schedule, we had put this exquisite work - packaged together with two other outstanding computer-generated auteur films, Simon Pummell's *Butchers Hook* and Keith Piper's *Go West Young Man* - into a season that also went behind the scenes at Pixar and various other hot names among animation studios. Maybe our efforts were lost on most of the young computer fans we were courting with this season - but who knows whether one or two were moved, were excited, whether they decided as a result to take a new direction in their bedroom Amiga experiments…

We felt like royalty when Many Happy Returns won the Fantoche Grand Prix
Courtesy Marjut Rimminen

165

Pond Life
Series 1 1996/13 x 11mins

Director/script/design
Candy Guard
Voices
Sarah Ann Kennedy
Emma Chambers
John Thomson
Charlotte Mitchell
Brian Murphy
Dominic Guard
Elizabeth Rider
Animation director
Geoff Loynes
Colour designer
Bunny Schendler
Music
Chris Guard
Sound
Wild Tracks
Editing
Reelworks
Producer
Ed Bignell
Executive producer
Trevor Murphy
Animation production
Telemagination
Production company
Pond Life Productions
for Channel 4 and S4C
in association with EVA
Entertainment

Pond Life: Mr Wrong

Dolly Pond lives in a suburban cul-de-sac, surrounded by her 'crap' family and friends who are, she is sure, holding her back. The series follows her attempts to achieve her true, fantastic potential.

When Candy Guard brought her *Pond Life* proposal to Channel 4 she was welcomed with open arms. We had loved her vignettes for the 1988 *Woman in View* series, including *Alternative Fringe* and *Fatty Issues*, and a further group, *Moanologue*, *What About Me?* and *The Wrong Type*, commissioned by S4C for a youth programme of theirs but co-funded by C4. All featured women, but they were obviously not driven by the politics of the women's movement.

The crucial influence that Candy acknowledges, and which she claims as the direct inspiration for Dolly Pond, could not have been more different: it was female characters such as Minnie the Minx and, especially, Beryl the Peril in the comics she was obsessed with as a child (until she 'gave in and read a novel at the age of 15'[230]). Beryl, drawn in the 1960s by David Law in *The Topper*, was *feisty, naughty, easily bored, moody and charming - and easily as funny as Dennis the Menace. She was the original ladette [...] I wondered what Beryl would be like if she'd had a chance to grow up. She became the inspiration for*

my own female characters, Dolly Pond [...] and Edie Dudman.[231]
Another favourite, later on, was the cartoonist Claire Bretécher, whom she admired for her humorous treatment of Everywoman, in everyday situations. (She also has a lot of respect for Posy Simmonds' witty observations, but the latter's humour derives from the foibles of a far more restricted social group.)

Pond Life: Boyfriend. At the pub

Pond Life: Bitter and Twisted. Dolly seeks help from a therapist

At Newcastle Polytechnic, with most of her fellow-students specialising in the more elitist skills of painting or sculpture, 'all I wanted to do was to be funny'. Yet she did not immediately turn to animation, which might have seemed the logical discipline to choose, given her constant reading of comics and drawing of cartoons. Instead, she wanted to be a photographer - of ordinary people. 'I wanted to be Cartier-Bresson. I didn't really fit in. But not fitting in suited me. I grew in a more natural way.' She did eventually make an animated film at Newcastle (about a bag lady), yet by the time she had graduated and gone on to a further year at St Martin's School of Art, she had decided she wanted to be a live action film editor. Around the time of *Woman in View* she was also writing live action scripts, including co-writing the 1990 feature film *Women in Tropical Places*. We begin to divine another model for Dolly Pond's erratic ambitions.

But by the time Candy brought the *Pond Life* proposal to us in 1992 we knew she was a wickedly funny animator-scriptwriter with a brand of humour - dialogue-dependent and visually sparse - that could adapt well to the series format which she wanted to try. I was sure it could work on the Channel in our 9.45pm post-*Dispatches* slot. The pilot episode, *Boyfriend*, has Dolly meet an ordinary sort of chap in a pub, laugh and joke with him in an easygoing manner... until she starts to wonder whether perhaps he fancies her. In a trice she is lovelorn, tongue-tied and has imagined a life together in such detail that it gets to feel oppressive - and breaks it up before it has actually started. The production was fairly painless, the minimalist animation done in the traditional way by a team of five people. The Channel liked it, the head of scheduling declared it good for the desired slot - however, series production being expensive and this series, unlike *Crapston Villas*, potentially appealing to co-production partners, the Channel would only put in 55 per cent of the budget. Executive producer Trevor Murphy battled tenaciously to assemble the balance and eventually S4C and EVA Entertainment were brought in as co-production partners; scripts were commissioned in 1995 and the series finally went into production in 1996.

The first step was recording the voices. Sarah Kennedy, Candy's Newcastle Poly contemporary, seemed the obvious choice for Dolly and had voiced most of Candy's earlier films:
I did think about using a "name". But Sarah's good - very funny and a natural performer. She always understood the scripts - the mood and the emphasis. And she knows how I speak. People often think it's me, because she gets the intonation. I don't think I could have got an actress to do that.

Pond Life: Fit. Dolly's new regime

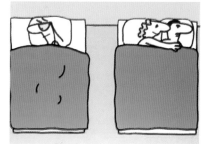

Pond Life: Holiday

The rest of the cast were equally felicitous choices: Emma Chambers (Belle) and John Thomson (Nobby) were rising sitcom stars at the time - now they have risen and might not be able to find time for an unknown quantity such as this series then was. The family rallied round, with Candy's actress mother Charlotte Mitchell voicing Dolly's mother and brother Dominic Guard contributing some bit parts. Trevor Murphy's father Brian (of *George and Mildred* fame) played Dolly's father, and an assortment of friends played the rest. All were brilliant. Candy's soundtracks are very full, in contrast with her sparse visuals:

I treat it like a radio play. If it works that way, it'll work as a film. My technique is very simple, very economical. Because the soundtracks are so busy - I use a lot of voice over, characters' thoughts - it would be distracting if there was a very full visual style.[232]

Based on these voices, Candy then did all the character sheets and storyboards (an enormous workload, but this production just could not afford more staff).

But by the time it finally came to animating the series, a succession of problems surfaced. The only way for the chosen animation company, Telemagination, to do it in this country (and animating in the Far East was not then such a tried and tested route as it is now, especially for the group of first-timers making *Pond Life*), and on the extremely tight budget allocated, was to employ some young, inexperienced and cheap animators to work on the series, along with a few more experienced hands. Candy now feels that the company had looked at her simple style and made the mistake of assuming that it was simple to draw. Veteran animator Geoff Loynes emerged as the hero of the day, totally dedicated, taking others' less professional work home and re-doing it correctly - though Candy still feels that some scenes betray a slightly amateur hand. The other problem was that by the time the series was commissioned technology had progressed and computers could colour animation far more cheaply than human hands. But Candy's drawing style had been formed years earlier, when hand-drawing was the only option, and had been used for the pilot for this series. She employed very little colour and it did not necessarily occur in discrete areas - hair, for instance, consisted of a few lines radiating from the top of her characters' heads. Now, all areas to be coloured had to be joined up so that the computer could read them (but in a blue pencil so as not to show). Obviously, if one were setting out to do a series today it would automatically be computer-coloured and the design would have to reflect this requirement.

After a fairly stressful production, the series was successfully completed and I thought it excellent - just right for the 9.45 slot it was commissioned for. But problems arose, seemingly stemming from the findings of a series of focus groups and the well-known preference of advertisers for young male rather than female audiences. *Pond Life* was slotted instead at 5.45 after a housewife-oriented talk show, *Ricki Lake*. (See chapter 9 for more details of this sad story.)

Pond Life: Glastonbury

Pond Life: PMT

It remains, however, to celebrate the real success of the series. 'Best thing of the whole evening', said Lynne Truss in *The Times*, '… gloriously funny… the scripts are brilliant.'[233] 'An animated sitcom with more wit and bite in 12 minutes than most television programmes offer in an entire series', said Cristina Odone in the *Telegraph*.[234] Dolly Pond was 'destined to become the heroine of '90s womanhood', opined Fiona Morrow in *Time Out* - '*Pond Life* deserves to be on your must-see list.'[235] And there were many more in the same vein. But perhaps the series' greatest achievement was that it consolidated *Crapston Villas'* success in bringing animation out of the ghetto to which it had usually been confined: Candy's scripts were considered to be on a par with the best of live action comedy writers. Well, almost on a par in the case of the Royal Television Society. Kirsty Young, when announcing the winner in the Situation Comedy and Comedy Drama category, prefaced the announcement with the comment: 'The jury remarked on the very high standard this year and noted the cleverness of the animated series *Pond Life*, which would have won a prize for animation had there been one' - but drew the line at actually nominating an animated sitcom. The Writers' Guild and the *Broadcast* magazine awards both went further and nominated Candy alongside star sitcom writers of major hit programmes. She did not win. But she did make a clean sweep of the animation festivals, winning best primetime TV series and best director thereof at the Los Angeles Animation Celebration and best series prizes at Annecy and Ottawa.

This was not the last of Dolly Pond. She inspired a pregnancy testing kit commercial (the people at the agency must have seen the *PMT* episode) and Channel 4 did finally commission a second series, this time produced by Collingwood O'Hare, after another struggle to find funding partners. It did not, however, have quite the verve of the first, largely because a half-hour format was imposed this time, thanks to the standardisation of the schedule into half-hour blocks. Dolly has now been reincarnated in the character of Edie Dudman, heroine of Candy's novel *Just a Little Disco on an Open-Top Bus*[236]. Edie has trouble making up her mind, boyfriend problems, no job and is continually making lists. She also ends up leaving the friends and family who are holding her back, to study art in Newcastle…

Images © Channel Four Television Corp/S4C

Death and the Mother

1997/10½mins

A film by
Ruth Lingford
Based on a story by
Hans Christian Andersen
Animation assistance
Lisa Flather
Michèle Smith
Alex Potts
George Lingford
Narrative adviser
Caroline Leaf
Performance adviser
Linda R Scott
Digital adviser
Timo Dan Arnall
Music
Nigel Broadbent
Story editing/sound
Larry Sider
Producer
Dick Arnall
Production company
Ownbrand for Channel 4

A mother is nursing her sick child when Death knocks at the door, disguised as an old beggar, and snatches the child away. The distraught mother follows, determined to defy his power.

Ruth Lingford trained as an occupational therapist, working with mentally ill, mainly old people, and brought up a family before embarking on a career in the visual arts. She completed her BA in fine art and art history at the age of 37 and then moved on to the Royal College of Art for an MA in animation. Her student films manifested considerable originality and an interest in sexuality, which would remain with her. From the RCA she went on to do a few odd jobs in the industry including some medical animation and some animation on TV Cartoons' *Beatrix Potter* series. Being weak at pencil rendering, she was fired from *Beatrix Potter* and would certainly have abandoned animation had she not, on the same day, heard that she had won an Arts Council/Channel 4 Animation (later Animate) Award to make *What She Wants*, a film about female sexual fantasies.

Her ambition was to remain in the area of personal, short films, but funding for such films was hard to come by. Even Channel 4, almost the only funding

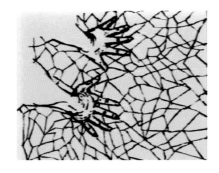

source, was more likely to go with an experienced director than a semi-novice. So the next step seemed to be an application for the MOMI/C4 Animator in Residence scheme, which was open to new animators within five years of graduation. Since a condition of this scheme was that the filmmaker must work for three months in a glass-fronted booth in the Museum of the Moving Image, in full view of museum visitors, projects needed to be child- and parent-friendly. It also gradually came to be assumed that straight narrative was required for eligibility to this scheme. This was not in fact the case although, given that Animate was focusing on edgy and experimental work, it would perhaps have been sensible to see storytelling - often a big problem in animation - as a skill to be nurtured by AIR. In the event, the scheme drifted into narrative of its own accord.

So Ruth prepared to break new ground, for her, and looked for a child-friendly theme with a straightforward narrative - though she would not, it turned out, be abandoning her penchant for taboo subject matter. She started, by her own admission somewhat cynically, by leafing through a book of Hans Christian Andersen fairy tales, which she had assumed would be safe and cosy. The first story she came to, *Death and the Mother*, was anything but safe and cosy. 'My God that's a horrible story - I can't possibly do that,' was the first reaction.[237] But its effect was 'viral'. It kept nagging at her and she felt the need to pass on to others this tale of a mother whose love is such that she allows her child to die rather than suffer a potentially horrific future. The Andersen text did have one major advantage to the animator: the story is told entirely visually. Sadly, she would have to cut out, for reasons of length, a particularly beautiful scene in Death's greenhouse, where the sightless mother has to find the emaciated plant that is her own child. She would also tone down the Christian morality which pervades the original, but otherwise the film was to be completely faithful to Andersen.

A partial storyboard was done and submitted with the application, this was accepted and Ruth began her three-month stint in the glass box, watched over by the scheme's production adviser, Lisa Beattie. The technique chosen was the same as that for *What She Wants*: Deluxe Paint in an Amiga computer, but a more powerful version this time. It still did not have enough memory to handle a wide range of colours, however, and this partially dictated the eventual look of the film. Another, equally helpful, technical limitation was that the digitising tablet on which she drew her animation was not pressure-sensitive as the newer models are, so she needed a scraping movement to produce a mark. This produced a print-like effect and inspired her to look to the German printmakers of the 1900s and 1910s: the influence of the young Expressionists, with their penchant for primitivist woodcuts, is obvious. Probably even more so is that of Käthe Kollwitz, who also used a variety of printing techniques and, unlike the Expressionists, was also working in similar subject areas, with motherhood and death ever-present. Whenever Ruth was uncertain as to how

to approach a particular scene, she would look at these artists' works and try to guess how they would have approached it.

The development work was outstanding and the film was duly commissioned (though none of the material produced at MOMI would make it into the final version, and this was typical of the scheme - it was the thought and experimentation which would inform the film). The production would take about a year, in the congenial atmosphere of the Clerkenwell Studios, a warren of different-sized spaces which normally housed a few animators along with all sorts of other craftspeople. Ruth had very much enjoyed the support of Dick Arnall on her Animate film *What She Wants*, and now opted for him to produce this new project. She rhapsodises about his qualities as a producer, pointing out that not only was he 'very knowledgeable and passionate about film and animation but he also has a playgroup leader's qualification'. He liberated the child, the dreamer, in his directors, nurturing them while at the same being stern if they tried to take any easy way out. 'The trouble is that he spoils you for any other producer afterwards.'[238] Dick for his part found working with Ruth 'a real treat. Not the world's best animator but her passion transcends that.'[239] He also shared her 'digital persuasion' and the two, together with Marjut Rimminen (also a convert, as was demonstrated by her 1996 *Many Happy Returns*) and others would gather for late-night discussions of computer developments and potential glimpsed. The computer technique did not merely appeal to Ruth's spirit of adventure - it was also a valuable solution to the complexes which had inhibited her while animating by traditional methods. Digital marks can easily be undone, and this knowledge liberated her.

Narrative did not come easily to Ruth, who claims to have completed an animation MA and made two student films plus *What She Wants* without learning any film language whatsoever. Her great saviour in this sphere was Larry Sider, well known for his sound creations on the Quay brothers' films but here also taking on the role of story editor. He came in at the animatic stage and taught Ruth all the basic rules of storytelling plus one extra: 'that an audience will without fail misunderstand anything that seems to you, as the filmmaker, impossible to misunderstand.' So Ruth set about doing all she could to help an audience, with the last section remaining ambiguous, as in the original story, but trying to spell everything else out clearly. Narrative support also arrived by fax from Caroline Leaf (teaching at Harvard at the time), whose films *The Street*, *The Owl Who Married a Goose*, *Two Sisters* and others are models of animated storytelling.

A further major contribution was that of composer Nigel Broadbent. The original intention was to use Arvo Pärt, but suddenly Pärt's melancholic tones were everywhere, so Ruth turned instead to London Symphony Orchestra violinist Broadbent for an original score, his first work for film. Aside from some conflict as to the extent and use of the music - Ruth wanted it composed 'like lengths

of cloth I could cut and edit', whereas Broadbent, like most composers, would have preferred to produce a finished soundtrack, with sound effects composed in - Ruth was delighted with the emotional quality of the music. At this stage Larry Sider did the track-laying and the sound effects. It was he who found the sound of the sika deer's heartbreaking call, a sound which seemed to encapsulate the emotional quality of the whole film and the devastating choice the mother must make.

Expectedly, given the film's graphic, technical and narrative qualities, it took multiple festival prizes including best graphic direction at Annecy 1997, best film 6-13 minutes at Espinho 1997, best film over 10 minutes at the British Animation Awards 1998 and an unprecedented special jury prize at the Cartoon d'Or, among others. The film has obviously had a strong influence on young animators, as can still be seen at animation festivals. But the most pleasurable result for Ruth has been the response from ordinary people. Rather unexpectedly, as audience votes tend to go to lighter films, the film took top prize in the public awards section of the 1998 Stuttgart Festival. And following its screening on Channel 4 (in January 1998, in one of the sought-after 9.45pm slots) and others elsewhere, she received and still receives the most heartwarming responses, the most surprising perhaps being from a Spanish policeman who wrote to say the film had moved him to tears.

Ruth characterises her work as 'feelbad'. *Pleasures of War*, which followed *Death and the Mother*, was about Judith and Holofernes and women's potential for extreme violence, and was initially titled *The Worst Thing*. But the mother's predicament in this heart-wrenching tale could equally well compete for that title.

Silence

1998/11mins

Directors
Sylvie Bringas
Orly Yadin
Narrated by
Tana Ross
Music
Noa Ain
Animation direction
Tim Webb (Sweden scenes)
Animation
Ruth Lingford (camp scenes)
Ron MacRae (Sweden scenes)
Painting co-ordinator
Mark Shepherd
Rostrum camera
Begonia Tamarit
Editor
Tony Fish
Dubbing mixer
Nigel Heath
Producers
Orly Yadin
Sylvie Bringas
Production company
Halo Productions for Channel
4 in association with Rockfilm
(Sweden) and Swedish Film
Institute

The end of the story: leaving Sweden with a bundle of letters

Tana Ross recounts how she spent her childhood in Theresienstadt concentration camp, constantly dodging transportation to Auschwitz. After liberation she was sent to live with relatives in Sweden, muffled in a conspiracy of silence.

The project originated in the friendship of documentarist and animation producer Orly Yadin with Tana Ross, a survivor of Theresienstadt (Terezín) concentration camp. Silence had been imposed on Ross's memories during her subsequent life in Sweden, from the age of 5 to 20. Later, with the help of family correspondence, she had managed to reconstruct her early life and understand both the nightmares she had constantly experienced and the reason for her relatives' guilty silence - though even then she did not feel able to speak out about her past. Finally, in late middle age, Ross saw that such reticence was counterproductive: silence was contagious, and the public too found it far more comfortable not to discuss unpleasant events now long gone.

This was particularly true in Sweden which, neutral during the war, had occasioned many dubious incidents like the behaviour of Ross's relatives, who had ignored pleas for help from Tana's parents. A survey taken in the early 1990s had shown that 60 per cent of Swedish teenagers did not believe the holocaust ever happened, prompting a national campaign, instigated by the prime minister, to educate young people about it. So it was a Swedish event, entitled Culture and Barbarism, that persuaded Ross to break her silence in 1995. There she told her story in the form of a poem, conceived together with composer Noa Ain and performed within a specially created cello concerto. Convinced of the need to tell the story more widely, she tried to persuade Orly to make a documentary - but the latter could find no way of shedding new light on the survivor's experience.[240] In the absence of relevant personal documents or any previously unseen film footage, she would have to resort to yet another interview, with the concomitant risk of voyeurism. Strangely enough, given the outstanding examples of animated documentary already made in the UK by that time, including Marjut Rimminen's moving *Some Protection*, which Orly herself had produced, it took some time for the penny to drop. Animation would, in fact, be the best - the only - way to do justice to the story, to tell it with due respect to the protagonist, but in a way which would abstract it to a universal level.

The beginning: Tana is snatched away from Berlin

At school in the camp

The original plan was to use the actual poem as the film's voice over, and development work began, using the poem to dictate the film's structure as well as its visual style. Ross's story reminded co-director and co-producer Sylvie Bringas of the work of Charlotte Salomon, a Jewish girl whose history was not dissimilar, and who had chronicled her middle-class life in Nazi Germany in a series of over 700 paintings before being captured and sent to her death. Her brightly-coloured images portraying the unsullied surface of life under the Nazis inspired a similar limpid style for Tana's superficially wholesome Swedish childhood.

The structure dictated by the poem was, however, not conducive to a clear narrative. The first script I received took the moment the 20 year-old Tana left Sweden as its present tense and structured the narrative as a series of flashbacks (to the Swedish childhood and, further back, to life in Theresienstadt) and flashforwards to a life in New York when the adult Ross would continue to suppress her memories. After drawing myself a fairly complex chart to try to understand the story, I admitted defeat. Possibly it would all have worked out fine in the animation, but neither the filmmakers nor I wanted to take that risk, and the structure was simplified and the whole of the New York life removed. After all, it was not the specific experience of one Tana Ross in later life that was at issue here, it was the wider question of engineered silence. Better to leave the end more ambiguous and thereby of more universal application. In fact, the structure would continue to develop throughout the production period.

The film now had two main time frames, in Theresienstadt and in Sweden, plus an introductory section of archive footage, this being subject to various digital processes 'so as to create a sense that the footage serves an atmospheric

Tana was good at hiding

purpose and is not trying to establish a historical, authoritative "voice" of its own'[241]. The two main sections were entrusted to two of the country's best animators and directors in their own right: the versatile Tim Webb would animate the Swedish scenes in a style inspired by Salomon, while Ruth Lingford, who had just finished *Death and the Mother*, was asked to bring a similarly severe black-and-white look to the camp scenes. While the directors had complete control of the structure and the voice over, the two animators were fully involved in stylistic decisions. Ruth's task was to evoke the misery of Tana's situation without resorting to horrific images of concentration camp atrocities and instead she was encouraged to introduce telling images, such as that where the children in the camp change into cockroaches and are swept away by a broom. 'Animation's access to the language of metaphor and transformation allowed, I think, a subtler and more concentrated portrayal of the situation than would have been possible using live-action drama.'[242]

The production processes of the two sections were entirely different. Ruth animated her sequences

… on an Amiga computer, drawing straight into the computer with a digitising tablet and pen and a simple programme called Deluxe Paint. In some sequences, I started from photographic reference. After I had finished the animation, the frames were transferred on to a Mac, which Sylvie then treated with a glow-effect. The decision to apply the glow-effect came late in production, and I was rather put out, as a lot of my detail was lost. But looking at the film from this distance, it seems like a good decision and had worked well.[243]

Although the computer was not used to animate the inbetween phases of movements (as it often is in low-budget commercial animation), nevertheless the animation can be 'stretched' somewhat by this technique, with cross-fades between the frames.

Tim's section was more complicated, in that his more labour-intensive technique needed a team to assist in animating and painting. Even the storyboarding was complicated. This would normally be done in pencil, to provide an accurate guide for the animators. But the pencil drawings simply did not work for Tim and he ended up with a storyboard of small gouache paintings, which then had to be redrawn in pencil when it came to animating them. The animation was done on paper and, once approved, these pencil drawings were placed on a light-box under watercolour paper and the art workers painted over the pencil images, using the original colour paintings of the storyboard as a guide, although 'the painting style had to be tightened for animation, as the image would have "boiled" if each frame was as loose as the storyboard or Salomon's painting'[244]. Unlike traditional cel animation, with separate backgrounds which can remain constant while elements of the foreground are animated, this style required a new painting, on paper, every two frames, with the background as well as the foreground re-drawn each time.

Thus, a complex process from start to finish for this deceptively simple look.

Of course, marrying the two starkly different styles was never going to be easy, especially when it came to the sequences where the repressed memories of the black-and-white camp world momentarily intrude on the serene and colourful present. In fact these sequences, such as the moment when a kindly Swedish conductor reaches into the train to help little Tana off and transforms into a concentration camp guard, are among the most successful of the whole film - and of course they escape the practical problem of juxtaposing the two totally different Tanas because they are, naturally, presented from Tana's own point of view. On the dissimilarity in styles in general, co-director Sylvie Bringas calls it 'usefully confrontational', both because it chimes with Tana's split life and also because it 'allowed us to create an "abstracted" representation of Tana, avoiding characterisation altogether.' The periodic emergence of the black-and-white past into Tana's present also implies that she will grow up as 'an irreconcilable composite of the two girls'.[245] An original decision to include a live-action scene of Ross reading the letters, at the moment in the film when she decides to break her silence, was abandoned, both from a fear of potential voyeurism and also from the conclusion that the animated, abstracted, composite Tana was the appropriate heroine for this film.

Storyboard panel: a kindly guard reaches to help Tana out of the train

He reminds Tana of a camp guard

As with most animated first-person documentaries, *Silence* features the protagonist's own voice telling her story. But, unlike most others, *Silence*'s soundtrack consists of a scripted performance rather than the more natural-sounding, conversational voices of the Aardman vox pop films, *A Is for Autism* or *Abductees*. Yet, given that these latter interview tapes are guided by the interviewer and then, of course, edited to fit, could it perhaps be that - just as animation can be considered more honest and upfront than selected and edited live action as a vehicle for documentary - a performed text, written by the protagonist and using 'the artifice of poetic speech to express a deeply personal story'[246] could come closer to distilling the truth? This, at any rate, was the intention of the filmmakers.

The film was completed in 1998, but by this time the 15-minute peaktime slots had disappeared from Channel 4's schedule and the only place for serious animation was in the block following the magazine show *Dope Sheet*, which itself started at a variable time somewhere around midnight. After many delays, mostly in the vain hope of being offered a better slot, the film was finally transmitted in September 2000 in a midnight slot in the context of an Animation Week. Not good for the premiere of an outstanding film, but we can hope the Animation Week context alerted people to set their videos. The Channel did, however, find the film to be of value and it had a dozen or so screenings on its satellite film channel, FilmFour. Festival prizes were plentiful, including major awards at Hiroshima, Odense (Grand Prix), Chicago and Melbourne and the best film over 7 minutes prize at the British Animation Awards (2000). The film

Storyboard panel

has also featured in numerous school and museum events, mostly in the UK and USA, and a print was purchased for the permanent collection of the film department of the Museum of Modern Art in New York.

But it made its greatest impact in Sweden, where it was shown in cinemas and, as part of the prime minister's campaign mentioned above, the government bought 900 copies for distribution in high schools. The newspapers also picked this up and it sparked a series of articles urging Swedes to question their complacency. The theme of the film is, of course, of international application and is becoming more and more so with the passage of time. The film, already available on a British Animation Awards DVD, has now been released on an individual DVD with various extras filling in background material relating to the moral questions raised as well as the technical processes. By this means it will, with any luck, reach the wider audience it deserves.

The Man with the Beautiful Eyes

1999/5½mins

A film by
Jonathan Hodgson
Poem by
Charles Bukowski
Design
Jonny Hannah
Additional animation
Kitty Taylor
Lucy Hudson
Bunny Schendler
Martin Oliver
Artwork
Mark Shepherd
Rostrum camera
Peter Tupy
Voices
Peter Blegvad
Louis Schendler
Recorded by
Liam Watson
Produced by
Jonathan Bairstow
Production company
Sherbet for Channel 4

A male voice recounts an incident from his childhood when, with a group of friends, he had come across a drunk living in a dilapidated house. When the house burned down the boys decided their jealous parents did it, 'because it was all too beautiful.'

Jonathan Hodgson had studied animation at Liverpool Polytechnic under charismatic teacher Ray Fields. An artist with connections to the St Ives school, Fields had encouraged a style which was 'semi-abstract, loose, painterly, semi inspired by children's drawings'[247]. When he graduated (after an MA at the Royal College), the energy and spontaneity of Jonathan's work struck a chord with advertisers and his career took off immediately. He took some time off the commercials treadmill to make his Animate film *Feeling My Way*, but returned to commercials until, luckily for us, he encountered a slack period in late 1997 and decided that a Channel 4 commission would hit the spot.

A year or two previously he had been back at Liverpool Poly doing a day's teaching and was introduced to Jonny Hannah, a talented young man about to graduate from the illustration department and start his MA at the Royal College of Art. Like Jonathan, Jonny was fascinated by American culture. He was particularly inspired by artists who identified with the working class - paintings by Ben Shahn and the writings of Charles Bukowski, for example.[248] The latter had also deeply affected Jonathan. He was intrigued by Bukowski's Angeleno hell-raising persona, his boozing, his womanising, his alienation. 'I understood where he was coming from. His dislike of the herd mentality and the values of

most of the human race.' While Jonny was still at the RCA the pair searched for the right poem to provide the basis for a collaboration but, realising that some of Bukowski's violence and sexism might be too much for more sensitive viewers, dismissed the most extreme material. They finally came up with *The Man with the Beautiful Eyes*, a late piece, written only two years before the writer's death in 1994, which was gentler and more reflective, but still very much embodying his characteristic world view. Jonny did some drawings and they sent the proposal to me at Channel 4.

I was delighted to hear from Jonathan - I thought we had lost him to the world of commercials - and loved the poem and the designs, which looked a bit like 1950s Steinberg. I had no hesitation in accepting the proposal, though I do remember harping on a bit about the pitfalls of animating to a pre-existing text. I had seen many animated films come to grief by either slavishly illustrating the text or by going to the other extreme so that text and visuals conflict and a viewer is unable to take in either. This was to remain a concern throughout the production and Jonathan would adopt various strategies to solve the problem. Sometimes he would avoid synchronising the visuals to the text, coming in either before or after. Sometimes an illustrative section would dissolve into extreme stylisation and abstraction or sometimes into Jonny's distinctive hand-rendered typography. And he would avoid cuts wherever possible, avoid sudden new worlds requiring rapid adjustment, using instead animated transitions which allow the viewer to 'float through the film' and to 'get lost in the drawing and painting quality'. Finally, at the end of the production period, the right voice and the right tone of voice would do a lot to help. Jonathan feels that, taking such precautions, 'you can go a long way from the text as long as you pull it back every so often. I feared it was following the text a bit too much, but it didn't seem to bother anyone else.'

The film went into production a week after Jonny left the RCA. The actual production was a very organic process. Jonny and Jonathan each made individual rough storyboards and then decided which bits would work best. *Jonny had a lot of brilliant graphic ideas and I tried to use as many of them as possible. Some of his ideas needed some adaptation and some of my ideas possibly worked a bit better in animation, so we dovetailed our respective ideas to make something that I could see working. [...] Once we had agreed on how each scene would be visualised, Jonny then made a more resolved black and white line drawn storyboard from which I edited a black and white animatic. [...] Once the black and white animatic was complete, Jonny got straight on to the colour keyframes and he painted up practically every one of the 120 frames in the black and white storyboard.*

Jonathan was bowled over by the freshness of Jonny's paintings and his exceptional speed. He managed the 120 keyframes in two weeks. Once the colour version of the animatic was complete Jonathan, helped mostly by

Kitty Taylor, animated the film in pencil, after which Jonny, together with Mark Shepherd, produced the final artwork. The majority of the art work was painted on to paper, with a small amount done on cel, using acrylic paint on top of the cel rather than on the back, so as to reveal the paint texture. They managed all the artworking in about six months - again, an amazing achievement. Apart from a bit of not very interested dabbling in his first year at Liverpool, this was Jonny's first experience of animation, and he took to it like a natural. For Jonathan 'it was very much a collaboration - I can't overestimate Jonny's contribution to the process.'

When the animation was complete, Jonathan started looking round for an American to do the voice over. He found Peter Blegvad, a UK-based American singer-songwriter and cartoonist, whose comic strip *Leviathan* was at that time running in *The Independent*. The first attempts were in Blegvad's usual style, which is bright and quite jocular. Jonathan found it was fighting with the visuals but it took him some time to realise what kind of delivery he actually did want. After several attempts he hit on it: 'Quite dreamy. Almost as if he was lying on the psychiatrist's couch, telling something half-remembered…' Each new recording was more laid-back, but not laid-back enough. Finally, after Jonathan had advised Peter to 'just imagine you're talking in your sleep', a tape arrived which was perfect. Peter had done it first thing on a Sunday morning, with a bad hangover. His voice was two tones lower than normal, very slow, with lots of heavy breathing. Finally Jonathan, who writes his own music, added a

music track, but then realised it was superfluous. The sound had to be sparse - nothing should detract from Peter's masterful mumbling.

The film was a success on all fronts, cultural and commercial. It took a massive number of festival prizes, notably the BAFTA award, the best film under 7 minutes at the British Animation Awards, top prizes at Bourg-en-Bresse, Toronto and Valencia and a nomination for the Cartoon d'Or. Jonathan Myerson in *The Independent* called it 'a staggering sideways look at childhood fears and misunderstandings, more profound and beautiful than most feature films'[249]. It also brought in a lot more commercials to the studio, some of which would involve Jonny. One, in fact, for an American investment company, was specifically based on *The Man with the Beautiful Eyes* and would also involve a rather bemused Peter Blegvad, whose usual, vaguely alternative lifestyle does not normally involve eulogising pillars of the capitalist system.

TMWTBE was not to be animation's last word on Bukowski. J J Villard did *Son of Satan* in 2003, an urgent, raw painting of youthful violence and its causes with great visual style - but it does illustrate its powerful text a bit too literally for my taste. In early 2007 Johnny Depp and Gabor Csupo announced a feature-length compilation of four Bukowski-based pieces, to be entitled *How the Dead Love,* but as this book goes to press it is still not in production. Jonathan, meanwhile, is shedding his 'painterly' persona - and the painstaking labour that style involves - with a series of low-budget, mixed-media works with a more personal, documentary orientation.

Home Road Movies

2001/12mins

THE HENLEY COLLEGE LIBRARY

Director/animation
Robert Bradbrook
Script
Ian Sellar
Editor
Tony Fish
Father
Bill Paterson
Narrator
Phelim McDermott
First assistant director (live action)
Lesley Manning
Director of photography (live action)
Sam James
Audio edited/mixed by
Hackenbacker Audio Post Production
Music
KPM Music Library, and 'Split Level'
written by Warburton
Producer
Dick Arnall
Production company
Finetake for Channel 4 in association
with Arts Council of England

Dad buys a car and starts taking his young family around Europe: camping holidays of a lifetime, using the latest hi-tech equipment. But as children, dad and the car all age, the holidays become less harmonious.

Robert Bradbrook's first degree was in geology and cartography and, although a film fan, he had no particular interest in animation. He did have one notable passion as a youngster, though, and that was pottery. He would build whole villages out of clay, 'which is very much what I do now, but in the computer'[250]. However, in order to earn a living he took his cartography skills to *The Independent*. This was the time of the Gulf War, and Robert was employed producing maps, diagrams and illustrations, to aid understanding of the news stories. Being dyslexic, Robert had always avoided writing wherever possible and instead turned to drawing. 'I knew I could explain things a lot better by doing a diagram than writing a page of explanation.' Gradually, he realised that on television diagrams were nowadays being made to move, and this realisation, along with a chance viewing of the early John Lasseter films on a BBC *Horizon* programme about computer animation, spurred him to return to college, this time to Coventry University for an MA in electronic arts and graphics. When he arrived there and saw people making personal films, the TV moving graphics job suddenly looked rather less alluring, and he too decided he must make a film. He was able to take that option as part of his degree.

His initial idea for the degree film was the story of his father and the family car. His father had recently died and Robert and his siblings were regularly

Before the car

Dad plans the route

All mod cons

meeting up at the family home to sort out his affairs. Two things became plain: firstly, that their father - ex-Royal Air Force - had kept punctilious records of the family's history, with boxes full of holiday photographs, guide books and maps; and secondly that the siblings could between them write a whole book of anecdotes about dad and his car. It was also obvious that there was a good story there: the early days, when the impressionable children had seen the vehicle as a huge, glitzy sports car; then the teenage years when they had constantly ribbed him about the old car's shortcomings; and the last, guilt-ridden act, when their mother had died, the children had all left home and their dad was left alone to take the bus to the hospital where he himself would die. Furthermore, the children (except at that stage Robert) were by then parents themselves and so felt all the more keenly the emotional aspects of the tale.

Robert started work on the project at Coventry, first of all presenting the story of his dad and the car as a slide show.[251] It included some animation, but he decided that the challenge of this particular subject as a film was too much for him at that time. This was before the advent of Power Macs, and computers then did not have the storage capacity for colour - and this film would demand a really dynamic colour scheme. (It appears that among the favourite films of Robert's youth were the Bond movies - not so much for the technical gadgetry as for the sumptuous colouring of the high life locations, the casinos, etc.) He also felt that his own skills were not at that stage up to the task. Apart from anything else, most of the story took place in bright daylight, whereas Robert was at this time usually animating dark or night-time scenes, with plenty of shadows, which he knew would conceal a multitude of modelling problems. So he made a different film for his final piece (a film he says is dreadful), graduated from Coventry and almost immediately won an Animate award, to make another dark, shadowy, black and white film, *End of Restriction*.

It was via the Animate experience that he met Dick Arnall, who would become his producer and close collaborator on *Home Road Movies*. Robert was not brimming with confidence at the time, and remembers undergoing a somewhat aggressive interview for the Animate award - and as I, sadly, do not remember the interview at all I cannot defend myself - before being ushered through to talk to Dick. As production adviser, Dick would take candidates through the technical and financial aspects of their project to make sure it was feasible. When the latter began his own gentle and courteous questioning, Robert decided that this must be a 'good cop, bad cop' routine, and that Dick was 'out to get me'. I must admit I was similarly sceptical when I first met Dick. However it was, amazingly, all for real.

Robert made the very successful *End of Restriction*, after which he desperately needed to earn a bit of money and spent four years doing animation for the then-booming CD-ROM industry. But Dick had remained a good friend and was constantly urging Robert to make another personal film. When Robert told

Holiday snap
Photo Arthur Charles Bradbrook

Wire frame version

him the story of his father, Dick became passionate in his belief that this film must be made. Robert's enthusiasm for the project had also burgeoned during the four years of CD-ROMs: he was fed up with animating for a tiny screen. 'I wanted to make an animation for a big screen that had big music. *Home Road Movies* was a film about my family and I wanted it to feel like a big budget movie, not a video art piece.' Together they put together a proposal to bring to me at Channel 4. The proposal was, of course, very full thanks to the years of thinking and experimenting that had gone into it, and it seemed irresistible - especially because there was now matching lottery funding available for good projects, administered by the Arts Council. *Home Road Movies* was thus a bargain in comparison to the kinds of budgets we had regularly funded: we and the lottery would each pay £42,500.

The first step in the production was a visit to the pub, with Robert recording his and his brothers' reminiscences, mostly car-related. It was also an opportunity to check family reactions. Since their father had taken all the photos, he did not feature in them. His role would be played by an actor. They would not be upset, would they, when via computer trickery they saw photos of their mother standing with a strange man? No, not at all. And how would they feel if Robert changed the boringly-shaped Peugeot the family owned for a more interesting model such as a Citroën? Impossible! The Peugeot had to stay, and it must retain its authentic, eye-popping bright blue colour.

The second major step was a decision as to the elements and look of the film. The original idea was that the whole of the holidays section would be photo-montage, based on the hundreds of holiday photos his dad had taken. But somehow, despite the extra skills and time it would need, a decision was taken to model almost the whole film in the computer instead - a decision which would, unbeknown to me, add an extra year to the production schedule at one fell swoop. The challenge was initially aesthetic and then technical.
It took me quite a long time to come up with a method of lighting that gave the images an atmospheric feel that hid the bad modelling and stopped it having the very 3D plastic feel that was common at the time. A lot of this was done by taking cues from old Super-8 cine film and looking at the way it colours the scenes.
The software Robert used was Form-Z, to create all the 3D sets and models, and ElectricImage, into which the models were imported, along with family photographs and video footage of the actor playing the father, for the scene to be constructed and lit. It seems this was, at the time, the only good programme for use with the Macintosh. But it all needed to be learned.

Another priority was selecting and filming the actor who would play the father. An initial thought was Tom Wilkinson - but he suddenly disappeared to America and was unavailable. Bill Paterson was a last-minute inspiration, and even bore a disturbing physical resemblance to Mr Bradbrook. Dick sent him a

Actor and blue screen incorporated into image

The final version

dossier about the proposed film, including photos of the modelled European architecture. It seems that Bill Paterson's wife, a designer of opera productions, was so intrigued that she persuaded him to take the job. It was a tough assignment, acting against a blue screen, with no clues as to where computer-generated props were supposed to be except for marks on the wall where he would have to direct his gaze. Robert was nervous, having never directed an actor before, and was additionally somewhat spooked when Paterson appeared on set, made up to resemble his father and wearing one of the latter's old jackets. 'It was like bringing my dad back to life. I thought, "Am I doing the right thing here?" ' But, once recovered, he was delighted with Paterson's contribution of various insights which helped the film tremendously. He cites the wink, when driving through the tunnel. The voice-over script had become bogged down at that stage, in a long-winded attempt to demonstrate that dad loved the family, the family loved dad and all was right with the world. When filming that section, Paterson had simply looked up to where the car mirror was supposed to be and given a cheerful wink which, they realised, said everything and superseded reams of dialogue.

Robert had assumed that, this being a personal film - and a very personal film at that - he would be writing the script himself, but Dick was concerned about this plan, partly because of Robert's dyslexia. When Dick proposed Ian Sellar to work with Robert, the latter was very much against it, Sellar being a professional writer[252] - but one who had no experience with animation - and a senior tutor at the National Film and Television School. 'I hate people correcting my spelling. I thought it was going to be like school.' In fact, the partnership went brilliantly. Sellar imposed some rules. The story must build up logically and economically. Everything that happens must do so for a reason ('Why does dad buy a car?'), and extra anecdotes could not be accommodated, no matter how delicious, if they did not illustrate anything new. Thus the time the car door fell off had to go, as did the tidal wave that would wash over passengers' feet when dad braked, once the rust had started letting rain in. Sellar was continually pruning and Robert 'learned such a lot about how to write. And it was really enjoyable'. The result was a model of compression, with every word pondered over, yet sounding utterly spontaneous.

It was not only the dialogue that needed pruning. Robert just got carried away with some of his favourite scenes, and actually animated several minutes of material for the brief car ad near the beginning. He had also constructed a Danish brewery (plus Copenhagen waterfront, cafés and little mermaid) and a whole section for the end of the film, showing the children returning to the house and discovering the car and the boxes of mementoes. This was the moment when editor Tony Fish came into his own. Tony has a great understanding of how best to tell a story and exactly what elements, in what order and, crucially, at what length are required to make a point. One of Tony's contributions was the transition from 1960s Europe to 1970s UK,

which had completely stumped the writing team. His simple solution was to use the cable car shadow to mask the father's ageing, and to change the real mountain scenery into a photograph on the wall. Likewise, there was no need to emphasise the barrenness of Mr Bradbrook's later life by that extra scene. The ending is sad enough as it is, and all agreed that the upbeat music had to be brought in swiftly, to stop it getting too heavy. Even so, Dick Arnall reckoned that 'you always hear a sob at the end, usually from a bloke'[253].

The final stage of production - and another delay in the schedule - was Phelim McDermott's voicing of the narrative (Robert's) voice. Robert had originally done the voice over himself, but somehow the tone had always sounded a bit sarcastic. When they started looking for an actor to do the job, all the tapes that came in were 'too actorly, too mannered'[253] - until they heard a voice that was 'completely fresh and authentic'[253]. The only problem was that its owner, Phelim McDermott, was totally committed for the next six months. Robert by this time was desperate to finish the film. What had seemed a reasonable budget for the one-year schedule originally estimated had long since run out and he was now sleeping on a friend's floor to save money. Dick, however, was determined to wait, though he later conceded that 'hanging round for perfection consumed a lot of time and a lot of money. It's not the way you're supposed to do it'[253]. So Phelim McDermott was booked and duly arrived six months later to do the recording. On arrival he revealed that he had lost his own father that very week, but was still anxious to go ahead with the recording. It must have contributed to the performance.

By the time the film was delivered to Channel 4 in 2001, there were no longer good peaktime slots for 12-minute films, but it seems the film premiered in a late-night block of British animation in the 2001 Animation Zone. It has screened several times since then, but never before 1am. Yet still people get home late and come across the film by accident and Robert still gets responses. People write describing their dad, their car… He was surprised to get a letter from someone who had seen the film on a British Airways flight and been moved to tears. In France, however, the film gets far more exposure and Robert has recently had to order six new prints for French cinemas, where it was going out with a feature.

But the real success of this film is on the international festival circuit, where it is still active years later. Apart from a small minority who take the computer modelling for live action, audiences and juries have been alert to this film's combination of a great story well told and a unique conception (pre-dating *Sin City*, which would pull off the same trick) of computer-generated space as an integral part of the narrative. Dick was proud to note[253] that *Home Road Movies* won more top awards (best film or best in category) in 2002 than any other short film. The total was 24 and they included the Cartoon d'Or for best European animated film, the Grand Prix at Ottawa, the Annecy special

The last act

jury prize, best animated film at the Rushes short film festival and a BAFTA nomination. There was talk of a theatrical release but, given the film's relatively long duration and cinema chains' determination to fit in as many programmes as possible, this did not happen. However Robert was not, ultimately, deprived of the chance of seeing his family epic on the big screen he had always had in mind while making the film: the London Film Festival selected it to support a feature film - the British thriller *Happy Now* - and it screened at the Odeon, Leicester Square.

Images © Finetake/Channel Four Television Corp/Arts Council England

City Paradise

2004/3mins and 6mins

Director/script/design
Gaëlle Denis
Music
Joce Mienniel, Joanna Newsom
Editing
Tony Fish
Sound design
Fabrice Gerardi
Live action director of photography
Sarah Bartles Smith
Cast
Hiroe Takei, Robert Stevenson
Lighting/texturing
Antoine Moulineau
Executive producer
Andrew Ruhemann
Producer
Erika Forzy
Production company
Passion Pictures for Channel 4
Animator in Residence scheme

Tomoko flies into London and arrives in the dingy street where she will stay. English for Beginners does not immediately aid communication but a trip to the swimming pool yields magical results.

Gaëlle Denis, talking about the fantasy scenario of a commercial she made recently, described to me one of the technical tricks used in it and concluded: 'I like playing with things like that. And I like to keep learning all the time'[254]. Her career to date, marked by an eagerness to experiment and a passion for travel, is the proof of this. She studied graphic design at Paris's prestigious ENSAD (or 'les arts décos'), which included an exchange visit to Central St Martins College of Art and Design in London. She was impressed by the innovative animation she saw here both in commercials and on Channel 4, and a visit to the Museum of the Moving Image and the Animator in Residence booth there inspired her both to take up animation and to return to the UK as soon as possible. In her final year at ENSAD she opted for animation, producing a graduation film which was painted in oils on glass and composited in AfterEffects. Supported initially by an au pair job, she returned to the UK to study for an animation MA at the Royal College of Art and was able to spend four months of the course studying in Japan, at the Kyoto University of Arts. This was the inspiration for her RCA graduation film, *Fish Never Sleep*. By this time she was using another technology, drawing on to a digitising tablet to generate her animation in the computer.

Londoners: slightly scary yet comical

Catwalk fashions were an inspiration for the aliens

Fish Never Sleep was to prove highly successful, taking a rich haul of prizes including the BAFTA award. But as the RCA course was drawing to an end this was all in the future and Gaëlle was concerned that she may not find a job. The Animator in Residence scheme, which she had first observed in action at MOMI some years previously, seemed to beckon, and she made a concerted effort to get on to the scheme. She had already started sketching an underground world peopled by strange beings arriving via tunnels under Hyde Park. That summer she began developing these ideas for her AIR application and saw that this fantasy could link up with her own story, that of a foreigner in a confusing metropolis. 'I wanted to give life to my own vision of London, a lively and beautiful yet surreal city. A slightly scary yet comical place populated by creatures with strange walks.'[255] So Gaëlle spent the summer preparing a scenario, a partial storyboard and some visual and technical research. She remembers the application coming to about fifty pages. It was successful, and she moved into the AIR booth, which was by now located in the BFI's Imax cinema on the South Bank, to start developing a project entitled, at that stage, *The Girl Who Talks with Aliens*.

She knew she wanted to diversify yet again in this film, and decided to add some new technologies - 3D, as well as a live component - to the 2D CG she had already mastered on *Fish Never Sleep*. But, given her lack of experience, her 3D ambitions were initially limited, and the live component was to be still photos representing the characters rather than live action. She recognised that it is harder to generate emotion from still photos, but also realised how difficult it is to integrate live action into a 3D world - it is often tried but rarely looks right. Fellow RCA graduate Siri Melchior had completed her own AIR film, *The Dog Who Was a Cat Inside*, two years earlier, combining 2D and 3D by using flat squares on which she added a texture, and Siri was now recruited to help Gaëlle with the technical research element of this development. Gaëlle also produced a 3-minute animatic - by this time all AIR films had to be of 3 minutes' duration since the year's crop was transmitted, stripped across a week, in the slot following the news, at 7.55pm - and further development of her design ideas for the film.

Her inspirations are varied, and intriguing. Her underground aliens were partially inspired by some Alexander McQueen creations she had seen on a catwalk, and she is a great admirer of the inventive spirit of Issey Miyake and the way such designers incorporate movement, shapes and texture into their fashions. She is also obsessed with human movement, from silent comedians, Jacques Tati and *Monty Python* to theatre director Philippe Genty and choreographer Philippe Decouflé, and their influence would find its way into, especially, the Londoners' funny walks. Gaëlle found the three months in the booth rather trying. Her first meeting there with production adviser Chris Shepherd, the two cowering together in the tiny booth while a giant Winnie the Pooh and a horde of children danced outside, seemed to set the tone.

Tomoko in blue skirt, cut out and pasted
into a modelled version of the room
Courtesy Passion Pictures

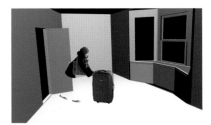

With blue skirt keyed-off, she is placed into
the 3D scene
Courtesy Passion Pictures

The final version

Tomoko incorporated into untreated photo
Courtesy Passion Pictures

Since the development work was obviously of high quality, Channel 4 (it was Ruth Fielding who was handling the AIR films) gave the go-ahead, and Gaëlle started looking round for a congenial company to house her and the production. Passion Pictures stood out: it was well known for its experience in combining animation with live action and had staff skilled in all the various technologies Gaëlle wanted to use. And she was sure by now that there must be a far greater live element than the still photos she originally proposed, as she really wanted her actress's emotions to come into play. When she arrived at Passion she was given a computer and three months in which to learn 3D animation. Using LightWave, Gaëlle modelled in the computer all the spaces to appear in the film, and then shot the actors, in blue rooms constructed to the correct dimensions. They also had to wear blue skirts, as she was planning to replace their legs with 2D legs resembling, in the words of a *Digit* magazine piece[256], 'al dente spaghetti'. The live action footage was then imported into the computer and edited into the probable shape of the final film before adding in the textures. But not all could be 3D - it is extremely expensive and time-consuming - so some crafty subterfuges were used. In the scene where Tomoko sits on her window-sill looking down at the street below, this is a still photograph taken from the window of Passion. But the addition of some 3D buses seems to suggest that the whole lot is 3D. The al dente legs were achieved by time-remapping the live action in AfterEffects, varying the tempo to create comic effects.

As soon as live action replaced the still photos, it had become apparent that the 3-minute running time would pose a problem. Whereas the stills could be animated rapidly, in cartoon style, live actors needed more time to walk, to breathe, to react. Gaëlle begged Channel 4 to allow her a longer running time, but the post-news slot was obviously not elastic - it could only accommodate 3 minutes. Finally it was decided that there would have to be two versions, one for broadcast and the longer one for festivals. The running time was reduced largely by cutting out two of the most charming and significant scenes, those where Tomoko meets her neighbour, but there seemed to be no alternative.

In view of the longer-than-expected running time and the abundance of hi-tech processes needed, it was plain that C4's £40,000 budget - standard for the 3-minute AIR scheme films - would not suffice. However, this was obviously going to be a prestige project which would bring great credit to all concerned, so Passion felt it worth donating staff time, and various other facilities and labs contributed favours. Their confidence was justified: the film took top prizes at Annecy, Los Angeles, Resfest, Imagina and many others, as well as two audience prizes and nominations for the BAFTA and Cartoon d'Or. The 3-minute version duly ran in its post-news slot in November 2004 and was seen by around 1.4 million viewers. Advertising agencies loved the film, Saatchi and Saatchi running it in their New Directors Showcase at the Cannes Lions advertising festival.

Soho street awaiting transformation
Courtesy Passion Pictures

Final version, with the arrival of Tomoko

Gaëlle has now completed several commercials at Passion. But *City Paradise* was a one-off, for few commercials could allow the luxury of so much research time. They are mainly live action and rather less complex mixed-media pieces. She has completed a live action short, has taken various directing, acting and playwriting courses and is currently developing a live action feature script. Why is she, seemingly, moving away from animation? Well, for the moment she 'just wants to keep learning' - about structure and character - until such time as circumstances, notably funding, are right for her true ambition, an animated feature.

Rabbit

2005/8½mins

A film by
Run Wrake
Original illustrations by
Geoffrey Higham
Animation assistants
Martin Morris
Barnaby Hewlett
Online editor
Rich White
Dubbing editor
Craig Butters
Re-recording mixer
Cliff Jones
Music
Howie B, Craig Richards
Production company
Sclah Films, funded through
Finetake by Arts Council England
and Channel 4

Two children, the picture of innocence, decide to kill a rabbit. The discovery of an idol in its gut leads to several strange plot twists and a field full of animal cadavers.

Run Wrake spent his youth in rural Leicestershire and Sussex, in a milieu vastly different from the music scene which he would later inhabit in London, but not so far removed from the pristine environment of 1950s and 60s children's books as evoked in *Rabbit*. His father being an army chaplain (Run was actually born while the family was posted to the Yemen), Christian values were to the fore. And while 'like many offspring of the clergy I spent a large part of growing up actively rebelling against all that it stands for'[257], some things did stick. It was his father who instilled in him the respect for nature which is key to the film. There was no particular interest in art, still less animation, as he grew up. Going fishing and digging up old bottles[258] were favoured pastimes, as was prowling junk shops, a hobby which would later throw up the 50 year-old stickers, designed to help children learn to read, which would become the basis of *Rabbit*.

A third interest - movie-going - later took him to see Alan Parker's *The Wall*: 'The animation sequences were like nothing I'd ever seen before, proper grown up stuff it seemed to me. Instrumental in turning me into an animator.'[259] Thus, he took an art foundation course and went on to study graphic design at the Chelsea School of Art and animation at the Royal College. Influences picked up on the way included Dada, the collages of Max Ernst and John Heartfield and the free-form, music-led animation of some of the best music videos. Vintage medical textbooks also proved endlessly fascinating. From now on found materials and body parts would jostle for position in open-ended, surreal, spontaneous-looking 'walk' films closely synchronised to a strong music track, such as his RCA graduation film, *Anyway* (1990), and *Jukebox* (1994), his first film for the Animate scheme. The latter was spotted by Glaswegian musician/record producer Howie B, who commissioned Run to make an animated video for the single 'Music for Babies'. This has led to an illustrious career in the music business, with many more videos for Howie B, The Charlatans, Stereo MCs and Manu Chao among others, and animated backdrops to live shows for artistes including Oasis, U2 and Paul McCartney.

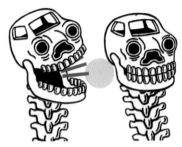

Body parts in Run's first Animate film, *Jukebox*

What, then, prompted such a change of direction for *Rabbit*? Pure chance, it seems. Run had decided to apply for another Animate award and was playing around with a totally different idea when he happened to open up a drawer and come across those old stickers he had bought years earlier in a Sussex junk shop. Though Run's primary education was in the late 1960s, the Dick and Jane design and ethos were still in evidence, so the stickers inevitably took him back to his own rural youth and very correct upbringing, and invited comparisons with the present.

We live in such greedy times. The images in Rabbit *hark back to a time when it didn't seem so important to be greedy. [...] Now we admire people who are ostentatious with their wealth and we all seem to aspire to it. Clearly it doesn't make you happy, so why? [...] The past always seems a bit more rosy, but it genuinely did seem to be a simpler time, where simpler values were admired. It's a very unfashionable thing to say, but I think it's worth thinking about.*[260]
So the stickers offered him the chance to say something he wanted to get off his chest. They also offered a pleasurable challenge: to construct a narrative (his first) around a predetermined set of concepts - and a strange group of concepts they were too. Why infants of an age to learn the words 'mother', 'jam', 'tree' and 'horse' were also offered 'idol' is unclear. But to Run, laying out the stickers and looking for connections, 'idol' became his trump card. It would be his agent of change, able to transform objects and mould the predetermined concepts into the moral tale he was seeking. He would be able to bring in several of his interests, with the medical illustrations coming into their own in the beautifully diagrammatic innards, devoid of blood, of the bisected rabbit, and his love of nature and of animation loops coming together in an ending where order would be restored.

The Animate scheme demands a partial storyboard as part of the application. Run's previous storyboards had been sketchy, and liable to change en route. This would be his first detailed and fixed storyboard, and in fact what he produced was scarcely partial. It comprised eleven pages of beautiful, detailed storyboarding, with only the final scene not storyboarded but instead clearly

A girl watches a rabbit run past

and dreams of a lovely muff for the winter

Extract from the storyboard, showing the stickers in their entirety

explained in words. It was obviously planned down to the most minute detail and indeed would change very little in the course of production. Of course, the iron rule imposed by the stickers did generate some strange plot twists. In the lead-up to the final, apocalyptic scene, we read that:

In town the boy and girl find a shop. Inside, they negotiate with the man who runs it the exchange of their feathers and ink for a vanful of jam. The man, seeing the potential market for quills, and thus ink, agrees.

It seems the Animate selection committee was bowled over by the proposal. 'Never had the selection been so unanimous,' recalled Dick Arnall[261].

So the production went ahead, in Run's home studio. He began animating, very much according to the storyboard, though with two main design changes. Firstly, he had originally planned to show the stickers in their entirety, right up to their edges, but this made for crowded images, so the stickers themselves were removed, leaving only the object and its name. Secondly, he had planned to use simple flat colours as backgrounds. However, by eliminating the clutter of the stickers he was able to clear the way for a detailed environment. The original stickers were scanned into Photoshop and then carefully cut out, with moving arms and legs all given their own layer. The elements were then composited in AfterEffects. There was very little original drawing. Run had, of course, used AfterEffects before, but this time his use was more ambitious, creating in the computer extra depth and a sense of space which would have been quite impossible by traditional methods.

By the time of *Rabbit*, Animate's rules had changed and a strict one-year production schedule was imposed. Run found this an excellent discipline, though it put him under pressure towards the end of the year, especially when he discovered that a scene near the end, with flies crawling all over dead bodies, which he had expected to be relatively simple, actually turned into a technical nightmare. For the first eight months he had been working alone but then employed an animator for the last four, and finally another to assist with the closing scenes.

The music was courtesy of Howie B, but the process was quite unlike previous collaborations, where Run had based his animation on pre-existing tracks. This time he took his completed film to Howie B, together with a record of a piece of Mozart, and asked for 'something minimal' based on a particular group of chords. 'He grabbed the record, stuck it on the turntable and sampled it and came up with that little melody. Bang, five minutes.'[262] Run was equally delighted with Craig Butters' detailed sound effects. This short film boasts, at times, up to 79 different levels of effects tracks, meaning that almost every fly had its own effect.

Jukebox

It is a deeply shocking film, and Run concedes that he does hear from people who hate it - though these are mostly the type who make that elementary mistake of believing animation, especially animation featuring children, must be wholesome kids' entertainment. But with the vast majority it has really struck a chord - perhaps for that very shock value but also for its endearing moral as well as the perverse logic of the narrative and the persuasiveness of design and animation. Most importantly, his father 'got it straight away', as did the rest of the family. At the British Animation Awards it took both best short film and best film at the cutting edge, at Edinburgh the McLaren award for best animation, and it garnered major prizes at Annecy, Hiroshima, Rotterdam, Soho Shorts Festival, Leipzig, Holland Animation Festival, the Imago Young Film and Video Festival in Portugal and a 2006 BAFTA nomination - among very many others. It has been seen on giant outdoor screens - in Trafalgar Square for the London Film Festival and in Hyde Park as part of *Time Out*'s Park Nights event - and in the back of a solar-powered London taxi at the Glastonbury festival. It was shown on Channel 4, packaged with the other Animate films of the year, just after midnight - but, given the current lack of slots for short films, this was the best that could have been hoped for. But it has done well in TV sales overseas and, luckily, fits admirably into today's short film distribution systems: it has travelled the world in theatrical packages such as onedotzero, The Animation Show and ResFest. Run has tried to avoid the film being included in too many DVD compilations, instead issuing it himself as a limited edition, a beautifully produced collector's item with lots of extras.

In fact, his animation, his music connections and his commercial philosophy seem tailor-made for the new conditions. He is still much in demand in the music world, mainly in the area of backdrops to live tours. However, if *Rabbit* was a big step after the music films, Run's next project is a far bigger challenge. He is planning a debut in the expanding world of animated features, dialogue and all, with a project based on that character in *Jukebox* with a pork chop for a head. With Run's sure feel for public taste, he might even bring it off.

Images © Run Wrake

Peter and the Wolf

2006/32mins

Director/adaptation
Suzie Templeton
Music/original libretto
Sergei Prokofiev
Music director
Mark Stephenson
Supervising director of photography
Hugh Gordon
Director of photography
Mikołaj Jaroszewicz
Production design
Marek Skrobecki
Jane Morton
Lead animator
Adam Wyrwas
Editors
Suzie Templeton
Tony Fish
Co-writer
Marianela Maldonado
Music performed by
The Philharmonia Orchestra
Producers
Alan Dewhurst
Hugh Welchman
Co-producer
Zbigniew Żmudzki
Executive producers
Lars Hellebust
Simon Olswang
Luc Toutounghi
Production company
BreakThru Films and
Se-ma-for Studios in association
with Channel 4, Storm Studios,
Archangel SA

Peter and his grandfather live alone, at the edge of a Russian forest. In grandfather's absence, Peter leaves the compound to play on the frozen pond. Soon the wolf comes prowling…

Peter and the Wolf is a lavish and complex production, extremely unconventional in its creative approach to a family classic. It is an extraordinary achievement, especially in the current difficult climate for the financing of unusual properties, and as such merits close attention.

The individuals involved are also somewhat unconventional. It was conductor Mark Stephenson who initiated the project. Stephenson is passionate about bringing classical music to new audiences, especially children. In 2001 he approached a young producer, Hugh Welchman, recently graduated from the National Film and Television school, with a proposal: to collaborate on a film based on something from the classical repertoire, which would lend itself to live performances in concert halls. He suggested *Peter and the Wolf*, a great piece of music which would be 70 years old in 2006, and thus ripe for some anniversary celebration.

Hugh introduced Mark to the talents of Suzie Templeton. Suzie had come to animation after a science degree and nine years of indecision, spent mostly travelling and temping in a variety of strange roles. She had always made things (hats, clothes, furniture) but was sure she did not have the talent to study art. It

Peter's house

was only when she saw pictures of Wallace and Gromit and their contraptions - in India, strangely enough, where she was working in a women's refuge - that she had the idea of training as a model-maker, and so applied for the animation course at the Surrey Institute of Art & Design in Farnham. Her films were dark and deep: her Farnham graduation piece, *Stanley* (1999), focused on an elderly couple in a troubled marriage, her Royal College of Art film *Dog* (2001) - winner of a BAFTA award and several festival Grands Prix - on a traumatised boy whose mother and dog die in quick succession and whose equally traumatised father is unable to help. Not the most obvious director to choose for a family classic; and her experience of short films with tiny teams hardly equipped her for the proposed extremely elaborate, half-hour co-production. But Hugh was 'fairly obsessed'[263] by *Dog* and took Mark Stephenson to see it at the London Film Festival. Five seconds into the screening the air was rent by the latter declaring at the top of his voice that Suzie was amazing and that she absolutely had to do the wolf.

However, before Suzie was recruited and the project started, Hugh had to raise some finance. The original hope was to make the film in the UK, but it soon became plain that cost would rule that option out. Even shooting in Russia, the Ukraine, Estonia, Hungary - all of which were investigated - or, the final choice, Poland, the budget was likely to be substantial. The first potential funding partner approached was Channel 4. Jan Younghusband, the commissioning editor responsible for music and performance, knew Suzie's work and felt that Suzie's 'understanding of darkness' would deliver a more profound interpretation than the previous, cartoony versions of *Peter*.[264] C4 funded the team and worked with them to develop the project. However, the budget was around £1.4 million and, with no other partners on board at that stage, Jan could not commission the film outright, but suggested that the Channel would deficit fund the film in due course. This enabled Hugh, now armed with the development work, to embark on what would amount to 700 meetings over the course of three years and would finally enable him to stitch together finance from no fewer than seventeen different sources.

Most people he approached viewed him with considerable suspicion, partly because this group was so new on the scene and partly because they were intending to do something different with an old favourite. It would have to be shot abroad for cost reasons, and this lent a further element of risk in the minds of the money people. On the plus side, a deal had already been done for the film to be premiered at the Royal Albert Hall, and arrangements were in place to offer the work to orchestras world-wide. Finally, the tide began to turn. The National Endowment for Science, Technology and the Arts came in with a grant and more finance would be generated by the tried and tested means of producers' deferrals and pre-sales. A couple more grants made a further sizeable chunk and then, thanks to these inputs, the deal was looking more manageable for C4, which was now able to put up a quarter of the budget. But there was still over a quarter missing, a gap which Hugh was able to plug by the use of two innovative funding formulas - sale and leaseback and the Equity Investment Scheme - both based on tax concessions to encourage private investors.

In town

Hooligans bully Peter

Prokofiev had been commissioned to write *Peter and the Wolf* for the Central Children's Theatre, with the aim of inculcating musical taste into children of primary school age. The commission was, it seems, completed in record time. Some sources say four days, others two weeks. Given the quality of the music, one has to assume that the story took Prokofiev a very small proportion of those four days or two weeks, and it does seem a rather perfunctory plot, constructed around appearances of the characters personified by the specific instruments of the orchestra. The original narration, taking up only three minutes of the total piece, does not attempt to give any detail of Peter's life, save that he is (like most Soviet children of that period) a member of the Communist youth organisation, the Pioneers, and emphasising that 'Pioneers are not afraid of wolves' - thus fulfilling Socialist Realism's requirement of a positive hero to be emulated. The duck quacking in the wolf's stomach at the end was interesting musically and a sweet joke, but not a very satisfying denouement to the drama.

Over the years many film adaptations have been produced, all attempting to make it more appealing to contemporary youngsters, perhaps the best known being Disney's, which first appeared as a segment in the 1946 *Make Mine Music*. BreakThru was determined to retain the film's educational aspect and also to introduce some major ethical as well as musical issues. And a half-hour animated film, especially for children, would need a lot more than three minutes-worth of action. Prokofiev's words had been recited down the years by an extraordinary range of artistes, from John Gielgud to Boris Karloff, and more recently Sting, Lenny Henry and even Dame Edna Everage, in a quest to reach new audiences.[265] But the text was too limiting and was abandoned early on, providing the freedom to create a story with more action than the original, with which children could identify, which would reflect various contemporary issues and would also include a good few laughs. There was always to be dialogue however, until Suzie's epiphany: the Pet Shop Boys' concert in Trafalgar Square, where they accompanied *Battleship Potemkin*. Amazed at the power of the music plus images formula, she immediately dropped the dialogue. The constraints of the score would, of course, still be observed: the bird's activities would be represented by the flute, the duck's by the oboe, the cat's by the clarinet, grandfather's by the bassoon, the wolf's by the French horns and Peter's by the strings. Liberated from Prokofiev's text, the BreakThru team could take new inspiration from the music.

The script would go through fifteen drafts before the team was happy with it. Suzie, with co-writer Marianela Maldonado, would change the season from

Peter: Suzie's first concept sketch
Courtesy Suzie Templeton

Ewa Maliszewska's maquettes of Peter and grandfather
Courtesy Suzie Templeton

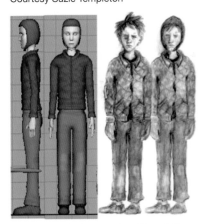

Character sketches translated into CGI
Courtesy Suzie Templeton

summer to winter - great for the dramatic opening in which grandfather has to repair a roof during a blizzard and for comic routines on the frozen pond - and change Peter the confident Pioneer to a lonely boy struggling in the modern world. They would include scenes set in his poverty-stricken home and others among the peeling Stalinist architecture and rusty cars of the nearby town. They would emphasise the solitary nature of Peter's life and give him trouble with a gang of bullies. Instead of taking the captured wolf off to the zoo at the end, a more ecologically-minded Peter would finally release it back into the wild, after an adversarial but respectful relationship has built up between the two. We are still left with the oboe, at the end, representing the duck quacking in the wolf's stomach - for the score was of course sacrosanct - but no reference is made to this in the story. Musical viewers, recognising the continued presence of the eaten duck, will take it that she lives on in her friend Peter's memory.

The writing was nourished by considerable research, including trips to Russia and to the UK Wolf Conservation Trust. Fairly early in this pre-production period, Alan Dewhurst applied himself to setting up the co-production. Alan's production experience dates from the early 1980s heyday of British animation and encompasses commercials, long form and auteur shorts in all techniques and working with partners across Europe and North America - yet nothing had been as complex as what he was about to embark on. Looking for a studio to house the production, he advertised worldwide and received hundreds of showreels. The Se-ma-for studio in Łódź sent a film called *Ichthys*, directed by Marek Skrobecki. According to Alan, when he and Suzie watched it for the first time 'the hairs stood up on the back of our necks. We immediately felt that its makers had a sensibility that could be perfect for *Peter and the Wolf*.' So they visited Łódź in the summer of 2004 to check them out. Se-ma-for was extremely impressive. Founded in 1947, it is celebrated both for its festival-winning auteur shorts and for its children's series using all animation techniques as well as live action. Its creative stars have included Daniel Szczechura, Piotr Dumała and Zbigniew Rybczyński, who won the studio an Oscar® with *Tango* (1981) - and now Marek Skrobecki. A deal was concluded and the UK team would move to Poland in September 2005.

Meanwhile, now that scripting was well under way, Suzie began working on a storyboard. But this film was not to be the normal kind of stop-frame animation, with a static point of view. For *Peter and the Wolf*, the camera was to be as mobile as for a live-action film, and a traditional, drawn storyboard would struggle to represent these moves in three dimensions and would require constant re-drawing when the choreography changed. So Suzie started working instead with computer artist Martin Clapp to produce a CG animatic, a simply animated version of the whole film. Maya software made it easy to work out camera angles, where the characters were on set, how big the set needed to be, etc, providing a reference for the whole crew. It also helped

Peter and bird in the CGI animatic
Courtesy Suzie Templeton

The final Peter
Courtesy Suzie Templeton

Suzie Templeton and animator Krzysztof
Brzozowski
Photo Paulina Majda

Suzie to work out body language. It took over a year for the animatic to reach its final form, which was fine cut to a music track recorded by the Philharmonia Orchestra. Transcribed on to a bar chart, this provided the structure to which the animators would synchronise their movements.

During this period, production designer Jane Morton was researching, brainstorming with Suzie and beginning her detailed designs. Sadly, she would later become ill and when the crew moved to Poland Marek Skrobecki would take over the role. Suzie was also at this time working on the all-important design of the Peter puppet. She had always sculpted her own maquettes and she certainly knew the kind of look she was after. Her inspirations included Augustus John's portrait *Robin*, the sullen young face on the *Angela's Ashes* poster and Christian Bale doggedly making his way in the prison camp of *Empire of the Sun*. She had produced some sketches. Yet when she started to sculpt she could not seem to get what she wanted: 'My sculpts were too realistic and complex.' Then, suddenly, the film was green-lit and Suzie, Alan and the rest of the British crew had to move out to Poland, where they would remain for a year (a year which, incidentally, would see both the coldest winter and the hottest summer in 30 years). Over there, Suzie would have no time to sculpt. So an open competition was held for the job. She ended up with thirteen sculptors 'trying to find Peter' under her direction. Ewa Maliszewska's work stood out right from the beginning. Fascinated by Suzie's sculpts for the boy in *Dog*, she tried to combine these same exaggerated proportions with Suzie's Peter sketches.

She did a few sculpts and then suddenly there he was. My Peter! Exactly as I'd seen him in my head. I was amazed. It's so expressive. As soon as we had Peter I felt much more relaxed about the quality of the film itself and also my ability to direct other people!

The Polish crew numbered over a hundred and they would be responsible for set design and production, model-making, animation and digital post-production. It was a mammoth job. The forest set was 60 feet long and comprised 1,700 real baby trees from the forests outside Łódź. All sets, props and puppets were accurate down to the tiniest detail. The wolf's hair and birds' feathers were laboriously implanted in small tweezerfuls. The bricks in the railway arches were all individually laid with a tiny trowel (in the UK they would almost certainly have been done with sheets of standardised brick patterning). 'We're miniaturising the world,' said Skrobecki in a *Kino Polska* report[266], but the realism was of the kind favoured by both Suzie and Marek - tempered with poetry. They even designed each set using a different colour palette to achieve different atmospheres.

The puppets were another major job. Since they would be shooting on up to eight sets at the same time, many duplicates were needed - making a total of about fifty puppets for the nineteen characters. They were constructed in

Adding feathers to the duck
Photo Paulina Majda

Suzie Templeton and Mikołaj Jaroszewicz
filming in the house
Photo Paulina Majda

Hugh Gordon photographing Peter
Photo Paulina Majda

accordance with Suzie's armature designs, and most of them were of normal puppet size, ie about one fifth of life size. However, Skrobecki has a penchant for extremely large puppets. (I had first become aware of him in 1992, via an amazing film called *D.I.M.*, for which he had deployed life-sized puppets. I later learned that he had at this stage just returned from a British Council-sponsored visit to the UK, during which he had worked as an intern at Jim Henson's Creature Shop - I wonder if there is a connection.) He now suggested larger puppets, one third of life size, for the interior scenes and all close-ups. In the *Kino Polska* report, lead animator Adam Wyrwas demonstrates the advantage of these large puppets in the extraordinary detail possible. While the grandfather sleeps, his hands move slightly - but just moving the hand would produce a lifeless result: each finger is, he says, 'like a character' and has to be moved separately. An enormous job, but it does create an amazingly life-like puppet. On the other hand, large puppets are much heavier - grandfather was particularly top-heavy - often demanding rigging to support them, which would have to be removed digitally in post-production.

After five months spent constructing sets and puppets, shooting the film took a further five months. As well as being detailed, the animation was also unusually full of action scenes in which it was not only the large puppets which would have to be rigged to stop them falling over. Given the need to project on to giant screens, the film was shot with digital stills cameras which generated extraordinarily detailed images at nearly 13 megapixels per frame. These are small and light and can shoot from unusual positions, so are far more versatile than 35mm cameras.

Given the complications inherent in the production and its financing, it was perhaps to be expected that some things would go wrong, and they did. But the determination of the production team, with a lot of background support from Channel 4, always got the show back on the road. It was really up to the wire, though, with the crew working day and night to be ready for the 23 September 2006 premiere at the Royal Albert Hall.

There were obviously going to be a few disapproving voices among the classical music purists, but the majority 'got' what the film was trying to do and liked it. Classiquenews.com called it '30 minutes of pure magic and spell-binding enchantment.'[267] *Classic FM* magazine felt Suzie's adaptation was more successful than any other in making sense of the original in terms of character, atmosphere and location.[268] Neil Fisher, reviewing the Albert Hall premiere,

Peter returns with the captured wolf

noted 'delighted gasps' from the audience and 'many giggles from the duck's high-spirited exploits', and even suggested that the two other pieces from the Russian classical repertoire which the Philharmonia 'ploughed through' before *Peter* would have benefited from the Templeton treatment.[269]

It is undeniable that one or two children's giggles at the duck's exploits turned to tears when she was then so suddenly gobbled up. It was always a concern, but unavoidable if the adaptation was to remain at all faithful. Suzie was relieved that so few children did actually get upset. It seems the worst casualty in this respect was animator Adam Wyrwas. Obviously the wolf puppet could not be sufficiently capacious to accommodate the duck puppet it was supposed to be consuming. So the beautiful duck had to be gradually sliced up, one slice removed for each frame to simulate its gradual disappearance into the wolf's gullet. After animating this shot, Suzie recalls, Adam 'couldn't move for hours - just sat there and smoked with a horrified look on his face!'

The film has triumphed at both TV and animation festivals, winning among others a Golden Rose at the world's most prestigious TV festival, in Lucerne, the Grand Prix as well as the audience award at Annecy, a British Animation Award, and culminating with an Oscar®. It was aired at 4.30pm on Christmas Eve 2006 on Channel 4, attracting a very healthy 1.8 million viewers, putting it among C4's top-rated shows of the Christmas period. The orchestral rental scheme appears to be working: as this book goes to press 27 orchestras in eleven countries have already performed the piece with the film or have booked to do so. The future seems rosy.

Given the difficulty of financing all but the most commercial animation at the current time, I was wondering whether Hugh sees this complex patchwork of sources as a template for future projects. He sounded a bit tired: 'Hopefully, future films will be more straightforward to finance.' But he still insists that the choice of a good project will always take precedence over ease of financing. So there are more struggles to come - but that Oscar® win will certainly help.

Stills and production photos © BreakThru Peter Ltd and Se-ma-for

9   Changing contexts

Animation had fared surprisingly well during the first half of the 1990s. Yet this was a period of change, and some of those changes would have an effect on the animation department which would only later become apparent. Several areas of the Channel's more challenging programming were already doing less well, notably the experimental work championed by the independent film and video department, which had begun to suffer budget cuts and less congenial scheduling[270] quite soon after Michael Grade's arrival in 1989. This was a function of his determination to make the Channel's output appear more professional, as well as the recession of the early 1990s and consequent decrease in advertising revenue. And independent film and video was particularly vulnerable to budget cuts, having started out with £1.5 million in 1981/82 and reached a global sum of £10 million by 1990[271] (whereas animation never went far above £2 million). As early as March 1993 David Curtis of the Arts Council was writing to John Willis, director of programmes, with a plea for greater support and regular programme slots for more experimental work. He based his letter on 'the now widely expressed view that Channel 4 has lost its automatic association with innovation, and that it's become safer and more predictable than of old.'[272]

The 1990 Broadcasting Act, which had changed Channel 4's status so that we would be selling our own advertising, also took some other, discreet steps to forestall any plunge downmarket that this change might set in train. The Channel 4 remit, previously so delightfully vague - we were simply to be innovative in form and content and cater for viewers whose needs were not met by ITV - was tightened up. Subject areas which were thought to be important (current affairs, educational, multicultural and religious programmes, etc) were highlighted in the Act and a minimum number of hours' programming per week specified. A further Act, in 1996, would add more detail. Animation, not a subject area but a group of technologies, did not benefit from such protection.

Another development, which had initially seemed to be a godsend but ultimately proved extremely damaging, was the BBC's gradual entry into the field. Alan Yentob, then running BBC2, had observed Channel 4's success and, according to BBC insiders, decided to mount some competition. In 1988 he commissioned Irene Kotlarz to programme an Animation Week in the context of BBC2's *Def II* youth programming strand, and in 1989 he hired Jayne Pilling to consult on acquisitions and other animation projects. She, rather irritatingly, nipped in while I was still searching for the red card index and bought up the short films of Jan Švankmajer (whose 1987 *Alice* had been co-financed by Channel 4), while Michael Jackson (then head of arts at the BBC) commissioned Švankmajer to make *The Death of Stalinism in Bohemia* (1990) for a major season devoted to Czech art and politics. At around the same time BBC Bristol's formidable *10 x 10* series, initially conceived for junior ranks within the BBC to cut their directorial teeth on short documentaries, began to include some fiction and, finally, occasional animation projects. One of these turned into the pilot for Dave Borthwick's 1993 *The Secret Adventures of Tom Thumb*.

The Secret Adventures of Tom Thumb
© Bolex Brothers

Despite the competitive nature of this entry into the (totally un-televisual) field, I felt it as something of a relief, as C4 had until then been the only possible funding body for such work. Now, if I regretfully had to turn down a good project through lack of funding, at least I knew there was another port of call. Further, the BBC ethos was different from our own and would tend to serve a different clientele. Whereas Channel 4 was conceived in the publishing house style, as a very benevolent but totally hands-off patron, BBC Bristol's production, because it had always been in-house, was far more hands-on, and that would remain the case for its animation projects. Colin Rose, the instigator of the Bristol end of this expansion, would be intimately involved with scripts, financing, production management, setting up and running studios, and would work mainly with filmmakers from the Bristol area.[273] He would be freed of his live action work in about 1993, to concentrate on animation alone.

Sadly, however, the BBC soon saw that short films were a mug's game. Dave Borthwick's *The Secret Adventures of Tom Thumb* (1993), originally a 10 minute short, then proposed as a 10-minute series, finally became a one-off, 1-hour programme. Colin Rose realised that for more easily schedulable and saleable formats such as series and specials he would be able to tap various other sources of funding within the BBC including, notably, BBC Enterprises (predecessor to BBC Worldwide) to supplement his own meagre resources. This realisation came to him at about the same time that Aardman, thrilled with the success of their *Lip Synch* series on Channel 4, had decided that Nick Park, whose *Creature Comforts* had been the runaway success of that series, should work up the Wallace and Gromit characters from his Film School piece, *A Grand Day Out*, into a second half-hour show.

In the early 80s Aardman bosses David Sproxton and Peter Lord had been happy with the C4 funding for *Conversation Pieces*. It had paid the production costs and an additional fee on top of that to keep the studio going while developing further projects, a formula which was uniquely generous in television practice of the day. However, C4 did retain all rights (as they did for all programmes they 100 per cent funded) and the studio's share of income from overseas sales, for example, would have been in the order of 30 per cent. By the time of *Lip Synch*, Aardman had wanted to invest more, to retain more rights. They now hoped to fully-fund the next film in order to retain all rights and subsequent income, and asked Channel 4 to agree a modest licence fee for a couple of transmissions. So this was firmly allocated in my budget. Things started to go wrong a few months later, when they came to me for urgent funding of a short film by their young director Jeff Newitt, for which I had no funds allocated. Desperately wanting to keep my star studio on side, I hoovered up every penny of unspent funds, to provide approximately £70,000 for *Loves Me... Loves Me Not*; which left nothing whatsoever for a rainy day. But the rainy day did, inevitably, come. Aardman discovered that they were unable to raise the budget for *The Wrong Trousers* entirely alone, and asked us to come in as co-producer. They were at that stage asking for a similar amount to what I had just committed to the Newitt short. It was a derisory sum - the studio was still not very experienced in the business aspects - and would have been a drop in the ocean proportional to the total budget (which Colin Rose, then head of the BBC's animation unit, remembers finally amounted to about £600,000[274]), but once hooked into the project Channel 4 would certainly have put in more. However, my budget did not contain £70,000, nor any uncommitted funding at all. I set up a meeting for Andrea Wonfor, head of the arts and entertainment division, and programme finance chief Colin Leventhal to discuss the problem with David Sproxton and myself. But to no avail – sadly, the Channel could not find that £70,000.

Aardman went to the BBC, where they would remain, only coming to C4 for short film funding. The BBC was probably the right place for them, given the variety of funding sources within the Corporation and its clout when seeking overseas co-producers. The higher viewing figures possible on BBC1 were certainly another attraction. *The Wrong Trousers* would start off on BBC2, but when its second transmission achieved that channel's second highest rating (after the men's final at Wimbledon) it moved up to BBC1. On Christmas day 1994 it would be seen by nearly 10 million viewers.

Later, the financial support which BBC Enterprises and later BBC Worldwide had furnished to Colin Rose's Animation Unit would become more problematic. Having at one stage been prepared to take a punt on riskier-seeming projects such as *The Wrong Trousers* and Sylvain Chomet's 1997 *The Old Lady and the Pigeons*, they would later become more commercial and spurn the quirkier material. By that time, however, the damage to Channel 4 was already done. We had lost our star performer and with it perhaps the delicate balance I had tried to maintain between popular and challenging work.

However, the modest expansion into series detailed in chapter 8 did seem to be going well and we pursued it further. Sarah Kennedy's *Crapston Villas*, having gone into production without needing to wait for co-production partners, was completed during this halcyon period, given a perfect slot in the schedule (Friday evenings at 11.15) and launched in October 1995 with a gratifying amount of on-air promotion. Press reactions were, predictably, mixed, but there were plenty of favourable reviews, some from surprising sources - the *Daily*

Telegraph called it 'vulgar, relentlessly modern - and rather entertaining'[275]. The programme even won a major award, *Broadcast* magazine's Best New Programme award. Not 'Best New Animation Programme' but 'Best New Programme'. This was one of the few times that animation was able to leave its ghetto and take its proper place alongside mainstream programming. A second series was commissioned immediately.

Pond Life and *Bob and Margaret* would fare less well. The whole of 1994 having been spent looking for coproduction partners, series scripts for the former could not be commissioned until 1995 and the series was not completed until the following year. By 1996 the attitude to animation at the Channel had changed. Dawn Airey, whose strategy had been an almost blind trust in her commissioning editors, and who had supported me to the hilt, left the Channel that year to become director of programmes for Channel 5 and had been replaced as head of arts and entertainment by Stuart Cosgrove. Michael Grade was still around in 1996, but his heart was no longer in the job. He was perhaps getting a little bored, having polished the Channel's image to the smooth finish he had striven for and succeeded totally in his campaign to secure its finances. But this political campaigning had taken him further and further from the production process.

The Channel's schedule was virtually being run by John Willis, who did it so brilliantly as to raise increasingly in my mind the question: assuming that our political and financial base is secure does the Channel really need me any longer?[276]

Well, the animation department did need him, and suffered without his patronage. John Willis, then director of programmes, had come up through documentaries. He is one of the cleverest, wittiest and most likeable people in television, and a genuine innovator. But he seemed to have a blind spot where animation was concerned. The problem first became apparent at our weekly programme review meeting, when the schedule for the forthcoming period was about to be circulated for discussion. John was chairing the meeting and began by chiding the assembled company for a dearth of fresh comedy projects in the schedule. I was feeling pretty smug, knowing that my own fresh comedy, *Pond Life*, was about to be revealed, the exception to that generalisation, in the post-*Dispatches* slot. But it was not. A season of student documentaries followed *Dispatches*.

After some prevarication and more delays, we were told a search was on for the very best slot, which would help *Pond Life* with a good number of inherited viewers. It was not considered possible that, over thirteen weeks, the series might create its own audience by word of mouth, in the slot for which it had been commissioned and initially accepted. Following the focus groups, in which some - but by no means all - of the 18-24 year-old men had reacted badly, the series had been declared a 'women's programme' and the decision

Crapston Villas
Courtesy Channel 4 Television Corp

Candy's reaction to the slotting of Pond Life: a cartoon in Televisual magazine
© Candy Guard 1997

made that it needed to follow another 'women's programme'. To give the focus groups their due, they were asked for recommendations as to the scheduling of the series, and their ideas were not at all bad. One suggestion was 8.30pm, following a popular soap, *Brookside*, another was 8.45, and there was even discussion of a 9.45 slot on a Friday, between *Roseanne* and *Cheers*.

However, it was finally scheduled at 5.45, following *Ricki Lake*, a 'sub-*Oprah Winfrey* talk show' [277], after which - as we already knew from the viewing figures we received every week - its audience (mostly housewives) always departed en masse for BBC1 where *Neighbours* was just starting. The audience *Pond Life* was actually targeting was still at work at 5.45. The problem was compounded by the fact that, instead of a weekly slot, which would at least have allowed word of mouth to alert potential viewers to set their videos before leaving for work, the whole series was stripped daily across weekdays (as was *Ricki Lake*), so it was all done and dusted in just over two weeks. Then, of course, there were the problems caused by scheduling a series conceived for an adult, post-watershed slot in a slot when children could be watching. At great cost and considerable effort, the whole series had to be filleted and the rude words cut. Two episodes were beyond the pale - in one of them Dolly, at Glastonbury, inadvertently drops some acid and behaves extremely badly; in the other, after a sleepless night before her driving test, Dolly overdoes the caffeine pills the following morning - so an 11.30pm slot was found for just these two episodes.

Even so, many parents phoned in complaining at the adult subject-matter to which their children were exposed (and let us not forget that animation, unless scheduled in an adult slot, is automatically assumed by viewers to be for children). Director Candy Guard was naturally angry, her anger exacerbated by the ease with which her Newcastle Poly chum had slid into a plum slot with *Crapston Villas*. This row was the occasion of my first resignation from the Channel.[278] The press were thoroughly confused. All gave the series rave reviews and all reviews were peppered with comments about the scheduling, ranging from the polite 'bizarre' (*Observer*) and 'inept' (*Independent*) to 'stupid' (*Time Out*), via a whole range of other expressions of disbelief (*The Times*, *Evening Standard*, *Televisual*, *The Daily Telegraph*)[279]. Many of these reviews were by women, but by no means all: Peter Waymark in *The Times*, Daniel Paddington in *Time Out* and Boris Johnson in the *Telegraph* loved it, as did Victor Lewis-Smith, who gave it a whole page in the *Standard*.

Perhaps we should have given up on animated series then, but with one successfully transmitted and as yet only one disaster it seemed to be worth trying again. In retrospect, though, it seems clear that my only chance of getting the necessary support in this would have been to brief a studio to produce something in the *Simpsons* mould or another post-pub gross-out for 18-24 year-old males. But the property which had actually turned up, via the time-honoured Channel 4 'publishing house' route, was the extremely low-key adventures of a middle-aged, childless couple, a dentist and a chiropodist. Put like that, or put any other way, it did not sound like a big pull for that all-important demographic group. There was initially no plan to make *Bob's Birthday* into a series, but even before the Oscar® win, heartened by a clutch of major prizes at festivals around the world, I commissioned six scripts, just in case... After the Oscar® its directors, Alison Snowden and David Fine, were pursued by American studios wanting to partner them, and us, in a series. American co-funding would be guaranteed. We were hooked. But this enthusiasm came to nothing. We would eventually find a partner in the Canadian company Nelvana. The series was given the go-ahead in July 1997, the month in which Michael Jackson became our new chief executive.

10   Animation on the slide

To some at C4 Michael Jackson's arrival seemed to herald a welcome return to our founding principles. The younger Jackson had been a prime mover in one of the groups lobbying parliament for the Channel's creation and defining its remit. When, years later, he felt Michael Grade was betraying this remit, and was asked to speak at the Royal Television Society in the spring of 1996, he did not mince his words. In a time of rapid media expansion and consequently less loyal audiences, he said, all established channels were suffering a loss of the respect which had been their due, but Channel 4 had lost the most: 'Am I alone in thinking that the pursuit of demographics - in particular, young, lager-drinking, upwardly mobile men - has led to a sapping of Channel 4's originality?'[280] And he went on to berate specific examples, singling out *The Girlie Show*, 'a late-night jamboree featuring drunk women shouting in nightclub toilets'.[281]

Jackson's approval rating in the television community was high. He had risen rapidly through the ranks of the BBC to become its director of television. His programming instincts were impeccable and he had riled Channel 4 no end by a constant poaching of talent and programme ideas. All in all, the denizens of Channel 4 felt it would probably be better to have him with us than against us.

And so, indeed, it came to pass. A year after the RTS speech Jackson would accede to the top job at Channel 4 and have the opportunity to put right the faults he had identified. His first actions, however, appeared to have remarkably little effect on the nature of the programming. His aim, according to a *Variety* article of 8-14 February 1999 was 'nothing less than the transformation of the feisty pubcaster into a branded media empire, marrying its unique creative element with a commercial agenda more aggressive than at any time in its history'.[282] It involved a major restructuring of the commissioning body (large numbers lost their jobs) and the creation of new channels FilmFour and, later, E4 - and a betting channel was planned too, though that idea finally came to nothing. A new strategy unit was created and, as staff were pruned in the commissioning area, there was a corresponding increase in the marketing department.

Michael Jackson was more willing than most chief executives to invest large sums of money and significant slabs of airtime in high profile arts projects. These included a live *La Traviata*, taking place in real time across a weekend (2000), a controversial Matthew Bourne ballet *The Car Man* (2001) and the equally controversial John Adams opera *The Death of Klinghoffer* (2003). Yet the overall proportion of popular, unchallenging material in the mix seemed,

Bob and Margaret™: Friends for Dinner
Series 1 1998
© Nelvana Ltd/Channel Four Television Corp

if anything, to increase. He had wanted to reduce the Channel's reliance on extremely expensive American series, yet *Frasier*, *Friends* and *ER* remained, and were supplemented by the perhaps less accomplished but more sensational *Sex and the City*. *The Girlie Show* was indeed replaced, but it was by the likes of *Something for the Weekend* and *Ibiza Uncovered*. Jackson began to announce, as Michael Grade had before him, that remit programming (which had previously been defined as appealing to minority audiences) could also at the same time be popular programming. The truth is that it can, but only in very rare cases, usually when sex or some other controversial material comes into the mix. The theory worked well in the case of *Queer as Folk*, the ultra-explicit and very engaging chronicle of life among Manchester's gay community. *South Park* pulled off the same trick, with brilliant scripts attacking small-town and many other prejudices - but it was not the social criticism that brought in most of the viewers.

There were of course very few programmes like this, which could be groundbreaking in addressing a serious problem or appealing to a previously invisible group and at the same time attract high ratings. Many of the new programmes seemed popular, trendy (Jackson was keen to keep up with and indeed ahead of fashions) but a bit vacuous, while some of the less high-profile experimental programmes saw their budgets tightened and slots diminished. To some the programming seemed to reflect exactly what Jackson had protested about to the RTS: treating the audience as categories of consumers and, among those consumers, privileging the young males still sought by the advertisers.

Yet in truth, with new channels proliferating and competing for advertising, it is hard to see what could have been done except move towards more popular programming. But perhaps this could have been done more openly - in the same spirit, perhaps, in which Jeremy Isaacs had commissioned a dramatisation of Barbara Taylor Bradford's *A Woman of Substance* (1985). He simply acknowledged that many of the Channel's programmes would not suit the advertisers, and this and other occasional crowd-pleasers were designed to even the balance.

By the time of Michael Jackson's arrival, however, *Bob and Margaret*, which would not appeal to many of those young males, was already under way and scripts were being written. The series was completed and slotted into the schedule for mid-November 1998 in a 10.30pm Wednesday slot. It was an excellent time, though the slot followed the nth repeat of an ancient comedy series, *Rising Damp*. Alison Snowden and David Fine, the directors of *Bob and Margaret*, always felt this paralleled the *Pond Life* slotting, the idea being that animation always needed help from a large inherited audience - but the wrong audience tended to be chosen. *Rising Damp* viewers were rather old and fairly downmarket. In America, Comedy Central would slot *Bob and Margaret* between *Dr Katz* and *South Park*, where its ratings were outstanding.

The launch on C4 benefited from some on-air promotion and achieved 1.75 million viewers for the first episode - an identical rating to the first episode of *Crapston Villas* and exceedingly good for the still relatively unfamiliar genre of adult animation. We were delighted. As the on-air promotion dropped off, so did the ratings decrease slightly (as they had for *Crapston Villas*) for two weeks and then, in week 4, as word of mouth spread, they picked up again. However, in week 5 some notable figure sadly died and merited a tribute, so one programme in that week had to be dropped to make way. *Bob and Margaret* was chosen. It returned the following week, was taken off for two weeks over Christmas and then brought back in January - but in a different slot, on a Tuesday. This, we were told, was because our ratings, though very good for animation, were not good enough to remain in that prime Wednesday evening slot, in which programmes were expected to hit the 2 million mark.

It is worth noting that the programme which replaced *Bob and Margaret* in this slot, series 1 of the new US import *Sex and the City*, was promoted on hoardings and bus sides as well as an overwhelming on-air campaign. This, along with the presence of 'sex' in the title, translated into over 3 million viewers in the first week. The figure had halved by the end of the 13-week run. In truth, series 1 of *Sex and the City* was not great. However, the Channel stuck with it. Not until series 3 did that show hit its stride. *Bob and Margaret*, however, was dropped after its first series. Production would now continue for a total of 52 episodes, financed by Nelvana and the US channel Comedy Central, but without its originator, Channel 4.

But Michael Jackson did want to continue with animation series. He gave the go-ahead for a second series of *Pond Life*, though he insisted that this time they must be half-hours. The 15-minute slot following *Dispatches* was, anyway, about to disappear as part of a general neatening-up of the schedule. Scripts were commissioned in 1998 but production was much-delayed while co-finance was sought. It finally got underway in 2000. Candy found the longer running time a challenge. Her scripts for the first series of 11-minuters had been brilliant - she had even been nominated in the best sitcom category of the Writers' Guild awards, along with *One Foot in the Grave*, *Men Behaving Badly,* and *Only Fools and Horses*. But whereas she had felt she could follow sudden mad whims in the shorter format - such as a London driving test getting out of hand and ending up in Brighton - 'half hours make you get sensible. Suddenly it all goes turgid. With half-hours everyone says you need three acts. I overworked them...'[283] Actually the scripts were rather good, and they contained some wonderful gags. But they were not propelled by the desperate lunacy of the earlier series.

Despite the half-hour format imposed on it, the series would still not get a weekly slot in the peaktime schedule. Instead, its seven episodes were squeezed into two groups, shown daily in 11pm slots, the first three just preceding and the rest during the September 2000 Animation Week. But Michael Jackson apparently liked the series. In response to a barrage of criticism of his programming, he put up a spirited defence in the *Evening Standard*[284], in which he refuted claims of a golden age in the 1980s and responded to Tony Smith's challenge to find in the C4 schedule 'one programme that contributes towards a distinctive character' by listing eight distinctive shows which had been broadcast in the previous ten days. He included *Pond Life*, a 'feminist animated sitcom'.

Before I left, another outstanding proposal came our way, this time from our partner on *Bob and Margaret*, Nelvana. The project seemed to be tailor-made for Channel 4: it was the blackest of black comedies, a series finding its humour in a community of variously (and grotesquely) disabled characters and their relationships with the outside world. I thought it could be C4's Holy Grail, a series which could genuinely fulfil the remit while notching up high ratings. The writer and designer was the well-known cartoonist John Callahan, himself paraplegic since a horrendous car accident of his own making, having been drunk at the wheel. Callahan had already made an animated short, the wonderful *I Think I Was an Alcoholic*, which we had shown as part of an alcoholism season and which had provoked an enthusiastic response from recovering alcoholics phoning in to express their thanks. His cartoon books were also well known in the UK. The deal would have been as generous as that for *Bob and Margaret*: again we would put in only one third of the budget, and we would share in creative control. But this time the writers and voices would be American - a draw, I thought, as far as Channel 4 schedulers were concerned. But, no. The project was refused because part-funding could be found for a single animated series project only, and that had to be British. (*Quads* did get made, though, and C4 did eventually acquire it for a repeat screening in a late slot.)

We had a bit more success with series in the 5-minute slot following the *Channel 4 News* where, given that the small, serious news audience was anyway expected to turn off at that junction, there was little risk to the Channel. Barry Purves' *Gilbert and Sullivan: The Very Models* had worked well in the slot in 1998 (though I felt Barry was wrong to string the episodes together subsequently and present them at festivals as a rather long, episodic and too densely packed short). So had Tim Searle's *The Outlaw* (based on Michael Heath's cartoon strip about the last smoker in Britain) and Bob Godfrey and Steve Bell's *Margaret Thatcher: Where Am I Now?* (both 1999).

Now I wanted to try Joanna Quinn's *Beryl* in that slot. The character had progressed beyond the stages of innocent fun with a male stripper and political

Gilbert and Sullivan: The Very Models
Photo Jean-Marc Ferrière

gestures on the factory floor and was more mature, more thoughtful. She would create a video diary, each episode of which was to reflect on an aspect of her life and would, judging from the outlines Joanna brought to me, be hilarious. But it was not to be. The series would be too expensive for the slot.

Animation no longer had a patron at the Channel, a Jeremy Isaacs, Michael Grade or Dawn Airey with their own reasons for getting behind it. And times were now very much harder. I had always supposed that the Channel's support of animated shorts could not last and was a function of the extraordinary circumstances in which C4 had been created - with a public service remit, adequate income and no competition for advertising revenue. I had expected that our shorts production would eventually be phased out and I would be diverted into potentially more commercial areas, including series. Instead, series projects never really got off the ground at all and shorts were preserved - but in falling numbers and on smaller budgets. It was disappointing.

The Outlaw

But my reduced budget was not the only problem for shorts production in the period. There was a definite decrease in the number of good proposals. Festival director Irene Kotlarz, who keeps a finger on the pulse of the animation community and is in a prime position to spot trends, sensed a decrease in the buzz around British animated shorts at the festivals as early as 1990.[285] This syndrome took longer to filter through to my own activities, but by the mid to late 1990s the scene had indeed changed drastically. Gradually (in fact ever since Who Killed Roger Rabbit in 1988) animated features had seemed more and more feasible. Aardman had progressed via half-hour specials on to feature films and now only approached the Channel for funding of occasional shorts, often with a view to giving experience to the young directors who would go on to work on the studio's longer-form work. The Quay brothers had diversified into experimental feature films, mostly live action, as well as live-action shorts and stage designs. Barry Purves went to Hollywood for Mars Attacks, though he was back soon, after an unhappy experience. Others went and stayed. There was even a moment in the early 1990s when several of the Hollywood majors opened studios in London to avail themselves of the UK talent on their feature films. Animated shorts production experienced a distinct brain drain. Perhaps the decrease in critical mass led to fewer exciting projects. Perhaps - perish the thought - we needed some more mavericks of the kind produced by the old laissez-faire system of animation education in our colleges pre-1985. Or perhaps, like any movement of its kind, it was simply slowing down.

Yet even with this dip in the number of good proposals, there were still more than my diminished shorts budget could satisfy. And although we did not hit the hoped-for 100 per cent strike rate - 'hoped-for' because we didn't hear much about the 'right to fail' these days - a good few major successes were nevertheless achieved. Orly Yadin and Sylvie Bringas's Silence was completed in 1998 and won a host of prizes. We were able to partner veteran Belgian

Papillons de Nuit
© Anagram

animator Raoul Servais - the director of several seminal shorts, notably *Harpya* - in his magical tribute to Belgian surrealist Paul Delvaux, *Papillons de Nuit* (1997), which took the Grand Prix and critics' prize at Annecy. Two films which were finally delivered after I had left also brought honour to the Channel. *The Man with the Beautiful Eyes* (1999), based on a poem by Charles Bukowski, took BAFTA and BAA awards and was nominated for the Cartoon d'Or. Robert Bradbrook's *Home Road Movies* (2001) took a total of 24 awards around the world including the Cartoon d'Or.

During the late 1990s animation, the constant misfit, had continued its peripatetic existence within the Channel. Having started off in 1982 as an extra, allocated to the commissioning editor for odds and sods, it had then been moved into the purchased programmes department, before enjoying a period with a full commissioning editor looking after animation alone and reporting direct to the head of arts and entertainment. However, Michael Jackson dismantled this system. It had indeed become unwieldy, with too many minor departments reporting to the beleaguered heads of the factual and arts and entertainment divisions. Now the major programme areas were each given a supremo, with the minor commissioning editors reporting to them. In this restructuring animation now found itself in the drama department, reporting to Gub Neal. Later we were moved to the comedy department under Kevin Lygo.

I decided, early in 1999, that I personally could do nothing more to foster animation on C4, and that in fact my presence might be obstructing its progress. In the hands of a younger commissioning editor with a racier style, it might be possible to find a compromise and appeal to larger numbers of the young viewers the Channel sought, while still remaining open to the whole range of genres, techniques, directors and types of production unit. I told Kevin that I would be leaving that September and organised a series of meetings between him and some of the younger and livelier representatives of the animation world (one had even done a spell on *Eurotrash*[286]), ostensibly so that they could advise him about where we were at and where we should think about going in the future. I told him (though not the unsuspecting candidates) that these were the kind of people he should be looking at to replace me. All this was accepted and the meetings seemed to go well, except that out of the blue it was announced that Camilla Deakin, deputy commissioning editor for arts and music, with no experience in animation, would take on the job in addition to her existing responsibilities. Animation was back to its status of an 'extra'. However, she would be supported by Ruth Fielding, who had learned a great deal about animation and animators during her two years as my assistant and, thanks to a background in drama, was already handling a lot of the script work.

One of the projects I was to take on when I left C4 was a piece of research on the Russian animator Yuri Norstein for the newly-founded Animation Research Centre at the Surrey Institute of Art & Design. I needed a reference from Channel 4 and this was duly provided by director of programmes Tim Gardam. It praised my various virtues and characterised my championing of filmmakers' freedoms (at the expense, it implied, of the schedule) as old-fashioned.[287] It was absolutely fair. It also defined ultra-succinctly the changes at the Channel since I had been recruited in 1989.

11　Young blood

Ruth Fielding and Camilla Deakin
Photo Fiona Campbell

In appointing Camilla Deakin to take care of its animation, the Channel hoped to attract the younger viewers it so desperately sought. Camilla did not know very much about animation at the time, but then neither had Paul Madden when he was given the job. Both had to run animation as a part-time activity. With the support of chief executive Jeremy Isaacs and in the creative ferment that was the early Channel 4, Paul had succeeded in adding a slate of great works to the canon of British animation and in seasoning the schedule with some unorthodox and highly-praised programmes.

But the TV environment was now greatly changed and Camilla would ultimately encounter a far harsher climate. At first, though, all went well. She was reporting to a supportive head of arts, Janey Walker, and thence (as arts fell under entertainment) to Kevin Lygo. In her arts role Camilla had previously been urging Kevin to allow her to do a series for younger people with an interest in visual arts, and had been keen to look at aspects of design in contemporary life, such as computer games and album cover design. We were all aware by this time of the growing army of youngsters, mostly boys, who had been turned on to animation by the digital revolution and were now tinkering with CG on their bedroom computers. Likewise, American series such as *The Simpsons* and *South Park* had gained a tremendous youth following, so it was hoped that by focusing on these young fans and computer buffs animation might finally become the ratings-winner the Channel now craved. The young and very enthusiastic Camilla seemed to be the person to do that. According to an interview given by Janey Walker to *Broadcast* magazine shortly before my departure, the main thrust of animation policy would now be 'a renewed drive for a peaktime, British-made, half-hour animated sitcom'.[288] A short while later it was announced that the comedy department would collaborate in this search.

Camilla and Ruth set about talking to the animation community and trying to educate them as to general trends in broadcasting and the specific new focus of Channel 4 animation. They sent out a series of newsletters explaining what slots and budgets were available and what kinds of themes might be of interest. The slots were largely as before: occasional access to the 5-minute slot after *Channel 4 News*, longer slots in the late-night schedule at specific times of year to be allocated as Animation Weeks, some good half-hour daytime slots for Christmas specials plus, presumably, some peaktime slots for the sitcom. One difference now was that there was much less funding for the kind of personal shorts in which the Channel had previously excelled. Or, rather, the Channel would indeed continue to fund the Animate and Animator in Residence schemes and even initiate a third scheme, Mesh, which would generate a dozen or so short films a year between them. But two of these schemes were specifically for newcomers and the third focused on experimentation, and most works were only 3 minutes, which is a bit short to develop the kind of ideas usually found in a festival prizewinner. So - while the schemes would go from strength to strength - top awards would now become rather less frequent overall.

But the good news was that among the potential animation slots a new possibility was on offer. One tool in the hunt for the great British animated sitcom was a new arrangement whereby animation would now appear from time to time in *The Comedy Lab*, a series trying out new comedy talent with a view to development into individual series if successful. Ideas were solicited, both from animation studios and from a range of comedy writers. The four selected projects came from experienced teams. But, despite Camilla's high hopes, none of these pilots was deemed sufficiently successful to develop into a series.

Rolf's Animal Hairdressers

Tim Searle of Triffic Films, having tested out the then new, time-saving Celaction system on his *Comedy Lab* piece, *Rolf's Animal Hairdressers*, was convinced that even topical subjects were now within the reach of animation. But when he brought the Channel a proposal for a topical political satire, *2DTV*, to be written by satirists who had worked on *Spitting Image*, it was turned down, as the powers-that-be were at that time specifically looking for narrative sitcoms. It later became a major hit, running for five series on ITV1.

Another series project which failed to bear fruit was an idea from Sam Morrison, a highly talented writer/animator who had made one of the best Animator in Residence films (*Emma 18*) and was now funded to make a 12-minute pilot for a series to be entitled *Home*, a hilarious and uncomfortably plausible portrait of a dysfunctional family. The Channel would have supported this project, had producer Phil Davies been able to raise European co-finance at the Cartoon Forum. Sadly, those potential partners failed to get the humour. And, even more sadly, it had gradually become plain that the collaboration which had been announced, between the animation and comedy departments, was not going to work. When, some time later, Hat Trick's proposal for the animated series *Bromwell High* became available to the Channel, Kevin Lygo developed this from his comedy budget and commissioned it under the comedy aegis without any input from the animation department.

Bromwell High is set in an extreme version of the kind of under-funded, graffiti-daubed comprehensive schools which struggle these days to educate most of Britain's inner-city children. The stars were three foul-mouthed but endearing girls who could run rings around their desperate teachers. It aimed to be the UK's answer to *South Park*. Reviews were full of shock-horror, but that usually does nothing to harm a good show, and C4's head of comedy defended the series: 'We think *Bromwell High* is ridiculously funny, deliciously filthy and absolutely cutting edge'.[289] She was right, in that the scripts were indeed sharp. Yet something did not quite work. As a means of making the series affordable it was co-produced with Canada, much of the production taking place there. It has been suggested that it is this clash of cultures that somehow waters down the comedy - yet other such co-productions have worked brilliantly. Or possibly the budget was so tight that there simply is not *enough* animation, making it a rather static illustration of the marvellous script. Or perhaps the problem was that the scriptwriters - veterans of some of the best British TV comedy of recent years, such as *Goodness Gracious Me* and *The Kumars at No. 42* - were basically live action writers and did not appreciate the rich vein of visual humour to be mined in the medium of animation. Neither was the series lavishly promoted, and with only six episodes there was not much time for word of mouth to spread. Anyway, for whatever reason, in a good slot at 11.30 on Friday nights it notched up barely half a million viewers.

This failure signalled an end to peaktime, expensively-animated narrative sitcoms. Producers sending in proposals to the comedy department after this were told that, in view of the failure of *Bromwell High*, there would be no more investment in sitcoms of this kind for the foreseeable future. Now the Channel would embark on less risky, lower-budget projects such as *Fonejacker* and *Modern Toss*, which already had a guaranteed audience inherited from other media.

However, despite a depressing career for adult series, there was a great deal of activity in smaller projects throughout Camilla's tenure. AIR and Animate were producing some outstanding films - *City Paradise* and *Rabbit* being celebrated elsewhere in these pages - while Animate was also undergoing massive structural changes. The Arts Council was withdrawing from hands-on participation in such schemes, which were instead put out to tender. It was perhaps not unexpected that the best proposal was that of Finetake, ie Dick Arnall (with, initially, Maggie Ellis) which, with increased Arts Council funding, initiated an extraordinary expansion of activities. These include regional exhibition of selected programmes of Animate works, often accompanied by discussion events (eg with luminaries such as A S Byatt and Iain Sinclair at the National Portrait Gallery); international exhibition at festivals and elsewhere; the launch of a new award for innovation in the manipulated moving image; a new collaboration with Lux (an organisation set up specifically to support artists' moving image work); residencies at the London College of Communication, offering artists space and facilities to explore the manipulated moving image; and a DVD of Animate work to be released by the British Film Institute.

In 2008, as I am finishing this book, the scheme is still in a state of flux. As direct commissioning of shorts by Channel 4 has decreased, so has the variety of applicants to Animate widened. Many of these new applicants are from the more narrative end of the animation world and bring with them pressure to move in that direction. Yet the new relationship with Lux - which actively promotes work from the more experimental end of the range - is pulling the scheme in the opposite direction. Some animators perceive a move in the Lux direction, towards artists with an interest in animation rather than vice versa. Changes in Arts Council funding policies have continued to affect the scheme, as has the untimely death of Dick Arnall. Gary Thomas has now migrated from the ACE film and video department and, with the scheme's line producer Jacqui Davies and the blessing of the Arts Council and Channel 4, set up Animate Projects, to take the scheme forward into a new, more entrepreneurial, era. (They have also dispensed with the lower-case 'a' and the exclamation mark sported by the scheme's name over a considerable period.)

Camilla and Ruth's new production scheme, Mesh, was designed very specifically to bring to the Channel those new voices, people who had neither the traditional skills taught by college degree courses nor the artist's desire to experiment but nevertheless aspired to use the new technologies creatively. A supporter in the creation of the scheme was Stuart Cosgrove, who had failed to get me to focus to any great extent on this new community but now found there was an animation editor with whom he could do business. Stuart's division, named 'nations and regions', was set up to promote production outside the home counties. Since Scotland's 'silicon glen' housed numerous computer games companies, Stuart contributed - along with funding from the National Endowment for Science, Technology and the Arts - towards setting up the scheme, which would be administered in Scotland. The new project was originally designated the 'digital animation scheme' until, within a few short years, it became apparent that the vast majority of all animation had become digital. So it began to characterise itself in terms of its constituency: what were termed 'convergence' artists, ie games designers, graphic designers or people with computers in their bedrooms who were teaching themselves. People who were not coming through the animation degree courses. People operating at the point where animation converges with TV, the web and mobile phone possibilities. Run by Glasgow-based Blackwatch TV, the scheme did not restrict itself to just financing the four best narrative films per year, and many of the winning pieces also had an interactive element.

But the Channel was trying to kill two birds with one stone. As well as cool design, they were looking for strong characters. They needed these films to run in the slot after the news - which had been deemed a narrative-only slot - and were at this stage still looking for ideas with potential to develop into longer-form comedies. And so, as well as various seminars and masterclasses on subjects such as the art of the animated title sequence, mobile content and web design, a scriptwriting workshop also took place each year for the selected filmmakers. But the 'convergence' people were not strong on plot or character. In latter years it turned out that many of the successful submissions were coming from the animation courses at the RCA and other colleges - and were not that different from the constituency that was applying to the AIR scheme. Mesh, along with AIR, has now come to the end of its funding and C4 is rethinking its management and commissioning of new talent for the future.

Camilla and Ruth tried hard to make the animation fit in better than it had previously with what the rest of the Channel was doing. Always a tough nut to crack, given that animation production had always had a very long lead time and that sometimes pan-Channel seasons were dreamed up quite rapidly, this was becoming easier with the new possibilities offered by digital technologies. Now, with only 5-minute slots available, and with ever decreasing budgets and therefore more functional animation, it did become possible to commission some films for Caribbean Summer, a season which the Channel was able to plan well in advance since it had acquired the rights to televise Test cricket two years earlier. In 2000 Britain's five-match Test series against the West Indies was celebrated by C4 on and off screen with extraordinary exuberance and animation's contribution to this magnificent event was a series of shorts stripped across the week in the 7.55pm slot, showcasing the work of black filmmakers.

Camilla and Ruth were also charged with seeking to provide new Christmas specials and Tim Gardam had kindly asked me to act as a free-lance consultant in this area after I left Channel 4. I was only partially successful - the specials were never really my forte. The first was by Raymond Briggs (of *The Snowman*, *Father Christmas*, *The Bear* and *When the Wind Blows* fame) who had come up with the suggestion that he would like to write an original screenplay for a C4 Christmas special, rather than going via the normal route, after publication of a book. And Briggs was the kind of name one would not refuse. The resulting *Ivor the Invisible*, produced by Paul Madden for TVC and directed by Hilary Audus, who had done a great job on *The Bear*, was not quite as captivating as the previous Briggs-based films. On a lower budget, the design did not have that handmade look of the earlier films and, one of the two main characters being invisible, something seemed to be missing at the heart of the film. But it got good press and ratings and the Channel was pleased.

In my quest for other properties I started digging around in the children's fiction world. The only book I proposed for serious consideration, Ian Whybrow's *Little Wolf's Book of Badness*, was a great read and made me laugh out loud. But it too had a drawback: the story is told in the form of Little Wolf's letters home throughout the course of an action-packed adventure, and most of the humour comes from Little Wolf's idea of good epistolary style and his prioritisation of facts to be recounted - not to mention his spelling and grammar - and slightly less from the story itself, which of course is what is needed to carry a young television audience along with it. However, Ruth worked with the author to give

Little Wolf's Book of Badness. Director Karsten Kiilerich

Dominion. Director Tim Searle

it that stronger narrative and the resulting programme, animated at the Danish studio A. Film and Chinese studio Wang, also went down well.

In recognition of the fact that animation on C4 had been and would continue to be about short films as well as the hoped-for longer-form hits, slots were provided once a year for seasons covering the full range. We had started off in the early 1990s scheduling our treasures in a kind of festival format, over short periods twice a year, with slots where they could be found in the afternoon and late-night schedule. The schedulers had subsequently complained that these festivals were bringing down the ratings for the week and we were instead given half-hour slots, into which we were to package our shorts, scheduled weekly a couple of times a year. Now, finally, things had come full circle and animation was back to the festival format - only it happened just once a year now. Animation Week 2000 started with a bang on Saturday 23 September, with a programme designed to press all the youth interest buttons. After an hors d'oeuvre of *South Park* and a short interview with *Simpsons* creator Matt Groening, Groening's new series *Futurama* had its premiere at 9.40pm. Following that, *Our Toon* asked a bunch of TV and pop celebrities to name and introduce their favourite cartoon. At 10.40 two youth icons gave their own personal angle on a range of animation (and *Adam & Joe's Animation Adventure* would later be nominated for an Indie award), at 11.40 there was a package of four animated sitcom pilots and at 12.15 came four new short comedies. And so it went on until 4.10am. The problem was that *Futurama*, the supposed new *Simpsons*, which was to be the motor behind the whole evening, was actually no such thing and viewers did not stay with it, let alone wait around to see what would follow it.

The rest of the week included in its late-night slots some Japanese anime, a guide to subversive animation invitingly entitled *Cartoons Kick Ass*, an animation magazine show called *Sick and Twisted*, some episodes of *Pond Life* (the first group having shown the week before) and that year's productions from the AIR and the Animate schemes. The science fiction mini-series *Dominion* ran in the 7.55 post-news slot. The student promo competition which Phil Davies had run for us in 1995 and 1997 was revived to produce a variety of stings to promote and punctuate the Week. There was a lot of good material here, all oriented towards the desired young audience, if perhaps (as Camilla and Ruth acknowledge[290]) not forming as coherent a unit as they might have hoped. Yet the ratings were disappointing.

Animation Zone, in 2001, went better in terms of coherency. This time, it was spread over six weeks, with a weekly episode of *Sick and Twisted*, followed by late-night blocks of themed shorts. *Sick and Twisted* included some inventive elements, perhaps the most successful being the Cel-Mates strand, in which a group of animators were incarcerated, *Big Brother*-like, for 36 hours, during which time they were to make a piece of animation - watched by a good number of C4 viewers by webcam on a special website. The ratings for the whole Animation Zone were better than for the previous year's Week, and in fact very good for the time of night: but they were not good enough for the Channel. As Camilla points out[291], the late-night slotting disadvantages programmes in two ways. There are, of course, fewer viewers available. And, secondly, that slotting indicates to reviewers that the Channel itself is not particularly proud of whatever ends up in these graveyard slots, so they also elect not to watch/write about them. And as for promotion... The Channel calculated long ago that it can achieve higher overall ratings by concentrating massive press and marketing resources on a few programmes with obviously popular appeal rather than using those resources to support programmes which are not obvious ratings hits. Sadly, the maths is correct.

By the end of 2001, animation at the Channel was on the skids. After Janey Walker's departure from the department Camilla had been promoted to full editor and was reporting direct to the supportive Kevin Lygo. But when Janice Hadlow arrived to take over arts, the large department was split in two and animation was moved into her section - which was now named 'arts, history, religion, science and animation', the latter obviously a long way down in the pecking order. It had also become plain that, despite valiant attempts to attract new audiences with potential sitcoms and animation seasons very much attuned to young tastes, director of programmes Tim Gardam had by now given up on any such developments. All the Channel wanted was an occasional Christmas special and a few prize-winning shorts. As if to confirm this decision, the budget had declined from £2 million a year to 1.2 million, which was barely enough to finance the three schemes and part-fund a Christmas special. Furthermore, the Channel was increasingly suffering from a downturn in advertising revenue and a reduction in audience share. Staff who left were not being replaced, and it was announced that there would be 200 redundancies. People were being encouraged to leave. Animation, always considered something of a luxury, was in a particularly vulnerable position.

The most likely outcome appeared to be what I myself had feared back in 1999: that animation would gradually be starved of funding and disappear entirely. Camilla and Ruth saw an opportunity here and offered the Channel a solution which would take two members of staff off the payroll and enable them to start up their own production company, administer the three Channel 4 animation schemes and look after any other animation activity which the Channel would agree from time to time. For the Channel it was 'a relatively inexpensive and hassle-free way for them to keep up their brand association with animation'.[292] For TV viewers and animators it meant the preservation of a small amount of animation activity on the Channel (for seven years as this book goes to press) with the hope that in a different broadcasting climate this activity might one day increase. Yet some members of the animation community were angry at this turn of events. It was handled in some secrecy and by the time the closure of the department was announced it was a done deal. Animators were upset that they had not had a chance to lobby the Channel to change its mind - not that C4, or any other organisation in a similar position, would have changed its mind, no matter how much lobbying had gone on.

Wilde Stories.
Framework story directed by Sarah Cox

There was also concern in the industry over rumours that the pair had left the Channel with some commissions. In these days, when the only C4 animation commissions outside Animate, AIR and Mesh were for very occasional Christmas specials, the idea that these jewels in the crown could be commissioned as part of a leaving package rather than by the old system of seeking the best submission from an independent producer irritated such independent producers no end. In fact, though, the principle had been abandoned - or at least watered down - long before. It had been plain for a couple of years that the weird and wonderful ideas likely to be submitted by animator/directors would not satisfy the Channel's more and more prescriptive policies. When, in 1999 and 2000, the hunt had been on for the edgy British adult animated series, writers had been approached and briefed, rather than risk another middle-aged dentist or the like. The fruits of this prospecting were not, of course, produced in-house, but they were certainly engineered by the Channel. Likewise, my own consultancy was designed to find good properties in children's literature, with C4 then deciding how best to put them into action.

As it happened, the acquisition of *Little Wolf's Book of Badness* coincided with Camilla and Ruth's decision to leave the Channel to become independent producers under the name Lupus Films, and they came away with the commission and partial funding. They were also given development funding for a series of three stories by Oscar Wilde and indeed later (July 2002) received a commission for the project, though again not for the full amount. Presumably familiar with these moans, Camilla and Ruth are anxious to point out that the consultancy fee they received to cover their management of the three schemes was modest in the extreme and that, as of early 2008, no C4 programme commissions have been forthcoming since *Wilde Stories*. The company has survived on BBC and Channel 5 commissions.

On balance it would seem that the deal with Camilla and Ruth has benefited the animation world and the viewer rather more than the alternative, a gradual withering on the vine. The benefits are becoming apparent, now that animation again has a champion within the Channel in the person of Jan Younghusband, whose music and performance brief was extended in 2004 to cover all arts, including animation. Younghusband has been behind some of the most popular and innovative music projects first on the BBC and latterly on Channel 4 (including the seminal *Operatunity*). She actually likes animation and even, when at the BBC, came up with the original idea for Collingwood O'Hare's delightful animated music series for children *Oscar's Orchestra*, starring the voice of Dudley Moore as Oscar the piano. It was Younghusband who, in difficult circumstances, managed to find 25 per cent of the funding for Channel 4's Christmas 2006 success, Suzie Templeton's extraordinary *Peter and the Wolf*. Perhaps that film's Oscar® win will inspire the Channel to further such investments.

Oscar®-winner Peter and the Wolf
© BreakThru Peter Ltd and Se-ma-for

Another straw in the wind is an unexpected initiative from the scheduling department, which has come up with funding to commission some shorts for the daytime schedule. Fillers have always been needed for daytimes, to plug gaps, but these were traditionally filled by acquisitions or repeats of commissions. But the available shorts were not usually ideal. And the new terms of trade (as amended in the 2003 Communications Act) mean that the Channel now only receives two transmissions of even commissioned works, so they do not have the large stock they had previously. In addition to this increased need, commissioning has become cheaper for the Channel. Digital technologies are bringing budgets down and now that filmmakers retain all rights in their work it has become normal for them to raise co-finance themselves, or simply to contribute their labour in return for these rights. The daytime schedule is not the place for experiment or innovation, but it is nevertheless a valid showcase for British animators' talents. And it is reassuring to note that animation can be mobilised to fulfil a need which has arisen in the current broadcasting climate.

But Camilla and Ruth's major hope for C4 animation is the new broadband animation channel named, nostalgically, 4mations. It is built and designed by Aardman and modelled on the already functioning, and highly successful, FourDocs broadband channel. The new channel is to give equal weight to archive material (with classic films but also interviews, filmographies and curated seasons); work from Animate and the successor scheme to AIR and Mesh; information on such varied topics as software, festivals, games and colleges; and user-generated content. Viewers will be able to vote for their preferred UGC works, with the editors at C4 also giving their opinions on a selection. It sounds rather wonderful - though I hope this positive development does not mean the final vestiges of animation will now disappear from the main, terrestrial channel, where most viewers are currently to be found (though who knows for how much longer). Camilla and Ruth stoutly maintain that this is not an 'either/or' situation. Animation will, they say, continue to have its presence in the post-news slot and in occasional late-night blocks on the main channel. That, certainly, is their intention.

Chief executive Andy Duncan is keen on 4mations, not least because the regulator, Ofcom, wants the Channel's public service commitment enhanced and is particularly interested in digital expansion - for this is where the viewers of tomorrow are increasingly to be found. There are grounds for optimism.

12   A future?

In his recent book *A History of Artists' Film and Video in Britain*, David Curtis makes the point that the moving image as art has been, for most of its history, 'devoid of a sustaining economy'.[293] This is largely true, and the entertainment end of the moving image spectrum does offer more obvious economic incentives. But, as we have seen, there have been exceptions, moments when a rich sponsor - a governmental or business entity - has considered screen art of various kinds to be a useful tool. John Grierson used only the most innovative moving images to sell the General Post Office's services to 1930s Britain and advertisers and record companies have, at times, decided that the weirder, the more enigmatic the animated commercial or pop promo, the more frequently viewers would want to watch it. And if we extend the definition of art beyond David Curtis's extremely experimental interests to include films which tell a story or make a point - but in an unusual way, art-based and often using hybrid technologies - we could also cite the honourable history of the National Film Board Canada and even the governments of the Soviet bloc, which financed all production, often giving animators a freer rein than live action filmmakers.

Channel 4 - and the BBC and S4C which in the 90s also came to see that animation could serve a purpose - constituted another such blip in the flat line of funding for art animation. Channel 4 was able to support animation because its legal remit demanded innovation, and advertising revenue was in place to pay for it. S4C's circumstances were identical to C4's, with the additional practical incentive that animation was the only medium in which dubbing was not a problem, and so one in which the channel could comply with its remit quota of Welsh language broadcasting while still successfully selling other language versions abroad. The BBC had initiated TV's interest in grown-up animation back in 1979 with its *Animated Conversations*: by 1990 it felt that C4 had stolen a march, and re-joined the fray.

Yet animation for grown-ups has now almost disappeared from all three of these broadcasters' repertoires. It was, I believe, inevitable. The favourable conjunction of circumstances dissipated. The BBC, not dependent on advertising, could perhaps have continued a little longer. But the BBC has a very direct financial relationship with its viewers - it is funded by their licence fees and thus, in this era of competitive channels, is also having to court the mass market. But as far as the commercial channels are concerned there is, basically, not enough advertising revenue these days to pay for luxuries. (And for C4 animation has become more and more of a luxury, since successive Acts of Parliament have added to the remit, protecting specific subject areas but, understandably, not mentioning particular technologies.)

One reason for the decline in advertising revenue is the proliferation of new channels. These are cheaper for advertisers and are taking an ever-increasing share of peaktime viewing. But not only is TV advertising revenue now more thinly spread than previously: there is also a marked decrease in TV advertising overall. With the possibility of cheaper advertising on the Internet, with a success rate measurable in clicks, the trend is away from television and on to the web. The result is that the profits of all commercial terrestrial channels have declined along with the ratings. Furthermore, broadcasters have to turn off their analogue signal by 2012 and switch to digital - an expensive exercise. Channel 4 would like some funding from the government - and is hinting that, without it, it will need to abandon some key remit programmes still in the schedule. At a time of such pressure on programming budgets, remit-friendly but ratings-neutral-to-unfriendly genres like animation have to come last on the priority list.

We are currently in a period of rapid change, both technical and economic, making it all but impossible to predict a likely future for animation and the various platforms which might support it. Some commentators, including Jeremy Isaacs'[294], still see a future for 'quiet seriousness' on Channel 4 and clamour for a return to the remit. The regulator, Ofcom, is due to report on the results of a broad-ranging review of public service broadcasting. But it might be a bit late for that - or at least for the main, terrestrial channels. Now, amidst a proliferation of channels and a general move to more popular programming, it would be suicidal for a channel to buck the trend and return to 'quiet seriousness'. It could never attract enough viewers and hence advertising to survive.

Anyway, judging by the speed with which new satellite and cable channels, broadband channels and use of websites such as YouTube and MySpace have increased, terrestrial, linear[295] networks will at the very least continue to shrink if not eventually disappear entirely. And, as a medium for showing animation, such channels were never really that good. That ideal world in which a thought-provoking little short could be placed between TV programmes and be seen by a large audience hardly existed at all, except perhaps for a very brief period during the earliest days of C4. And, even when it did, television did not offer the possibility of repeat viewings, which the best animation cries out for.

So if linear TV can no longer be expected to support animation, are other media poised to mop up this country's abundant animation talent? Animators happy to remain at the functional end of the spectrum have an assured future: computer games are the place to be, with a sector turnover now higher than that of cinema distribution and set to overtake VHS and DVD sales. Mobile phone content is also likely to be big - or small actually, since the screen size and manner of use does rather dictate short, simple, design-led material with any narrative quite perfunctory. Animated feature films are proliferating and live action features are also demanding ever more CG input. These are the kinds of healthy markets where work can both get properly financed and be widely seen.

But innovative short films are far more problematic. The problems are two-fold, relating to both funding and distribution. The latter is the lesser. Despite the disappearance of the most natural home of the short film, the cinema (long gone) and now the declining support of its successor, TV, potential media for viewing short films are proliferating. Traditional cinema programmes, with shorts accompanying features, are being replaced by a whole range of different venues and formats, from festivals to cafés to bars to art galleries to rock concerts. The most experimental end of the range is thriving in the new age, with the Animate scheme involved in all sorts of activities alongside its commissioning, with tours, exhibitions and educational events. The relatively new onedotzero organisation (which proclaims itself a 'digital creativity initiative') has also adopted the Animate model, and its very splashy events are reaching huge numbers of young enthusiasts at home and abroad. Another mode of dissemination is the travelling shorts programmes which have sprung up, mostly in the US, touring programmes around cinemas and campuses. These formats, along with DVD sales, offer improving visibility but no serious income.

In the future the Internet may be the best bet for animation distribution - though it is clear that in this time of rapid technological evolution anything I say today will be wrong tomorrow. But, with that proviso, this would appear to be the situation as this book goes to press: As of now various websites are streaming animated shorts, but it seems that Video on Demand is a complex system and it is currently hard to make this work economically for short films. So animation streaming tends to be gratis for the time being, though the system is sure to improve. Channel 4, for example, has entered the VoD market in a big way. And, importantly, the technology now exists to transport downloaded programmes from our computer screens to the more relaxed viewing mode of television.

But this is no solution to the current problem of getting films financed. Budgets are of course lower these days thanks to the new technologies available, so funding should be easier. The UK Film Council is offering some support to the kind of work Channel 4, S4C and the BBC financed in the past, but until now it had no specific fund for animation, which had to take its chances alongside live action in the Digital Shorts scheme. This scheme's small budgets have been geared to live action, where production tends to be less labour-intensive and where low- and no-budget short films are often no more than stepping-stones for young people heading towards a career in features. Animators, and especially established animators, have had a hard time. For the moment there are still animators around who are willing to work for next to nothing in order to realise their personal visions, but this is no recipe for long-term success.

No funding body can currently make commercial sense out of commissioning any but the lowest-budget projects and, with the honourable exception of the experimental sector, this situation tends to favour work which is good to look at, fun but perhaps lacking substance. This was one of the major concerns which recurred in the interviews I conducted for this book. Talking about the gap left since the reduction in TV funding, about current trends and the seemingly inevitable future, many people saw a tendency towards: 'clips, segments, bits of something but never a whole', 'moving wallpaper', 'surface-fixated' work 'without anything to say'.

One of the big hitters. Joanna Quinn's
Dreams and Desires: Family Ties
© Beryl Productions International Ltd

This leaves British art animation in a fragile state. The decline in TV funding and growth in CG features and computer games means that young animators with the creative talent to make their own personal films are instead being diverted into more prosperous sectors. Though our short films are currently holding up surprisingly well at festivals, it tends to be the same few big hitters winning prize after prize. We are slowly losing critical mass.

Once again Channel 4 has a chance to step into the breach. By the time this book is published, C4 will have launched its broadband channel devoted to animation - an outline of the plan is given in chapter 11. Again, as in 1981, commercial gain will not be the prime motive, as this and other youth-oriented broadband initiatives are specifically encouraged by Ofcom as part of the Channel's remit work. This is crucial. In terms of production, the new channel aims to foster the whole gamut, including both user-generated work and the products of Animate. And, as this book goes to press, there is also encouraging news about a possible successor to the AIR and Mesh schemes. Channel 4 and the UK Film Council are in talks about extending the Digital Shorts scheme, and involving the Film Council's regional and national partner agencies to generate 3-minute shorts by new animators across the country. (The budgets, however, will still be fairly modest.) It is also hoped that - if 4mations goes well - C4, perhaps in partnership with Aardman, will be able to commission one or two more ambitious shorts per year.

Though small in scale, this is a wonderful opportunity. My only concern is lest this broad gamut should polarise to produce on the one hand exceedingly low-budget work - either highly experimental or else fun and stylish, with little substance - and, on the other, highly professional entertainment shorts of the kind currently financed by some of the major studios as a means of trying out their newer directors with a view to future work in more commercial areas. Room - and finance - have to be found for a little 'quiet seriousness', for thoughtful work using innovative means to say something of interest.

Moving pylons. The new generation of Channel 4 idents. Director Brett Foraker

Animation has come a long way. Once there were only cartoons. Then, in the 1960s, with the advent of animation festivals, a new strain of more serious work was seen. But some of this could be pretty turgid. Paul Vester once asked me: 'Do you remember when animated films were all about bald symbolic persons pushing stones up hills?'[296] 'Fraid I do. But the new animation is more sophisticated. Offering perhaps more food for thought, it is rarely symbolic in that painfully earnest way, and rarely straightforward (in terms of either content or technique) entertainment.

The new animation does still use frame by frame techniques but it can also encompass anything else that is not directly recorded by a live-action camera - and a lot of technologies can fall into that category. This animation combines innovative technologies in short films with a point - but it also spreads into almost everything else we see. It is interesting to compare the original C4 animated idents with the current generation: these look like live action, and that is a major element, of course. But those hedgerows, pylons, haystacks and rock formations did not move themselves into those fleeting 4 logos… The essence of animation is the creation of new worlds. Whether it makes use of live action or any of the myriad other media, and whether the whole is confected in the computer or on a light-box, in the hands of a talented artist it still achieves this magic. Critic Jonathan Myerson has written of this kind of animation that:

Reality becomes irrelevant: like the best painting it becomes a perfect fusion of story-telling and vision. […] Take the beauty out of animation, take the artist out - as Disney has done in the name of mass-production - and you have nothing. So, next time you see Channel 4 scheduling a block of animation at three in the morning, set the video and, at leisure, settle down to a true treat.[297]

That was in 2001. Unless such animation is carefully nurtured, it could disappear completely. Or, in tomorrow's world of new technologies and unlimited choice, and with a bit of luck, commitment and modest finance, we may have these created worlds on tap - and not even have to wait till three in the morning.

Notes

1 The 1979 Cambridge Animation Festival catalogue contains a series of informative essays on British animation history, decade by decade.

2 The mechanism whereby CIA funding found its way to the project is discussed in detail in Daniel J Leab's *Orwell Subverted: The CIA and the Filming of Animal Farm*, Penn State University Press 2007.

3 The first franchises were awarded in 1954 and the first commercial went on air 22 September 1955.

4 Stan Hayward email to the author 26 October 2006.

5 Richard Taylor 1979 Cambridge Animation Festival catalogue, p15.

6 Based on Stan Hayward scripts.

7 '50 Fascinating Facts That One Never Knew About the Queen', *Daily Mirror* 30 May 2002.

8 *The Animated Film*, p95.

9 Ibid.

10 Vera Neubauer email to the author 10 May 2007.

11 It would become the National Film and Television School in 1982.

12 It would later change its name to Surrey Institute of Art & Design, University College, and more recently to University College for the Creative Arts.

13 Candy Guard interviewed by Linda Pariser in *Women & Animation*, p88.

14 'Outrageous Proportions', October 1992, p26.

15 Jayne Pilling interviewed by the author 16 April 2007.

16 Jerry Hibbert interviewed by the author 7 August 2007.

17 Jerry Hibbert speaking at the Everyman cinema, London, October 17 1995.

18 More details in Stephen Lambert *Channel Four: Television with a Difference?*, p76.

19 21 April 1972.

20 Jeremy Isaacs *Storm Over 4*, p6.

21 This lecture is printed in an abridged form in *The Listener*, 6 September 1979, p298.

22 *Storm Over 4*, p20.

23 The Broadcasting Act 1980, available from The Stationery Office Ltd (TSO).

24 'Sins of Commission', *Screen* 33:2 summer 1992.

25 The title derives from a phenomenon for which Jeremy Isaacs coined the noun 'stormovers', denoting the frequent Channel 4-related newspaper stories headlined 'Storm Over TV Language', 'Storm Over Gay Film', etc.

26 *Storm Over 4*, p29.

27 Ibid, p41.

28 Jeremy Isaacs interviewed by the author 26 September 2006.

29 Jeremy Isaacs interviewed by Elkan Allan, 'The Wonderful People Who Will Bring You Channel Four', *The Sunday Times* 24 January 1982.

30 Promotional brochure preceding the Channel's launch.

31 Jeremy Isaacs *Storm Over 4*, p45.

32 Ibid, p51.

33 Jeremy Isaacs interviewed by the author 26 September 2006.

34 Found in files but unpublished.

35 Isaacs' words, according to Baldwin.

36 Eileen Baldwin phone conversation 13 October 2006.

37 Derek Hayes phone conversation 25 September 2006.

38 Email from Aardman's financial controller 8 August 2007. 2007 figures not yet published as this book goes to press.

39 David Sproxton interviewed by the author 21 August 2006.

40 Ibid.

41 Ibid.

42 Naomi Sargant interviewed in Peter Catterall (ed) *The Making of Channel 4*, p157.

43 Paul Bonner email to the author 29 October 2006.

44 *Leos Janáček: Intimate Excursions* and *Igor: The Paris Years*.

45 Roger Noake obituary to Phil Austin, *The Independent* 5 February 1990.

46 Ibid.

47 Ibid.

48 John Coates interviewed by the author 22 August 2006.

49 A preliminary impression, on film, giving an idea of each scene but using still images to represent the eventual animation.

50 Bob Swain *Electric Passions*, p17.

51 Paul Bonner with Lesley Aston *Independent Television in Britain*. Vol 6, p131.

52 Jeremy Isaacs interviewed by the author 26 September 2006.

53 Paul Bonner with Lesley Aston *Independent Television in Britain*. Vol 6.

54 Steve Bell email to the author 5 October 2006.

55 *Storm Over 4*, p179.

56 *Margaret Thatcher: Where Am I Now?* (June 1999).

57 *Storm Over 4*, p154.

58 Actors wearing markers at their joints perform the necessary actions, which are recorded by a computer to provide the movement for CG characters.

59 Annabel Jankel email to the author 11 May 2007.

60 Quay brothers interviewed by the author 8 December 2006.

61 *Women Call the Shots*, a publication accompanying a C4 season starting in February 1990, p19.

62 This diploma film was later finished and given a professional soundtrack with funding from Channel 4 and S4C.

63 C Taylor *Undercut* no 13, winter 1984-85.

64 Jayne Pilling (ed), *Women & Animation*, p89.

65 *Who Needs Nurseries? We Do!* (1978), *Risky Business* (1980), *Pretend You'll Survive* (1981), *Give Us a Smile* (1983), *Council Matters* (1984), *Crops and Robbers* (1986), etc.

66 *Women & Animation*, p36.

67 14 January 1988, p41.

68 Candy Guard email to the author 9 January 2007.

69 *A Midsummer Night's Dream*, produced by NOS-tv (Netherlands) and animated by Tissa David and Ida and Kalman Kozelka.

70 Before joining the NFT I had been John Halas's administrative assistant for ASIFA (the International Animated Film Association), programmed animation at the Los Angeles County Museum of Art and had various free-lance assignments for animation festivals.

71 Michael Grade *It Seemed Like a Good Idea at the Time*, p284. In 2008 he again recommended that C4 be privatised.

72 Ibid.

73 The Independent Television Commission, the regulatory body which succeeded the IBA.

74 At that stage it was the Arts Council of Great Britain. That organisation would be split up in 1994 and the scheme continued under the auspices of the Arts Council of England, with David Curtis still heading the Arts Council side of the arrangement.

75 This was during the period when he had dropped out of animation, acquired various manual skills relating to building and carpentry to refurbish his house, and looked after his small son while his wife, Marjut Rimminen, pursued her career.

76 'Why I'm Pleased to Have an Animate! grant', *Vertigo* summer 1999.

77 If I have not yet mentioned in this book the role of producers in Channel 4 animation – and I do not believe I have – can I here put on record how vital they always seemed to me, both in the creative way in which they supported their directors and also in their diplomatic mediation between Channel 4 and the talent.

78 Dick Arnall interviewed by the author 29 August 2006.

79 Ruth Lingford interviewed by the author 22 June 2006.

80 Ibid.

81 *Film: The Critics' Choice*, ed Geoff Andrew.

82 In a 2001 symposium, Holocaust, Genocide and the Moving Image, held at the Imperial War Museum in London and later published under the title 'But Is It Documentary?', an extra with the recently-released *Silence* DVD, pub. yadinproductions.com.

83 Most of the material in this piece is from interviews with John Coates by the author of 22 August 2006 and 19 December 2006. Any information from other sources is identified as such.

84 *The Snowman Special Edition* DVD includes a documentary detailing the production technique.

85 Iain Harvey email to the author 16 July 2007.

86 Jeremy Isaacs interviewed by the author 26 September 2006.

87 See Howard Blake's website for details of *The Snowman*'s afterlife: www.howardblake.com/the-snowman-history.php

88 Most of the material in this piece is from letters and emails from Derek Hayes to the author during the period September 2006 to July 2007. Any information from other sources is identified as such.

89 Derek Hayes quoted in 'Spoils of animated violence', *Creative Review* November 1985.

90 *City Limits* 27 March-3 April 1986.

91 *Time Out* 25 October-1 November 1989.

92 John Coates interviewed by the author 19 December 2006.

93 'Blowing Away the Myths', *Sunday Express Magazine* 11 January 1987, p20.

94 John Coates interviewed by Graham Fuller, 'On location: When the Wind Blows', *Stills* magazine February 1986, op cit.

95 Unless otherwise specified, all production details are from Jimmy Murakami emails to the author of May 2007.

96 *Stills* magazine February 1986, op cit.

97 Technical manager Peter Turner interviewed by David Jefferson and Geoffrey Mackrill, 'The Background to When the Wind Blows', *Animation Magazine* spring 1988, p29, reprinted from *Animator* April-June 1987.

98 February 1986, op cit.

99 Iain Harvey email to the author 4 July 2007.

100 5 February 1987.

101 20 June 1993.

102 19 June 1993.

103 2006 interview with the brothers in *Quay Brothers: The Short Films 1979-2003* DVD set, pub BFI.

104 Most of the material in this piece is from an interview with the Quay brothers by the author of 8 December 2006 and subsequent emails. Any information from other sources is identified as such.

105 Quay brothers interviewed by Kim Newman, 'The Doll's House', *City Limits* 25 September-2 October 1986.

106 It is reproduced in the booklet in the Quay brothers' short films DVD set.

107 Quay brothers interviewed by André Habib, http://www.sensesofcinema.com/contents/01/19/quay.html

108 Quay Brothers interviewed by Jonathan Romney, 'The Same Dark Drift', *Sight and Sound* March 1992.

109 Alison de Vere died in January 2001, so I have had to rely here on secondary sources, mainly published articles and interviews and the recollections of her son, Ben Weschke, as well as documents he was able to locate.

110 Alison de Vere interviewed by Kayla Parker, *Imagine* no 2 spring 2002, p59.

111 Alison de Vere interviewed by Lorenzo Codelli, *Positif* December 1989, reprinted in *Women & Animation*, p83.

112 'Putting Themselves in the Pictures: Images of Women in the Work of Selected Female Animators in the UK', *Animation Journal* autumn 1995.

113 Sean Lenihan phone conversation with the author 12 December 2006.

114 *Direction* magazine, special issue for 1989 Bristol Animation Festival.

115 Paul Madden email to the author 3 January 2007.

116 15 January 2001.

117 Richard Taylor phone conversation with the author 3 January 2007.

118 Most of the material in this piece is from an interview with Jan Švankmajer by the author at the National Film and Television School on 30 May 2007. Any information from other sources is identified as such.

119 Jan Švankmajer interviewed by Geoff Andrew at BFI South Bank 29 May 2007.

120 Ibid.

121 Ibid.

122 According to Michael Havas, Prague-based executive producer on *Alice*, filmmakers were never officially banned - it is just that all projects submitted for approval would be refused as a result of a specific misdemeanour. Email to Keith Griffiths 21 June 2007.

123 Ibid.

124 *The Cabinet of Jan Švankmajer: Prague's Alchemist of Film*, made as part of the *Visions* documentary series in 1984. It contained some animated linking sequences by the Quay brothers which were later reconstituted into a separate short film.

125 Keith Griffiths interviewed by the author 17 August 2007.

126 Ibid.

127 Ibid.

128 At Švankmajer NFTS interview 30 May 2007.

129 Ibid.

130 Michael Havas email 21 June 2007.

131 *Monthly Film Bulletin* November 1988.

132 *The Observer* 23 October 1988.

133 *The Sunday Times* 23 October 1988.

134 *Time Out* 19 October 1988.

135 Jan Švankmajer interviewed by John Mulholland, 'The Surreal Thing', *The Guardian* 5 March 1992.

136 Most of the material in this piece is from an interview with Joanna Quinn by the author at the Gothenburg Film Festival on 31 January 2007. Any information from other sources is identified as such.

137 Phil Davies email to the author 30 July 2007.

138 W Stephen Gilbert, 30 March 1988.

139 30 March 1988.

140 Don Perretta, 23-30 March 1988.

141 Most of the material in this piece is from an interview with Erica Russell by the author of 3 May 2007. Any information from other sources is identified as such.

142 Charlie Hart email to the author 7 June 2007.

143 Most of the material in this piece is from an interview with Peter Lord and David Sproxton by the author of 21 August 2006 and emails from Peter Lord of August 2007. Any information from other sources is identified as such.

144 Peter Lord in *Cracking Animation*, p172.

145 Ibid.

146 Ibid, p173.

147 Commentary on DVD *Aardman Classics*, Momentum Pictures.

148 The original credits on the film imply that Nick did all the animation. This was because Channel 4 had extremely strict rules on credits in order to limit the air-time they took up, and they decreed that the same person should not be mentioned more than once on the credits.

149 Peter Lord interviewed by Jeremy Clarke, *What's On* 21 November 1990.

150 Most of the material in this piece is from an interview with David Sproxton and Peter Lord by the author of 21 August 2006. Any information from other sources is identified as such.

151 Peter Lord and Brian Sibley *Cracking Animation*, p168.

152 *Aardman Classics*, Momentum Pictures.

153 'Park Life: An Interview with Nick Park', *Art & Design Magazine* vol 12 no 3-4 1997.

154 Jiři Kubíček, 'Aardman Animations Annecy '93', *Asifa News* 1993 vol 6 no 3.

155 19 November 2007, http://www.guardian.co.uk/media/2007/nov/19/mondaymediasection.advertising

156 Comprising the works of various animators, mostly British (Aardman, David Anderson, the Quay brothers) and two compilations of other Channel 4 commissions.

157 25 April 1991.

158 Nick Park interviewed by Ivanceanu, *Asifa News* 1994 vol 7 no 4.

159 Peter Lord email to the author 2 August 2007.

160 Most of the material in this piece is from an interview with David Anderson by the author of 29 March 2007 and subsequent emails. Any information from other sources is identified as such.

161 Edwin Carels, 'Meetin Mizzta Youniverss', *Plateau* vol 13 no 2 1992, p18.

162 Russell Hoban in *State of the Art* ep 2, dir David Jeffcock, prod Redwing, tx 25 November 1990.

163 Ibid.

164 Ibid.

165 Paul Madden email to the author 12 April 2007.

166 Carels op cit p18.

167 Ibid.

168 *State of the Art*, op cit.

169 Ibid.

170 Carels op cit p20.

171 Simon Pummell email to the author 19 June 2007.

172 He sought out as a tutor June Collier, who had studied under Frank Auerbach at the Slade and continued his tradition. Ibid.

173 Simon Pummell interviewed by Jayne Pilling *2D and Beyond*, p34.

174 Ibid, p28.

175 'Francis Bacon and Walt Disney Revisited', originally presented as a dissertation at the RCA, then revised for the 1993 Society of Animation Studies conference and again revised in Jayne Pilling ed *A Reader in Animation Studies*, p163.

176 *2D and Beyond*, op cit, p29.

177 Ibid, p28.

178 'Technical Notes' on Simon's website, www.pummell.com.

179 Simon Pummell in *2D and Beyond*, op cit.

180 Ibid.

181 British Animation Week programme, ICA April-May 1993.

182 Ruth Lingford *Under the Radar: A Study of Transgression in Animation*, unpublished MA thesis.

183 Quoted in Jeremy Clarke 'Post-Cyberpunk and Skeletal Gothic', *Starburst* issue 220 December 1996.

184 Sint Lukasgalerij June-July 2000.

185 Most of the material in this piece is from an interview with Tim Webb by the author of 9 May 2007. Any information from other sources is identified as such.

186 Dick Arnall interviewed by the author 29 August 2006.

187 Most of the material in this piece is from emails from Barry Purves to the author during May 2007. Any information from other sources is identified as such.

188 Barry Purves interviewed by Mark McNulty, 'Production Close-up: Screen Play', *Televisual* August 1992, p16.

189 Glenn Holberton email to the author 4 June 2007.

190 'Passion Plays: The Films of Barry Purves', catalogue for Animac animation festival, Lleida, Catalunia October 1999.

191 Ibid.

192 Paul Wells email to the author 29 May 2007.

193 'A Mix'n'match Made in Hell' 20 June 1993.

194 The material in this piece is from letters, emails and telephone conversations between Petra Freeman and the author during the period November 2006 to July 2007.

195 Snowden and Fine interviewed by Tristan Davies, 'Animation Is a Big Draw', *The Daily Telegraph* 29 March 1995.

196 Snowden and Fine interviewed by Eleanor Mills, 'Animation at Ease with Itself', *Observer Life* 11 June 1995.

197 2 April 1995.

198 David Fine email to the author 12 June 2007.

199 Ibid.

200 13 April 1995.

201 David Fine email to the author 12 June 2007.

202 Richard Meltzer 'Phil Mulloy:An Appreciation', http://www.bfi.org.uk/booksvideo/video/details/philmulloy/article6.html

203 Paul Wells 'The Films of Phil Mulloy', http://www.bfi.org.uk/booksvideo/video/details/philmulloy/article.html

204 *The Independent* 14 June 1995.

205 Most of the material in this piece is from emails from Phil Mulloy to the author during August 2007. Any information from other sources is identified as such.

206 'Phil Mulloy: An Appreciation' op cit.

207 A prize instituted by filmmaker Jo Menell, funded by proceeds from his film *Dick*, which consisted of footage of a wide range of penises.

208 Phil Mulloy interviewed by Matthew Sweet at the Vila do Conde Short Film Festival, 'Small Enough to Take on Godzilla', *The Independent* 16 July 1998.

209 Most of the material in this piece is from an interview with Mark Baker by the author of 14 June 2007 and subsequent conversations and emails. Any information from other sources is identified as such.

210 'Notes on the Making of *The Village*', www.astleybakerdavies.com.

211 Paul Vester in *Secret Passions*, dir Paul Madden, prod Screen First, tx 14 June 1995.

212 Most of the material in this piece is from emails from Paul Vester to the author during June and July 2007. Any information from other sources is identified as such.

213 *Understanding Animation*, p27.

214 Jonathan Hodgson interviewed by the author 21 July 2007.

215 Sylvie Bringas 'But Is It Animation?', an extra with the *Silence* DVD, pub yadinproductions.com.

216 Ryan Gilbey 'British Animation, ICA London', review section 14 June 1995, p9.

217 Most of the material in this piece is from an interview with Sarah Kennedy by the author of 6 July 2007. Any information from other sources is identified as such.

218 Sarah Kennedy interviewed by Jayne Pilling, *Women & Animation*, p95.

219 Ibid.

220 Ibid.

221 18 November 1995.

222 Tristan Davies 'All in the Worst Possible Taste', *The Daily Telegraph* 11 October 1995.

223 28 October 1995.

224 Ibid.

225 *Broadcast* Production Awards programme.

226 Most of the material in this piece is from an interview with Marjut Rimminen by the author of 3 April 2007. Any information from other sources is identified as such.

227 Jury report Tampere International Short Film Festival 5 March 1997.

228 Jury report Kraków International Short Film Festival June 1997.

229 Thomas Basgier *Animation World Network Magazine* l October 1997.

230 Most of the material in this piece is from an interview with Candy Guard by the author of 9 January 2007. Any information from other sources is identified as such.

231 Candy Guard 'Pictures with Meaning', *The Guardian Weekend* 24 June 2006, p102.

232 Candy Guard interviewed by Linda Pariser, *Women & Animation*, p88.

233 3 December 1996, p51.

234 4 December 1996.

235 No 1371, Nov 27-Dec 4 1996, p172.

236 Penguin Books 2006.

237 Most of the material in this piece is from an interview with Ruth Lingford by the author of 22 June 2006. Any information from other sources is identified as such.

238 This interview was done before Dick Arnall's death in February 2007.

239 Dick Arnall interviewed by the author 29 August 2006.

240 Orly Yadin 'But Is It Documentary?', an extra with the *Silence* DVD, pub yadinproductions.com.

241 Sylvie Bringas 'But Is It Animation?', ibid.

242 'Silence: The Role of the Animators', *Holocaust and the Moving Image: Representation in Film and Television since 1933*, p173.

243 Ibid.

244 Ibid.

245 Sylvie Bringas 'But Is It Animation?', op cit.

246 Ibid.

247 Most of the material in this piece is from an interview with Jonathan Hodgson by the author of 21 July 2007. Any information from other sources is identified as such.

248 Jonny Hannah interviewed by Martin Salisbury on the Association of Illustrators website, www.theaoi.com.

249 'How to Bring Poetry to Motion', *The Independent* 10 April 2001.

250 Most of the material in this piece is from an interview with Robert Bradbrook by the author of 22 June 2007 and subsequent emails. Any information from other sources is identified as such.

251 Holly Willis 'The Road Home', *RES Magazine* July/August 2002.

252 He wrote and directed the 1989 *Venus Peter* among others.

253 Dick Arnall interviewed by the author 29 August 2006.

254 Most of the material in this piece is from an interview with Gaëlle Denis by the author of 7 August 2007 and subsequent emails. Any information from other sources is identified as such.

255 Gaëlle Denis interviewed by Marisa Materna *Animation World Magazine* 30 June 2006, http://mag.awn.com/?article_no=2924.

256 'City Paradise', *Digit* January 2005, p49.

257 Most of the material in this piece is from emails from Run Wrake to the author during July 2007. Any information from other sources is identified as such.

258 *Chief Magazine* no 6, http://chiefmag.com/issues/6/

259 *1000 Films to Change Your Life,* Time Out Group London 2006, p100.

260 Run Wrake interviewed in *RES Magazine*, http://www.res.com/magazine/articles/killyouridolsrunwrakesvisualanarchy_2006-11-01.html

261 Dick Arnall interviewed by the author 8 August 2006.

262 *RES Magazine*, op cit.

263 Most of the material in this piece is from emails to the author from Hugh Welchman, Suzie Templeton and Alan Dewhurst during June and July 2007. Any information from other sources is identified as such.

264 Jan Younghusband email 6 May 2008.

265 See www.prokofiev.org for a list of recordings.

266 Transmitted 19 February 2006 and included in a promotional DVD for the film.

267 Alexandre Pham, 27 November 2006.

268 Jeremy Nicholas, March 2007.

269 *The Times* arts section, 27 September 2006.

270 An account of the changes in scheduling and presentation style for the independent film and video's experimental output during this period can be found in Rod Stoneman 'Incursions and Inclusions: The avant-garde on Channel Four 1983-93' in *The British Avant-Garde Film 1926 to 1995*, p285.

271 Rod Stoneman 'Sins of Commission', *Screen* 33:2 summer 1992, p127.

272 Letter (unpublished) of 5 March 1993.

273 Colin Rose interviewed by the author 21 August 2006.

274 Ibid.

275 Tristan Davies 'All in the worst possible taste', 11 October 1995.

276 Michael Grade *It Seemed Like a Good Idea at the Time*, p395.

277 *Sunday Mirror* TV listing 1 December 1996.

278 The phrase 'first resignation' might suggest that I was begged to stay and therefore graciously retracted. In fact, my letter hit John Willis's desk at the end of the day when, unknown to me, all hell had broken out at the Channel after it was discovered that programme-maker Chris Morris had secreted, subliminally, the legend 'Grade is a cunt' into a programme that had just been transmitted. John Willis's words, on reading my resignation, were in fact 'Don't be silly, Clare, where would you go?' Not very kind, but he'd had a hard day and he was right. I hastily retracted my resignation to plan a more dignified retreat at a later date.
279 *The Observer* 15 December 1996, *The Independent* 4 December 1996, *Time Out* 27 November - 4 December 1996, *The Times* 3 December 1996, *Evening Standard* 28 November 1996, *Televisual* February 1997, *The Daily Telegraph* 2 December 1996.
280 Michael Jackson quoted by Andy Beckett in 'Growing Pains', *The Guardian* March 23 2000.
281 Ibid.
282 'New Strategy Comes to the 4', p33.
283 Candy Guard interviewed by the author 9 January 2007.
284 'So much for those good old days of C4', 4 October 2000.
285 Conversation with the author 18 October 2006.
286 A very rude and very funny show presented by Antoine de Caunes and Jean-Paul Gaultier.
287 Letter of 1 November 1999 to the personnel officer of the Surrey Institute of Art & Design.
288 'Animation Chief Kitson Quits C4', 18 June 1999.
289 'New TV Show that Laughs at Teacher Abuse', *Sunday Express* 5 June 2005.
290 Camilla Deakin and Ruth Fielding interviewed by the author 7 March 2007.
291 Ibid.
292 Ruth Fielding, ibid.
293 p3.
294 *Prospect* magazine, December 2006, http://www.prospect-magazine.co.uk/article_details.php?id=7950. Lord Puttnam (C4 deputy chairman), Roger Graef and ex-C4 commissioning editors Michael Kustow and David Lloyd have also raised such concerns in talks and articles.
295 ie television with a fixed programme schedule.
296 Paul Vester email to the author 24 June 2007.
297 'How to Bring Poetry to Motion', *The Independent* April 10 2001.

Bibliography

Andrew G ed. *Film: The Critics' Choice*. Aurum Press: London 2001.

Bendazzi G. *Cartoons: One Hundred Years of Cinema Animation*. John Libbey & Company: London 1994.

Berger J. *Ways of Seeing*. Writers and Readers: London 1972.

Bonner P with Aston L. *Independent Television in Britain. Vol. 6: New Developments in Independent Television 1981-92*. Palgrave Macmillan: Basingstoke 2003.

Brown M. *A Licence to Be Different: The Story of Channel 4*. BFI Publishing: London 2007.

Cambridge Animation Festival catalogue 1979, with several essays about the history of British animation.

Catterall P ed. *The Making of Channel 4*. Frank Cass: London and Portland Oregon 1999.

Cook B and Thomas G ed. *The animate! Book: Rethinking Animation*. Lux, London, with Arts Council England: London 2007.

Curtis D. *A History of Artists' Film and Video in Britain*. BFI Publishing: London 2007

Faber L and Walters H. *Animation Unlimited: Innovative Short Films since 1940*. Laurence King Publishing: London 2004.

Grade M. *It Seemed Like a Good Idea at the Time*. Macmillan Publishers: London 1999

Haggith T and Newman J ed. *Holocaust and the Moving Image: Representation in Film and Television since 1933*. Wallflower Press: London and New York 2005.

Isaacs J. *Storm Over 4*. Weidenfeld and Nicolson: London 1989.

Isaacs J. *Look Me in the Eye: A Life in Television*. Little, Brown: London 2006.

Lambert S. *Channel Four: Television with a Difference?* BFI: London 1982.

Law S. 'Putting Themselves in the Pictures: Images of Women in the Work of Joanna Quinn, Candy Guard and Alison de Vere' in Pilling J. ed. *A Reader in Animation Studies*. John Libbey: Sydney 1997, reprinted from *Animation Journal* autumn 1995.

Lord P and Sibley B. *Cracking Animation*. Thames & Hudson: London 1998.

O'Pray M ed. *The British Avant-Garde Film 1926 to 1995*. University of Luton/John Libbey Media 1996.

Pilling J ed. *2D and Beyond*. Rotovision: East Sussex 2001.

Pilling J ed. *A Reader in Animation Studies*. John Libbey: Sydney 1997.

Pilling J ed. *Women & Animation*. British Film Institute: London 1992.

Stephenson R. *The Animated Film*. International Film Guide series, Tantivy Press: London/A S Barnes & Co: New York 1973.

Swain B. *Electric Passions*. Channel 4 Television 1996.

Vertigo summer 1999 including articles on Animate by Jo Ann Kaplan, Ruth Lingford and Samantha Moore

Wells P. *Understanding Animation*. Routledge: London and New York 1998.

Wells P guest ed. *Art & Design Magazine*. Vol. 12 no. 3-4 1997. Pub. Academy Group. *Art & Animation*, profile no 53.

Index